ADAM SMITH RECONSIDERED

Adam Smith Reconsidered

HISTORY, LIBERTY, AND THE
FOUNDATIONS OF MODERN POLITICS

PAUL SAGAR

PRINCETON UNIVERSITY PRESS
PRINCETON & OXFORD

Published by Princeton University Press
41 William Street, Princeton, New Jersey 08540
99 Banbury Road, Oxford OX2 6JX

press.princeton.edu

All Rights Reserved
First paperback printing, 2024
Paper ISBN 978-0-691-23494-6
Cloth ISBN 978-0-691-21083-4
ISBN (e-book) 978-0-691-23493-9
LCCN: 2022279048

British Library Cataloging-in-Publication Data is available

Editorial: Ben Tate and Josh Drake
Production Editorial: Jenny Wolkowicki
Jacket/Cover design: Layla Mac Rory
Production: Danielle Amatucci
Publicity: Kate Hensley and Charlotte Coyne
Copyeditor: Joseph Dahm

Jacket/Cover images: *(Top):* Dagger. ClipArt ETC / Florida Center for Instructional Technology © 2004–2021. *(Bottom):* 18th century pistol, Album / Alamy Stock Photo

This book has been composed in Arno

CONTENTS

ACKNOWLEDGEMENTS

I HAVE INCURRED numerous debts in writing this work. First and foremost, I owe thanks to my colleague Robin Douglass, with whom I have engaged in the most fruitful of conversations about political thought, and regarding Adam Smith in particular, that it is possible to imagine the privilege of having. Many of the ideas and interpretations argued for here were either originally Robin's, or had their genesis in conversations with him. Indeed, I am often no longer sure who came up with what first. He has also been an unfailingly sharp reader of drafts, who has always and significantly improved whatever I have written. If this book is judged a success, he deserves shared credit for that (and if not, the failings are mine).

Richard Bourke has similarly been a long-standing personal friend, professional supporter, and intellectual interlocutor. The existence of this book is dependent on my having an academic career, and for that I owe Richard more than anybody else.

Glory Liu I owe particular thanks to, both for her long-standing support of what I am trying to do in my work on Smith, but also for her generous and highly insightful reading of the draft manuscript, suggesting numerous changes that markedly improved the argument.

Two anonymous readers for Princeton University Press provided extremely careful and helpful comments on an earlier version of the manuscript. I have done my best to incorporate their suggestions and comments into the final version. Chris Berry and Barry Weingast offered insightful and instructive corrections and comments at the proposal stage, many of which went on to shape what became the finished draft.

I am also grateful to those individuals who have read portions (or in some cases, all) of this work, or discussed some of the ideas that now feature in it, and who gave various species of encouragement, as well as much-needed correction, along the way. The list includes (but is not limited to, and with apologies to whomever is unfortunate enough to have been accidentally forgotten):

Chris Brooke, Ross Carroll, Clare Chambers, Greg Conti, John Dunn, John Filling, Sean Fleming, Nick Gooding, Ed Hall, Ryan Patrick Hanley, Kinch Hoekstra, Rob Jubb, Duncan Kelly, Jacob T. Levy, Dan Luban, Tom Pye, John Robertson, David Runciman, Jason Sharman, Matt Sleat, Mike Sonenscher, Tim Stuart Buttle, Helen Thompson, Bart Wilson, and Bernardo Zacka. Special thanks must also go to Heikki Haara for organising the 2019 Early Career workshop in Helsinki, where a draft of chapter 1 was circulated and discussed. Tejas Parasher and Lucia Rubinelli I would like to thank for their valiant efforts to try to organise a half-day workshop dedicated entirely to the draft manuscript of this book. Sadly, industrial action, and then nothing less than a global pandemic, laid waste to the best of plans. Nonetheless, I am grateful for what they tried to do for me. I must also thank Ben Tate, who has been (as previously) a model of editorial support and encouragement, and with whom it has once again been a pleasure to work.

The ideas in this book grew out of the doctoral research I undertook at Cambridge, and what became in turn my 2018 monograph, *The Opinion of Mankind: Sociability and the Theory of the State from Hobbes to Smith*, likewise published by Princeton University Press. This book is very much a sequel to that one. Accordingly, it likewise owes a massive debt to István Hont, who supervised my doctoral work before his early death in 2013. What follows bears the unmistakable imprint of István's influence—but it also seeks to strike out in different directions, not all of which he would have supported. It is a great and continual source of sadness to me that the one person whom I really wish I could show my readings to—and, who knows, perhaps even convince to see it my way (who am I kidding?)—will never be able to judge them.

Since leaving Cambridge I have had the great good fortune of researching and teaching in the Department of Political Economy at King's College London. I cannot imagine a better place to read, think, and write about Adam Smith, and I am enormously grateful to the colleagues who have welcomed me there, and have been a pleasure to work alongside of. In particular I must thank Mark Pennington for his outstanding work as head of department during my first three years, and for the unfailing support and encouragement he has given me then and since. Similarly, Andrew Blick, Jeremy Jennings, and Frans Berkhout have been the best of senior colleagues. Jonathan Benson, Adrian Blau, Billy Christmas, Humeira Iqtidar, Steven Klein, Carmen Pavel, Diana Popescu, and Adam Tebble are all owed a debt of thanks. I was also fortunate enough in the spring semester of 2019 to organise an 'Advanced Texts' module devoted entirely to *TMS*, consisting of a close-reading workshop with a small group of KCL third-year undergraduates. This was a fantastic experience in and of itself, but reading and discussing *TMS* slowly and carefully with my students considerably sharpened my appreciation of many of Smith's arguments. I am grateful to those who took that class.

Much of what follows was thought up and/or written down in Bryn Brethynau cottage, Snowdonia, property of the North London Mountaineering Club. The book is dedicated to the NLMC for its role in helping me to remember, amidst all my philosophy, to be still a man. Finally, my love and thanks to Jess Williams, not only for putting up with me for quite some time now, but for holding the ropes, both metaphorically and literally.

ABBREVIATIONS TO ADAM SMITH'S WORKS

CAS   *The Correspondence of Adam Smith*, rev. ed., ed. E. C. Mossner and I. S. Ross (Oxford: Clarendon, 1987), 2 vols.

ED   'Early Draft' of Part of *The Wealth of Nations*, in *The Glasgow Edition of the Works and Correspondence of Adam Smith: Volume V—Lectures on Jurisprudence*, ed. R. L. Meek, D. D. Raphael, and P. G. Stein (Oxford: Clarendon, 1978).

EPS   *The Glasgow Edition of the Works and Correspondence of Adam Smith: Volume III—Essays on Philosophical Subjects*, ed. W. P. D. Wightman and J. C. Bryce (Oxford: Clarendon, 1980).

LJ(A)   'Lectures on Jurisprudence, Report of 1762–63', in *The Glasgow Edition of the Works and Correspondence of Adam Smith: Volume V—Lectures on Jurisprudence*, ed. R. L. Meek, D. D. Raphael, and P. G. Stein (Oxford: Clarendon, 1978).

LJ(B)   'Jurisprudence or Notes from the Lectures on Justice, Police, Revenue, and Arms Delivered in the University of Glasgow by Adam Smith, Professor of Moral Philosophy, Report Dated 1766', in *The Glasgow Edition of the Works and Correspondence of Adam Smith: Volume V—Lectures on Jurisprudence*, ed. R. L. Meek, D. D. Raphael, and P. G. Stein (Oxford: Clarendon, 1978).

LRBL   *The Glasgow Edition of the Works and Correspondence of Adam Smith: Volume IV—Lectures on Rhetoric and Belles Lettres*, ed. J. C. Bryce (Oxford: Clarendon, 1983).

TMS   *The Glasgow Edition of the Works and Correspondence of Adam Smith: Volume I—The Theory of Moral Sentiments*, ed. D. D. Raphael and A .L. Macfie (Oxford: Clarendon, 1976).

WN   *The Glasgow Edition of the Works and Correspondence of Adam Smith: Volume II—An Inquiry into the Nature and Causes of the Wealth of Nations*, 2 vols., ed. R. H. Campbell, A. S. Skinner, and W. B. Todd (Oxford: Clarendon, 1975).

ADAM SMITH RECONSIDERED

Introduction

IT IS NOW commonplace for work on Adam Smith to begin by remarking that there was once believed to be such a thing as 'Das Adam Smith Problem', but that this has now happily been overcome. In turn (we are standardly told) the door has been opened to more fruitful investigations, and a fuller picture of Smith as first-rank moral, political, and economic, thinker—who also had important things to say about the origins of language, rhetoric, the philosophy of science, and religious belief—has duly emerged. As a result (the story usually concludes) the crude popular caricature of Smith as an advocate of narrow self-interest, with a Panglossian attitude towards markets and 1980s Chicago-style suspicion of government, has been firmly discredited.

At one level, this is all true. The crudest version of Das Adam Smith Problem, as standardly attributed to German scholars of the late nineteenth century, posited that there was a fundamental incompatibility between Smith's first book, *The Theory of Moral Sentiments* (*TMS*), and his second, *The Wealth of Nations* (*WN*). This was because the former was allegedly based on an ethic of 'benevolence', the latter on a psychology of 'selfishness'. But given that these are contradictory starting points, how could the same man have written both books?[1] Whether anyone ever really believed in such a crude version of precisely

1. For more detailed discussion and on the historical background especially, see Leonidas Montes, *Adam Smith in Context: A Critical Reassessment of Some Central Components of His Thought* (London: Palgrave Macmillan, 2004), 15–45. See also James R. Otteson, *Adam Smith's Marketplace of Life* (Cambridge: Cambridge University Press, 2002), chap. 4; Pierre Force, *Self-Interest Before Adam Smith: A Genealogy of Economic Science* (Cambridge: Cambridge University Press, 2003), 256–63; E. J. Hundert, *The Enlightenment's Fable: Bernard Mandeville and the Discovery of Society* (Cambridge: Cambridge University Press, 1994), 235; Vivienne Brown, *Adam Smith's Discourse: Canonicity, Commerce, and Conscience* (London: Routledge, 1994), chap. 2.

this binary is questionable.[2] Regardless, more recent scholarship has made plain that *TMS* is based on arguments about 'sympathy' (a much more technical, and philosophically sophisticated, concept than mere benevolence), whilst *WN* pays attention to what modern commentators would class as 'self-interest' (which is not at all the same thing as selfishness). This in turn dispels any crude version of Das Adam Smith Problem, based as it is on straightforward mistakes about precise philosophical ideas, and the differing levels of analysis with which each of Smith's works is primarily preoccupied (the first being about individual-level morality, the latter about societal level systemic analysis, there being no inherent tension between the two). Furthermore, the discovery of the notes made by attendees of Smith's lectures in the 1760s, now published as the *Lectures on Jurisprudence* (*LJ*), comprehensively refutes earlier suggestions that the same man could write two allegedly contradictory books because he changed his mind between their composition. Earlier suggestions that *WN* was the result of an about-face from Smith following an engagement with the materialism of Helvétius (whom he encountered only after publishing *TMS*) became untenable following the recovery of *LJ*.[3] We now know beyond question that Smith was working on ideas that would form the backbone of *WN* almost immediately after publishing the first edition of *TMS*, which he anyway went on to meticulously revise for the rest of his life, both before and after publishing his great work of political economy. In turn, it is undeniable that the burgeoning and ever-growing scholarship on Smith of the past half century has produced a more accurate picture of him as a major contributor to the Scottish, and indeed wider European, Enlightenment.

Yet there is a sense in which Das Adam Smith Problem remains firmly at the heart of much current Smith scholarship. This is because the so-called Das Adam Smith Problem may be understood not as a worry primarily about textual inconsistency or suppositions that Smith changed his mind, but as a more fundamental concern about the ethical status of societies that rely extensively on markets tout court. Specifically, that a society in which there is widespread reliance on markets—and hence, on the unbridling of self-interest, and in turn pursuit of consumer and in particular luxury and status goods—must necessarily

---

2. On which see Keith Tribe, '"Das Adam Smith Problem" and the Origins of Modern Smith Scholarship', *History of European Ideas* 34, no. 4 (2008).

3. Montes, *Adam Smith in Context*, 29.

be to some degree morally compromised.[4] This of course is neither a new worry nor one that is unique to the supposed Das Adam Smith Problem. Versions of it exist in (for example) various strands of Christian moral and political thought, in classical republicanism's insistence on civic virtue and its deep hostility to the luxury and economic inequality generated by and in turn fuelling market activity, and in contemporary anxieties commonplace in our own day about the deleterious effects of consumer-driven postindustrial capitalism. The *real* Das Adam Smith Problem, we might say, therefore cuts deeper—and remains more urgent—than merely a matter of textual interpretation and historical consistency. How could a first-rate moral philosopher like Smith think that morality was not fatally compromised by the existence of the kind of market-reliant society that he set out not only to understand and explain, but in various ways to suggest could be improved?

Understood this way, what I am calling the Real Das Adam Smith Problem remains very much alive. This is most especially true in the large body of recent literature that reads Smith as to a significant degree responding to his contemporary Jean-Jacques Rousseau's incendiary assault on market-based societies, *The Discourse on Inequality* of 1755. In the current literature connecting Rousseau and Smith, Rousseau is standardly presented as the arch-critic of market-based society, whilst Smith is either its defender or qualified apologist. The template is thus set: societies that rely heavily on markets are presumed to be normatively problematic on a host of metrics, and the extent to which Smith agrees or disagrees is considered in turn, and the picture we get of Smith is thus of someone who accepted this basic framework, but simply came out on the other side of the debate on various specific points, whilst acknowledging that Rousseau asked the right questions, and may even have been right regarding some of the matters he raised (how much, why, to what degree, and with what significance vary between commentators).[5]

4. István Hont, *Politics in Commercial Society: Jean-Jacques Rousseau and Adam Smith*, ed. B. Kapossy and M. Sonenscher (Cambridge, MA: Harvard University Press, 2015), 17–18. In fact I owe this insight more directly to Hont's allowing me to audit his (in)famous Adam Smith class for Cambridge MPhil students in the autumn of 2010, where this point was made more explicitly in the preparatory reading materials, and which has stayed with me since.

5. For a helpful overview, see Dennis Rasmussen, 'Adam Smith and Rousseau: Enlightenment and Counter-Enlightenment', in *The Oxford Handbook of Adam Smith*, ed. C. J. Berry, M. P. Paganelli, and C. Smith (Oxford: Oxford University Press, 2013). See chapters 3 and 4 below for full references and discussion. Not all recent commentators, it must be noted, conform to this framework. Christopher J. Berry, for example, writes that Smith 'deflects or counters the

A central aim of this book is to challenge this way of thinking from the ground up. For it is my contention that Smith *did not* operate from the basic assumption underlying the Real Das Adam Smith Problem, that is, that societies which rely heavily on markets are presumptively normatively problematic and must be either criticised, or qualifiedly defended, on ethical grounds pertaining to concerns about self-interest, vanity, status-competition, consumerism, and so forth. Whilst the recent literature on Smith and Rousseau has been invaluable in decisively discrediting crude depictions of Smith as a narrow theorist of *Homo economicus*, bringing to light the complexity and sophistication of especially his moral, and to a lesser extent his political, thought, it has nonetheless now itself become an obstacle to a truer understanding of Smith's ideas, which are more intellectually audacious (and to my mind, more persuasive) than have hitherto been appreciated.

A fundamental contention of this book, then, is that Smith did not share Rousseau's anxieties about market societies. In that sense he was also firmly outside the classical republican and various Christian traditions that predated him, as well as more recent anxieties about the pernicious effects of consumerism. This makes Smith *unusual*: his starting point is not an innate normative suspicion of markets and their effects on human moral well-being, and which is the default for many, if not most, thinkers in the history of Western moral thought. Whilst Smith did worry—extensively—about human moral well-being, he did not think that market societies were a privileged locus for such worries, or that they were especially liable to exacerbate those real threats to human ethical health that do exist. The problem, Smith believed, was not the widespread presence of markets, but more fundamentally the human condition, and the many ways it could go well or badly depending on a wide range of factors. This did not make Smith blasé about the challenges posed by markets, and hence faced by societies that rely extensively on them. Far from it, as

---

accusation that commercial transactions (and by extension a society founded upon them) are ethically suspect' ('Adam Smith and the Virtues of the Modern Economy', in *Essays on Hume, Smith and the Scottish Enlightenment* [Edinburgh: Edinburgh University Press, 2018], 359). Although I disagree with Berry on a number of technical matters of Smith interpretation—as will be seen in the succeeding chapters—I share with him a basic estimation that Smith rejected the traditional view that commerce is inherently suspect and that market exchange represents an inferior mode of human interaction both morally and political speaking, as compared to supposedly more virtuous (usually Christian or republican) alternatives. See also Christopher J. Berry, 'Smith Under Strain', *European Journal of Political Theory* 3, no. 4 (2004), and 'Adam Smith: Commerce, Liberty and Modernity', in *Essays on Hume*.

we will see in due course. What I aim to show, however, is the hitherto under-appreciated extent to which Smith was more centrally concerned with the political, rather than the moral, dangers that such societies were vulnerable to, whilst also highlighting what he took to be their often unappreciated or unrecognised achievements.

These were achievements which a critic like Rousseau in the *Discourse* did not see or understand because, at least from Smith's perspective, Rousseau in many ways simply did not know what he was talking about. This was because the Genevan made his pronouncements based primarily on philosophical conjectures, whereas the Scot was convinced that in order to understand the ethical and political situation of modern European societies, one had to grasp at least the basic contours of the real (and not merely conjectural) history of human civilization in something like its entirety. At the beginning of the *Second Discourse* Rousseau famously moved on from the thorny question of whether his state of nature account was intended to be purely imaginary, was in fact meant to have some grounding in historical facticity, and if the latter then what its relation to biblical scripture was supposed to be, by stating that he would 'begin by setting aside all the facts, for they do not affect the question'.[6] Smith's point of departure in political analysis was the reverse: we *cannot* set the facts aside, for they absolutely *do* affect the question. Political theory had to be genuinely historical, Smith believed, or else it would be simply a series of postulations untethered to the reality of what it was supposed to account for, and thus not accounting for anything. (The widespread view that Smith relied heavily on conjectural history in his political thought is mistaken, as I argue in chapter 1 below.) In turn, from Smith's perspective Rousseau's

---

6. Jean-Jacques Rousseau, *The Discourses and Other Early Political Writings*, ed. V. Gourevitch (Cambridge: Cambridge University Press, 1997), 132. For discussion on this point, see Christopher Kelly, 'Rousseau's "peut-etre": Reflections on the Status of the State of Nature', *Modern Intellectual History* 3, no. 1 (2006): 75–83. Even if—as some commentators suggest—the 'facts' Rousseau meant to set aside pertained only to purported facts of sacred history and not to facts about natural and political history, the general point still stands: from Smith's point of view, if there are indeed facts to be had, they better not be set aside. Indeed, this difference between the two thinkers is signalled by what Rousseau immediately goes on to say: that his 'Inquiries . . . ought not to be taken for historical truths, but only for hypothetical and conditional reasonings; better suited to elucidate the Nature of things than to show their genuine origin' (132). Smith by contrast rejected the idea that the 'nature of things' could be elucidated by hypothetical conjectures, holding that it was precisely the 'genuine origin' that needed to be known and understood.

quasi-history—based on speculative philosophical conjectures coupled with reading Buffon's *Natural History*, plus what he gleaned from unreliable travellers' reports sent back from distant lands, and lacking any firm grounding in the real and known history of either human civilization as a whole or European development in particular—fell far short of the required mark. Below (in chapter 3) I argue that even upon his first encounter with Rousseau's thought when reviewing the *Discourse* in the short-lived *Edinburgh Review*, the young Smith—already in the process of composing *TMS*, itself a powerfully original work of moral philosophy—would likely not have been particularly impressed or perturbed with what he found in the *Discourse*. This was primarily due to the considerable advances already made by British theorists of sympathy in the previous three decades, plus Rousseau's relatively unoriginal (from Smith's perspective) ideas given what had already put forward by Bernard Mandeville. Yet in Smith's subsequent and hence more mature and developed perspective—as he worked through material in his Glasgow lectures that would eventually constitute the backbone of *WN*, as well as the great unfinished work on law and politics that he ensured was destroyed before his death—Rousseau's *Discourse* would have come to seem only more inadequate to the task of providing a satisfactory political understanding of modern conditions, given the scale of the historical framework that Smith came to believe was required. Over a lifetime of audacious intellectual endeavour Smith tried to inform himself of that vast history, and to build upon it in turn. By bringing this out more fully than commentators have so far done, I hope to show that the Real Das Adam Smith Problem is, at least when applied to Smith, revealed as a non-problem. However, doing so also allows us to simultaneously resist any unwelcome backsliding into earlier caricatures of Smith as somehow unattuned to the genuine complexities of the moral and political thinking that surround the theory and practice of markets, which it is a great and undoubted virtue of recent scholarship to have helped us leave behind.

Making this case, however, is complicated by the fact that at present the scholarship on Smith is bedevilled by fundamental and widespread misunderstandings of central aspects of his thought, which themselves help to generate the false assimilation of Smith's ideas to the logic of the Real Das Adam Smith Problem. This is most especially true regarding his use of the term 'commercial society'—now used ubiquitously by commentators, and as far as I can tell, universally incorrectly. Other major misreadings have also been allowed to prevail, regarding the so-called four stages theory, the place of conjectural history, Smith's attitude towards ethical corruption, and his understanding of what primarily powers large-scale market activity, to name but some of the most important. These however must all be put right, both as a matter of proper scholarly interpretation, but also because it is only by correcting various cumulative misreadings that a more accurate understanding of Smith's major contribution to the history of Western political thought can be attained. I must, however, beg the reader's patience: each of the next five chapters will have to be worked through, and then taken in light of each other, and only then will it be possible to draw all the strands together as one.

Chapter 1 begins via a fundamental reinterpretation of the role, nature, and importance of three aspects of Smith's political thought: 'commercial society', the 'four stages theory', and 'conjectural history'. Against the established scholarship, I seek to show that Smith was not a conjectural historian in his political thought; that his four stages theory is an economic thought experiment and not a conjectural history; that he does not think real historical development reliably follows a stadial progression; that 'commercial society' is not the fourth stage of the four stages model; and that as a result Smith's label of 'commercial society', when properly understood, radically underdetermines any political conclusions that might in turn be drawn (something proved by what Smith has to say about the commercial societies of the ancient world and China). This reworking of the foundations sets up the argument of the rest of the book.

Chapter 2 turns to the question of Smith and 'modern liberty'. Whereas it is well known that Smith thinks luxury brought down the feudal barons and reintroduced freedom to modern Europe, largely unexamined is the underlying theoretical question of what Smith thinks liberty *is*. My contention is that liberty for Smith is best understood as a species of nondomination, understood in terms of the personal security afforded to ordinary individuals regarding their physical safety as well as the stability of their holdings. However, for Smith liberty is something that can be adequately made sense of only in thick historical contexts, and where philosophical analysis alone will be inadequate to achieving satisfactory understanding. *Modern* liberty, for Smith, is specifically understood as security yielding nondomination, as achieved via widespread realisation of the rule of law—something unique to post-feudal Europe. Yet whilst Smith is a theorist of nondomination when it comes to freedom, he is categorically not a republican, instead aligning himself with Hume and Montesquieu as a theorist of the constitutional monarchies whom he believed owned the future of European (and hence global) politics. Furthermore, Smith's unorthodox conceptualisation of freedom as being irreducibly historicised places him outside of the recent attempts to theorize freedom as nondomination put forward by republican political philosophers such as Quentin Skinner and Philip Pettit. Instead, he offers us an alternative model of political theorising, one which recognises the importance of non-domination as a political value, but does so without undesirable republican baggage, whilst placing the emphasis firmly on history and political institutions, not abstract conceptual philosophical analysis.

Chapter 3 examines the extent to which Smith's ideas were formed in response to, or significantly influenced by, those of Rousseau. Against the mainstream of recent scholarship on this question, I argue that when we restore Smith's British intellectual context, we see that Smith would have registered Rousseau's ideas as neither particularly novel nor especially challenging. On the contrary, Rousseau's argument in the *Second Discourse* was far behind the best available work in English (principally that of David Hume, which unlike Rousseau, Smith had read and absorbed by the 1750s), whilst the challenges he issued were merely restatements of arguments that had already been made by Mandeville some three decades previously. This indicates that Smith was neither seriously influenced nor animated by Rousseau's *Discourse*, and engaged it not as a major challenge to his own thought but as collateral damage.

Chapter 4 builds on chapter 3 by turning to the question of moral corruption and the extent to which Smith thought 'commercial society' was corrupting of its inhabitants, as well as potentially *itself* a corrupt form of social organisation. I suggest that if we remove the Rousseauvian lens that has dominated much recent interpretation, we come to see that Smith *did not* view 'commercial society' as a privileged locus for concerns of moral corruption. In this regard, *TMS* in particular has been subjected to a great deal of misinterpretation, which is badly in need of correction, and which this chapter offers in detail.

Chapter 5, by contrast, argues that insofar as Smith did express major concerns about 'commercial society', these were based in fears about not moral but political phenomena. To show this, I examine Smith's famous attack on the 'conspiracy of the merchants' and his assault on the mercantile system, but locate this in his wider theory of opinion as the foundation of political order, the importance of wealth to psychological authority generation, and his account of why the ancient commercial societies of Athens and Rome were ultimately destroyed by worsening misalignments between wealth and institutional political power. The result is a Janus-faced assessment of the merchants' conspiracy, but also a stark warning to modern European peoples about the need for—but also the rarity and fragility of—good political judgement under conditions of the predictable rule of law.

The book concludes with a reflection on why Smith has so often been misread, suggesting that this is due to ahistorical conceptualisations of—as well as frequent conflations between—the distinct ideas of capitalism, the economy, and 'commercial society'. Putting these matters right should, however, allow many common misinterpretations of Smith to cease, enabling his true value as a political theorist of commercial society to emerge into view.

1

Commercial Society, History, and the Four Stages Theory

ADAM SMITH is now ubiquitously referred to as a theorist of 'commercial society'. Unfortunately this term is used by commentators in a variety of different ways, many of which are, when applied to Smith, deeply misleading. In part this is a function of a lack of attention paid to Smith's own technical, and highly specified, understanding of 'commercial society', one that we must grasp precisely if we are to make proper sense of his wider political thought. Yet it is also because of a persistent mistake about the relationship of 'commercial society' to Smith's so-called 'four stages' account of economic and political development, as well as his use of 'conjectural history'. For contrary to received wisdom, 'commercial society' *is not* the fourth and final stage of Smith's stadial account. (That is something subtly, but importantly, different: a 'commercial age'.) And also contrary to received wisdom, Smith's 'four stages' theory is *not* a historical account, and not even a 'conjectural' history—but something else. Such polemical claims will appear outlandish at this early stage. By the end of this chapter, I hope to have shown that they are nonetheless correct. The rest of the book builds on the reworked foundations laid here.

Commercial Society

At least three common, but misleading, uses of 'commercial society' can be identified in the existing literature, all of which have the effect of distorting, more or less severely, Smith's thought. First, 'commercial society' is sometimes used as a loose general label for the large eighteenth-century trading states of Smith's day, that is, advanced European nations engaging in commerce with both sovereign neighbours and colonial territories. On this understanding 'commercial society' may be implied to be an alternative to republican political organization, something taken to be more or less anti-commercial in orientation, in both its ancient and modern guises. As we shall see Smith did write—frequently—with regard to political entities characterised by, and in regard to their operations of, trade, but when doing so he consistently avoided the term 'commercial *society*' and wrote either of commercial 'nations', 'states', or 'countries'. We shall see below that this distinction matters.

Second, and sometimes in conjunction with the above, 'commercial society' is often employed by commentators as a rough synonym for a consumption-driven economy, of the sort widely prevalent in twenty-first-century Western societies. Preoccupation with luxury status goods, and individual material consumption at the expense of other human endeavours, is taken to be a paramount (and typically morally problematic) feature of such socioeconomic existence. This understanding predominates in discussions of Smith and 'corruption', including especially comparisons of his thought with that of Rousseau.

Finally, 'commercial society' is sometimes employed as a generic term for what is now known as liberal capitalism, but without the anachronistic, post-nineteenth-century resonances that this conjunction now carries, and that prevent its direct application to Smith. Whilst the rhetorical camouflage of substituting 'commercial society' for 'capitalism' rarely adds anything of analytic substance, it does generate problems of using an anachronistic notion that Smith had no conception of, and was not himself employing, often serving to impose alien concerns onto his work.[1]

1. For example, inter alia, and often moving back and forth between these three usages, Michael Ignatieff, 'Smith, Rousseau and the Republic of Needs', in *Scotland and Europe 1200–1850*, ed. T. C. Smouth (Edinburgh: Edinburgh University Press, 1986); Ryan Patrick Hanley, 'Commerce and Corruption: Rousseau's Diagnosis and Adam Smith's Cure', *European Journal of Political Theory* 7, no. 2 (2008), and *Adam Smith and the Character of Virtue* (Cambridge: Cambridge University Press, 2009); Dennis Rasmussen, *The Problems and Promise of Commercial Society: Adam Smith's Response to Rousseau* (University Park: Pennsylvania State University Press, 2008), and 'Adam Smith on What Is Wrong with Inequality', *American Political Science Review* 110, no. 2 (2016); Lisa Hill, 'Adam Smith and the Theme of Corruption', *Review of Politics* 68, no. 4 (2006), and '"The Poor Man's Son" and the Corruption of Our Moral Sentiments: Commerce, Virtue and Happiness in Adam Smith', *Journal of Scottish Philosophy* 15, no. 1 (2017); E. J. Hundert, *The Enlightenment's Fable: Bernard Mandeville and the Discovery of Society* (Cambridge: Cambridge University Press, 1994), chap. 5; Siraj Ahmed, *The Stillbirth of Capital: Enlightenment Writing and Colonial India* (Stanford, CA: Stanford University Press, 2012), chap. 4; Maureen Harkin, 'Adam Smith's Missing History: Primitives, Progress and the Problem of Genre', *ELH* 72, no. 2 (2005); Christopher J. Berry, 'Adam Smith: Commerce, Liberty and

There is nothing wrong, in and of itself, with using the label 'commercial society' to mean any of the above. The problem is that *Smith* used the term 'commercial society' with great theoretical precision, and for him it did not mean any of these things.[2] Thus, if we are to get clear on what Smith meant, we need to be much more careful in our handling. We can begin in this regard by turning to one of the only two occasions in his published corpus where Smith actually uses the exact term 'commercial society'. In chapter 4 of Book I of *WN*, Smith states,

> When the division of labour has been once thoroughly established, it is but a very small part of a man's wants which the produce of his own labour can supply. He supplies the far greater part of them by exchanging that surplus part of the produce of his own labour, which is over and above his own consumption, for such parts of the produce of other men's labour as he has occasion for. Every man thus lives by exchanging, or becomes in some measure a merchant, and the society itself grows to be what is properly a commercial society. (*WN* I.iv.1)

The only other time that Smith uses the precise term 'commercial society' is when discussing the need to provide public education so as to offset the

---

Modernity', in *Philosophers of the Enlightenment*, ed. P. Gilmore (Edinburgh: Edinburgh University Press, 1989); Craig Smith, 'The Scottish Enlightenment and the Challenges of Commercial Society: Adam Smith's Wealth of Nations', *Horyzonty Polityki* 8, no. 25 (2017); Samuel Fleischacker, *On Adam Smith's* Wealth of Nations: *A Philosophical Companion* (Princeton: Princeton University Press, 2005), 55. Many more could be cited—indeed, my own previous work has been guilty of much the same.

2. That Smith used the term 'commercial society' very precisely, in a way that is not treated by the majority of the commentary with sufficient care, was noted by István Hont, *Politics in Commercial Society: Jean-Jacques Rousseau and Adam Smith*, ed. B. Kapossy and M. Sonenscher (Cambridge, MA: Harvard University Press, 2015), 3. Unfortunately, Hont goes on in that work to use 'commercial society' in just the sort of imprecise way he himself warns against, in particular by conflating it with the connected, but importantly distinct, notion of commercial *sociability*. On this see especially Robin Douglass, 'Theorising Commercial Society: Rousseau, Smith and Hont', *European Journal of Political Theory* 17, no. 4 (2018). Hont's tendency to elide the distinction between commercial sociability and commercial society is evident also in his 'The Language of Sociability and Commerce: Samuel Pufendorf and the Theoretical Foundations of the "Four-Stages" Theory', in *Jealousy of Trade: International Competition and the Nation-State in Historical Perspective* (Cambridge, MA: Belknap, 2005). For a sustained discussion of commercial sociability (which for Smith is the basis of *all* large and lasting human societies), and which is hence connected to in complex ways, but is not identical with, commercial society, see Paul Sagar, *The Opinion of Mankind: Sociability and the Theory of the State from Hobbes to Smith* (Princeton: Princeton University Press, 2018), chaps. 1 and 5.

debilitating effects of the division of labour upon the mental faculties of ordinary workers (*WN* V.i.f.52). In both cases, the term 'commercial *society*' is restricted by Smith to the analysis of the *internal relations* of members of a community, with regard to how those members attain their 'wants', in the context of increasingly widespread and advanced realisation of the division of labour.[3] In Smith's technical usage, then, commercial *society* denotes how 'every many becomes in some measure a merchant' because the division of labour means that in order to survive, and indeed prosper, individuals for the most part enter into the exchange of goods and/or services via market mechanisms so as to satisfy needs and wants. What is 'properly' called commercial society is an advanced stage of economic interdependence where direct personal toil on the products of subsistence (e.g., hunting, pasturage, tillage) has been superseded by exchanges in webs of market relations. It is thus a term used to denote the *internal* relations of individuals to each other when it comes to the securing of both the necessities and luxuries of life. As we shall see below, Smith also discusses the *external* relations of various societies in great detail, when it comes to both trade and, in particular, warfare. But in those regards, 'commercial *society*' is not his preferred term, even when dealing with the most economically advanced cases. The significance of focusing precisely on Smith's technical use of the term 'commercial *society*' will become evident in due course. In order to make progress and get to that point, however, it is first necessary to undertake considerable ground clearing. For many accreted layers of misunderstanding currently prevent proper appreciation of Smith's position, and we must first remove this obstructing sediment.

The majority of Smith scholarship operates at present, either explicitly or by way of background assumption, with what may be termed a 'standard model' with regards to two aspects of Smith's political thought in particular: the 'four stages' theory and the role of 'conjectural history'. A recent, and helpfully explicit, statement of the standard model comes from Jesse Norman:

---

3. Dan Luban has suggested accordingly that 'the distinctive feature of such a society is not so much the expansion of commerce as the generalization of wage labor' ('Adam Smith on Vanity, Domination, and History', *Modern Intellectual History* 9, no. 2 [2012]: 298). This may not be quite right, however: Smith does not explicitly invoke the idea of *wage* labour, only living from exchange—the former being a particular subspecies of the latter, but is not coextensive with it. We risk reading nineteenth- and twentieth-century preoccupations back into Smith if we equate commercial society with wage labour, so ought to be cautious about Luban's gloss.

[There is a] kind of theorizing on display in the *Lectures* of which Smith is arguably one of the originators. This is akin to what Dugald Stewart described as 'conjectural history': the attempt to imagine how a particular institution or practice might originally have arisen, and to deploy that imagined history as part of a wider theory. In this case, Smith's target is nothing less than the origins of the political-legal realm. Based on his analysis of property rights, he introduces the idea of 'four distinct stages which mankind pass through.'[4]

Norman goes on to claim that 'Smith is quickly able to show the value of his stadial theory by applying it to property rights, and then to government itself', ultimately using it to explain 'what he takes to be the actual historical development of Government in Britain.'[5] To be sure, Norman's account is part of a popular work aimed at a nonspecialist audience, but something like his picture underpins the majority of interpretations of Smith in the existing scholarship, and upon which he is evidently drawing.[6]

---

4. Jesse Norman, *Adam Smith: What He Thought and Why It Matters* (London: Allen Lane, 2015), 69–70.

5. Norman, *Adam Smith*, 70.

6. For example, Nicholas Phillipson, *Adam Smith: An Enlightened Life* (London: Allen Lane, 2010), 108–13, employs the standard model as the basis for a discussion of Smith's jurisprudence lectures. Christopher J. Berry, *The Idea of Commercial Society in the Scottish Enlightenment* (Edinburgh: Edinburgh University Press, 2013), chap. 1, makes extensive use of a version of the standard model, applied not just to Smith but to other Scots such as Kames and Millar, as does his *The Idea of Luxury: A Conceptual and Historical Investigation* (Cambridge: Cambridge University Press, 1994), 152–58. (In his earlier *The Social Theory of the Scottish Enlightenment* [Edinburgh: Edinburgh University Press, 1997], Berry does not employ the standard model and instead helpfully focuses attention on the four stages as 'a tool to identify certain coherences in social institutions . . . a device that highlighted the central role that property played since it was how property was organised that gave the coherence' [114]. With this I am in agreement.) Craig Smith, *Adam Smith's Political Philosophy* (London: Routledge, 2006), chap. 4, explicitly appeals to the 'four stages' in Smith as 'a general schema of social development which is applicable to all societies' (49) and exhibits all three features of what I call the standard model, as does his *Adam Smith* (Cambridge: Polity, 2020), chap. 5. Andrew S. Skinner, 'Adam Smith: An Economic Interpretation of History', in *Essays on Adam Smith*, ed. A. S. Skinner (Oxford: Clarendon, 1975), is clearly using it and appears to be an important influence upon later iterations. James R. Otteson, *Adam Smith's Marketplace of Life* (Cambridge: Cambridge University Press, 2002), 283–84, uses it. Ryan Patrick Hanley, 'The "Wisdom of the State": Adam Smith on China and Tartary', *American Political Science Review* 108, no. 2 (2014), relies on something like the standard model (e.g., 376); Rasmussen, *Problems and Promise*, employs a version of it (e.g., 92–101), and although he qualifies its use with the observation that the 'theory [is] less a rigid framework for how societies must develop than as a loose outline or heuristic device that provides a means of

The main components of the standard model are (roughly; there is inevitably variation between particular scholars) as follows:

1. Smith's four stages theory is a conjectural history.
2. Smith's four stages theory is nonetheless intended to correlate to, and help explain, all real historical periods of human political and economic development (even if this correlation is in practice imperfect).
3. The fourth, and final, stage of economic development is 'commercial society', and the four stages theory is intended by Smith to help explain

---

comparing different forms of society' (100), I show below that is not going far enough; Eric Schliesser, *Adam Smith: Systematic Philosopher and Public Thinker* (Oxford: Oxford University Press, 2017), chap. 6, offers a more nuanced picture than most but remains within the standard model; Harkin, 'Smith's Missing History', 433–34, 445, endorses it; Peter Stein, 'The Four Stage Theory of the Development of Societies', in *The Character and Influence of the Roman Civil Law* (London: Hambledon Press, 1988), 406–9, appears to be assuming something like it; Gavin Kennedy, *Adam Smith* (London: Palgrave Macmillan, 2008), 63–74, employs a version of it. Jerry Evensky, *Adam Smith's Moral Philosophy* (Cambridge: Cambridge University Press, 2005), departs from the standard model somewhat by postulating that Smith offers 'two histories', a 'conjectural history' of four stages, and 'an analysis of the course of recorded history explaining why the unnatural twists, turns, stagnations, and declines of societies do not represent violations of his general principles but, rather, reflect peculiar distortions of those principles caused by human frailty' (17). However, Evensky nonetheless claims that 'humankind has been evolving', according to Smith, through stages', which he gives in turn as hunting, shepherding, agriculture, and commerce (10). Thus, whilst Evensky departs somewhat from the standard model, for reasons that will become clearer below he remains close enough to it to share its fundamental mistakes. Knud Haakonssen, *The Science of a Legislator: The Natural Jurisprudence of David Hume and Adam Smith* (Cambridge: Cambridge University Press, 1981), chap. 7, does not employ the standard model as a whole but does read Smith as viewing history as progressing stadially, and hence as using the four stages theory to structure his historical account; I suggest in what follows that this is not an accurate way to read Smith. Likewise Donald Winch, 'Adam Smith's "Enduring Particular Result": A Political and Cosmopolitan Perspective', in *Wealth and Virtue: The Shaping of Political Economy in the Scottish Enlightenment*, ed. I. Hont and M. Ignatieff (Cambridge: Cambridge University Press, 1983), 259–60; and István Hont, 'Adam Smith's History of Law and Government as Political Theory', in *Political Judgement: Essays for John Dunn*, ed. R. Bourke and R. Geuss (Cambridge: Cambridge University Press, 2009), 149, 167, as well as Hont, 'Language of Sociability', also treat the four stages theory as though Smith believed it to (largely) correspond to actual historical human development. Hont, 'Introduction', in *Jealousy of Trade*, 106, suggests that Smith thought a four stages model of development *would* have applied to modern Europe if the German barbarians who conquered Rome 'had succeeded in obliterating all traces of Rome's economy'. I suggest below that this is unlikely: Smith did not see the four stages model as applying *anywhere*, precisely because of the incessantly disruptive effects of a permanently hostile international arena. Not even the earliest commercial republics of Attica emerged according to the model's predictions, as will be explained in what follows.

how European modernity in particular has arrived at this most advanced point of development.

Textual evidence certainly exists for attributing the above to Smith. (Hence, in part, why it has become the standard model.) Nonetheless, it is mistaken. In what follows I offer reasons for why each of the three points should be rejected. In doing so, I aim to paint a different picture, which looks something like the following:

1*. The four stages theory is most usefully thought of not as a conjectural history, but as a simplified economic model characterising the anticipated path of development for individual societies absent political disruption.

2*. Only the first two stages of Smith's model widely correlate to any observable real human histories; after that, everything depends on contingent historical developments that the model cannot, and does not attempt to, predict (meaning in turn that Smith's actual historical account is for the most part not *stadial* at all).

3*. The fourth and final stage of development given in Smith's four stages model is that of a 'commercial age', which is not the same thing as a 'commercial society', and the four stages model is *not* intended to explain how European modernity arose, or what its distinctive features are.

Once this revisionist framework is in place, we will be able to return to the question of Smith's use of the term 'commercial society' and analyse it properly. What we will see is that as a technical label 'commercial society' is, from Smith's perspective, *highly indeterminate* when it comes to drawing any relevant political or normative conclusions. As a result, any satisfactory analysis of Smith's political thought will need to be shaped in reference not to the underdescriptive label 'commercial society', but to the *specific kind* of commercial society that is under consideration. To get to that point, however, considerable work is first required, as a great deal of misunderstanding presently prevails. To begin to correct this, we start with Smith's supposed use of 'conjectural history'.

Conjectural History

To begin the process of replacing the standard model with a more accurate interpretation, it is helpful to go back to what appears to be the original source of much confusion in these matters: Dugald Stewart's valedictory 1793

'Account of the Life and Writings of Adam Smith'. As is well known, Stewart there attributed to Smith the use of 'theoretical or conjectural history', something employed when for 'want of direct evidence, we are under a necessity of supplying the place of fact by conjecture; and when we are unable to ascertain how men have actually conducted themselves upon particular occasions, of considering in what manner they are likely to have proceeded, from the principles of their nature, and the circumstances of their external situation' (*EPS* 293). Stewart claimed that conjectural history had already been employed by Hume, D'Alembert, and, most excitingly of all, Montesquieu, who was later followed by Kames and Miller in applying the tools of conjectural history specifically to 'the modes of government, and to the municipal institutions which have obtained among different nations' (*EPS* 294). According to Stewart this was also a central feature of Smith's work. As evidence he cited not only Smith's essay 'Considerations Concerning the First Formation of Languages' and his early 'History of Astronomy', but also *WN*, where 'various disquisitions are introduced which have a like object in view, particularly the theoretical delineation he has given of the natural progress of opulence in a country; and his investigation of the causes which have inverted this order in the different countries of modern Europe'. Furthermore, although Stewart could not be sure (because he was never in attendance), he nonetheless wrote that Smith's 'lectures on jurisprudence seem, from the account of them formerly given, to have abounded in such inquiries' (*EPS* 295).

Stewart's influence has, in this regard, been tremendous. Generations of subsequent commentators seem to have simply accepted his claim that Smith made extensive use of conjectural history, and proceeded to recycle such a view in turn.[7] Crucially, with the discovery of the two sets of students notes now known as *LJ* (which Stewart did not have access to) Smith's 'four stages' theory has been integrated into the established picture of him as conjectural historian, indeed becoming one of its central components. And yet, this is all wrong.

Whilst Stewart's characterization of Smith's essay on the origin of languages as 'conjectural history' is largely justified, insofar as this work consists of speculation as to how our prehistorical hominid ancestors might have developed

---

7. Ronald Meek, in his pioneering, though flawed, study of the 'four stages' theory, noted that Stewart rather overstated the case. Ronald Meek, *Social Science and the Ignoble Savage* (Cambridge: Cambridge University Press, 1976), 114. By contrast, in an essay published the previous year, Andrew Skinner endorsed Stewart's characterisation uncritically and has been mostly followed in this regard: Skinner, 'Adam Smith', 154–55.

linguistic capacities over time, as is (to a lesser degree) his so-labelling of the 'History of Astronomy', when it comes to *WN*, and what we now know of the content of *LJ*, Stewart's claim that Smith made great use of conjectural history is deeply misleading. This is because, contra Stewart, in these works Smith rarely engages in *conjectural* history at all.[8] Instead, when Smith advances historical theses or claims in the course of his political and economic analyses, the vast majority of the time he takes himself to be reporting genuine historical facts and authentically verifiable causal linkages, and this is true both in *WN* and *LJ*.[9] The evidence that this is so—whatever Stewart claimed—is plain. In both *WN* and the *Lectures*, Smith might accurately be said to make use of 'conjectural' histories only regarding those peoples he describes as being in the age of 'hunters'. When discussing 'shepherd' societies, by contrast, he appeals to the known histories of (for example) the barbarian tribes who overran Rome, the Tartar (i.e., Mongol) hordes of the eastern steppe, or the Arab tribes descended from the Mongols who later conquered the Middle East. There is nothing *conjectural* about Smith's account of these shepherding peoples: all are a matter of recorded history, and intended by Smith to be taken as such.

8. I will not here enter into the complex debate as to whether and how Smith is properly regarded as *a historian*, as opposed to simply making use of historical facts. For present purposes, this distinction need not concern us: my contention is merely that Smith used, in the vast majority of cases, what he took to be historical facts, not conjectures. Whether that makes him a historian, as opposed to a mere user of history, is immaterial for present purposes. For discussion of these issues, see especially J. G. A. Pocock, *Barbarism and Religion, Volume 2: Narratives of Civil Government* (Cambridge: Cambridge University Press, 1999), chap. 20, and 'Adam Smith and History', in *The Cambridge Companion to Adam Smith*, ed. K. Haakonssen (Cambridge: Cambridge University Press, 2006), but also Jack Russell Weinstein, *Adam Smith's Pluralism: Rationality, Education, and the Moral Sentiments* (New Haven, CT: Yale University Press, 2013), chap. 10.

9. Another way to make this point is to note that Smith *names his sources*, be they reports of the Tartars and Arabs sent back from the east or the writings of Tacitus, Cicero, Thucydides, and even Homer. Although Smith is clearly not an archive historian, he is nonetheless attempting to draw on the best facts available to him from recognised authorities. Compare, by contrast, Rousseau's *Discourse on Inequality*, which is explicitly presented as conjecture, and fits Stewart's description of 'conjectural history' far more closely than Smith's political writings, although Rousseau himself also used travellers' reports and evidence from (e.g.) Buffon when compiling his conjectures (see for example Jean-Jacques Rousseau, *The Discourses and Other Early Political Writings*, ed. V. Gourevitch [Cambridge: Cambridge University Press, 1997], 159). Here is a point where reading Smith in the shadow of Rousseau is unhelpful: they are simply not writing the same kinds of histories, and treating Smith like Rousseau will distort, rather than clarify, the Scot's thinking. More on this in chapters 3 and 4 below.

Indeed, even with those peoples said to be in the condition of hunters, Smith often points to the experiences of the Native Americans (whose societies were not 'conjectural', but known to European modernity). And furthermore, it is not even clear that describing a stage or age of society as one of 'hunters' is a primarily *historical* claim. It looks rather more like a description of economic circumstance, and the conclusions that can be legitimately inferred from that regarding social and political organization (for example, that a nation of hunters must be very small due to the limited means of securing subsistence in a given territory, and in turn their notions of government very weak and limited [e.g., *LJ(A)* iv.37; *WN* V.i.a.2–5]). By the time in the *Lectures* that Smith starts to discuss the rise of the ancient city republics of Attica, he takes himself to be discussing *real historical events*, and sticks to such facts all the way through when describing the subsequent rise, fall, and rebirth of European civilization. In other words, *virtually none* of *LJ* is taken up with conjectural history but instead makes appeal to what Smith believes to be the known facts.

Likewise, the pivotal Book III of *WN* is not a *conjectural* history of how the feudal order of Europe both came to manifest itself and then eventually came to be undone, via the 'unnatural and retrograde' progress of post-ancient civilizational development. On the contrary, it is Smith's identification of what he believes to have been the actual historical events. The same is true of Book IV's account of the real histories of European colonialism in both west and east, and the subsequent capture of domestic European state interests by homegrown mercantile elites. As we shall see below, Book V is also preoccupied with real historical case studies, not conjectures. In other words, *virtually none* of Smith's historical discussion in *WN* consists of conjecture, either. Smith may not always have had the best facts available to him, but when writing about history, politics, and economics, in the vast majority of cases he did his best to use what he took to be the facts, and to appeal to historical events that he believed had actually happened. He rarely proceeded by way of conjecture.

This, however, brings us directly to the 'four stages' theory. For is this not quite plainly a *conjectural history*, one which underpins all of Smith's historical claims, and provides the frame within which he thinks that human societies develop? And does this not, in turn, vindicate Stewart's overall characterization? The answer is no. We see this if we pay careful attention to the only two places—both of them in *LJ*, and *not* in *WN*—where Smith explicitly invokes a *four* stages theory, and do so whilst leaving aside Stewart's distorting characterization of Smith as 'conjectural' historian.

The Four Stages Theory

Smith's four stages theory is best conceived of not as a 'conjectural history' of how things ever actually happened, but as an a priori explication of how human economic development might be expected to proceed in idealized circumstances under certain artificial assumptions.[10] To put the point differently: a moment ago we considered Smith's discussions of real history, which weren't conjectural at all. By contrast the four stages theory *is* conjectural—but it is not intended by Smith to operate as any kind of *history*. Instead, the four stages schema is explicitly invoked to imagine how a single, isolated human society would develop were it to progress peacefully, in conditions of sufficient resource abundance, and without external shocks. It is thus correctly thought of not as a conjectural history, but as a simplified economic model, or if one prefers (the distinction here is not important), a thought experiment.[11] Time is certainly a factor in the model, but what is important to register here is that Smith *does not* present the four stages as possessed of any historical facticity. This, however, tends to be obscured if we speak of Smith as employing the four stages as part of a framework of conjectural history, because that label implies that he sees the four stages as how human beings might, in real history, have

---

10. This has been previously noticed by Pocock, who also emphasises that Smith's account of real European history does not follow the four stages model and is never intended to nor presented as doing so. However, Pocock remains broadly wedded to the Stewart-initiated idea that Smith employed conjectural history in an extensive manner, which I suggest is not correct. See especially Pocock, *Barbarism and Religion*, 314–17, 322–25. Smith's use of a four stages account appears to have first been noted in R. Pascal, 'Property and Society: The Scottish Contribution to the Eighteenth Century', *Modern Quarterly* 1 (1938), whilst Meek, *Social Science*, chap. 4, represents the first sustained—and pathbreaking—analysis of Smith and the four stages but is an attempt to locate Smith in a Marxist prehistory, and by claiming that Smith used the four stages theory in the historical discussion of the rise of modern Europe, it must be left behind. See also Ronald Meek, 'Smith, Turgot and the "Four Stages" Theory', *History of Political Economy* 3, no. 1 (1971). For critiques of Meek's readings, see John Salter, 'Adam Smith on Feudalism, Commerce and Slavery', *History of Political Thought* 13, no. 2 (1992); H. M. Höpfl, 'From Savage to Scotsman: Conjectural History in the Scottish Enlightenment', *Journal of British Studies* 17, no. 2 (1978); Roger Emerson, 'Conjectural History and the Scottish Philosophers', *Historical Papers* 19, no. 1 (1984); Thiery C. Pauchant, 'Adam Smith's Four-Stages Theory of Sociocultural Evolution', in *The Adam Smith Review*, vol. 9, ed. F. Forman (London: Routledge, 2017); Haakonssen, *Science of a Legislator*, 181–89; Winch, 'Adam Smith's "Enduring Particular Result"', 254–62. Berry, *Idea of Commercial Society*, chap. 2, points out that a *four* stage theory is also much less common, both in Smith and in the writings of other Scots of the period, than Meek claims.

11. István Hont, 'Adam Smith and the Political Economy of the "Unnatural and Retrograde" Order', in *Jealousy of Trade*, 373–75.

really developed in some place or another. But as we will see below, he does not think that this has in fact ever been the case.

Smith signals the imaginary, thought experimental nature of the four stages device by asking his 1762 audience 'to suppose 10 or 12 persons of different sexes settled in an uninhabited island' (*LJ(A)* i.27), a scene upgraded in the 1766 lecture to their being 'shipwrecked on a desart island' (*LJ(B)* 149). This is thus not an account of anything that is supposed to have ever actually happened, conjecturally or otherwise, and Smith neither presents nor intends it as such. Nonetheless, he goes on to develop the thought experiment. Why? For two reasons. First—and most immediately in the presentation of the 1762–63 lecture—because doing so allows him to draw conclusions about various forms of property rights and acquisition, with which the initial discussion of man's rights 'as an individual' are concerned in the *Lectures*, something which is initially forwarded by considering how property regimes would differ given different levels of economic development (*LJ(A)* i.33–63).[12] But second, because the simplified modelling device of the four stages would in due course also allow Smith to identify why actual historical developments took markedly *different* turns from what might be expected by pure economic theory.[13] The real use of the four stages in Smith's more developed analysis is thus not that it elucidates how history *does* actually happen, but precisely that it helps us to understand why and how history so often *diverges* from what might be expected were human development to follow a more straightforward, economically logical (or in Smith's nomenclature, more 'natural') path than is the case in the real world. As a result, Smith's core position, as we shall see in more detail below, is that most of human history is *not* stadial at all, but the product of contingent events and unexpected consequences, in particular under the

12. It is worth noting however that Smith in fact discusses in any detail only hunter and shepherd societies, with the occasional allusion to the innovation of agriculture, and does *not* discuss the fourth 'commercial' age in these sections after having first introduced it. The likely reasons for this will become clearer below. See also Meek, *Social Science*, 119–22. For a discussion of Smith on property rights and their relation to the four stages account (although one which, in my view mistakenly, reads Smith as seeing the four stages as an explanation of real historical progress), see Paul Bowles, 'The Origin of Property and the Development of Scottish Historical Science', *Journal of the History of Ideas* 46, no. 2 (1985): 202–8.

13. Evensky comes close to seeing this, but his commitment to the standard view of the four stages account as a conjectural history leads him to claim—erroneously, in my view—that Smith attempts to fit the facts of real history into the stadial scheme predicated by the four stages. This, I contend, is the *opposite* of what Smith was doing: Evensky, *Smith's Moral Philosophy*, 15–19.

pressure of external military aggression.[14] Having the stadial picture in hand, however, first allowed Smith to work out why what was predicted by the logic of economic theory did not, in fact, happen in practice, as well as clarifying the basic aspects of property rights and acquisition, insofar as these must necessarily supervene upon a given level of development.

We can see all of this better by considering the basic aspects of Smith's account of the 'four stages' theory as supplied in the 1762–63 set of lecture notes. At first, the desert island inhabitants are imagined to survive by hunting, fishing, and gathering fruits: this is the 'age of hunters'. But it is a precarious existence, and over time the people learn to trap and tame wild animals, which gives rise to the 'age of shepherds'. In turn, however, 'when a society becomes numerous they would find a difficulty in supporting themselves by herds and flocks. Then they would naturally turn themselves to the cultivation of land and the raising of such plants and trees as produced nourishment fit for them. . . . And by this means they would gradually advance in to the age of agriculture'. Finally:

> As society was farther improved, the severall arts, which at first would be exercised by each individual as far as was necessary for his welfare, would be seperated; some persons would cultivate one and others others, as they severally inclined. They would exchange with one an other what they produced more than was necessary for their support, and get in exchange for them the commodities they stood in need of and did not produce themselves. This exchange of commodities extends in time not only betwixt the individualls of the same society but betwixt those of different nations. . . . Thus at last the age of commerce arises. (*LJ(A)* i.27–32)

We can make sense what Smith is doing in these passages by retrospectively employing his own terminology from Book III of *WN* (which is likely to be no accident: working through the implications of the four stages model helped Smith to arrive at his later analysis). In chapter 1 of Book III, when setting up

---

14. Realising that Smith did *not* think that real history progressed stadially means that we can abandon in turn the view of him as committed to a picture of inevitable developmental progress. This means that we can also abandon, as a pseudo-problem, the idea that Smith was simultaneously committed to a macro-narrative of progress that was incompatible with an admiration for primitive forms of society. Such a tension is argued for by Harkin, who, taking over a hint from Pocock, describes Smith as being incoherently a 'Rousseauvian elegist of a lost social harmony' who was incoherently wedded simultaneously to a view of stadial developmental economic progress (Harkin, 'Smith's Missing History', 437); similarly Ahmed, *Stillbirth of Capital*, chap. 4.

his analysis of how the 'unnatural and retrograde' modern European order came to be established, Smith makes a distinction between the 'natural course of things', and that affected by 'human institutions' (*WN* III.i.4).[15] In Book III Smith draws upon this distinction to highlight how Europe *should* have developed, were it to have followed what Smith terms a 'natural' (i.e., economically logical) and hence non-retrograde path, versus how it did in fact develop. What should have happened (at least according to pure economic theory) is for the countryside to have preceded the towns in order of development, with manufactures emerging only later, and international trade appearing last of all.[16] But of course what actually happened was that the 'unnatural' and economically deformed regime of feudalism came to settle across Europe after the fall of Rome, characterized by an imbalance of development between the town and countryside, and exacerbated by the injection of luxury goods via international trade with more economically advanced manufacturing bases in the city-states of southern Europe.[17] This was all completely out of line with what economic logic predicted should have occurred. But that is, nonetheless, what happened. What we can see in turn however is that Smith in the 1760s lectures was already employing, albeit implicitly, his later distinction between the 'natural course of things' and 'human institutions'. What the 'four stages' theory seeks to show is how human societies would have developed, according to the 'natural' progress of pure economic relations, had they not been subjected to the shock of 'human institutions'. In turn, Smith is able to consider how property rights emerge and change, relative to differing levels of development. But in actual historical reality—and as Smith knew full well, and made

15. On this see also Evensky, *Smith's Moral Philosophy*, 167–68, although I disagree with Evensky on Smith's 'moving' from 'conjectural' to 'narrative' history in these passages. It is *all* 'narrative'. For detailed discussion of Smith's idea of 'natural' development and the backwards emergence of modern Europe, see Hont, 'Adam Smith and the Political Economy', esp. 356–75. Hont notes that Smith 'well understood that commerce appeared on the European agenda before it was appropriate in terms of a purely "natural" model of economic stages' (373), but he does not appear to realise that this indicates that Smith therefore cannot have been a theorist of four stages when it comes to the real history of human development, remaining (inconsistently) wedded to that view elsewhere (see references above). See also Ahmed, *Stillbirth of Capital*, 106–8, 110–13; Giovanni Arrighi, *Adam Smith in Beijing: Lineages of the Twenty-First Century* (London: Verso, 2007), chap. 2.

16. Note that Smith's analysis here follows exactly what the four stages model in the *Lectures* predicts. More on this below.

17. Hont, 'Smith's History', 162–67; Evensky, *Smith's Moral Philosophy*, chap. 7.

central to his wider analysis—things rarely, if ever, went the way that 'natural' economic development predicted. In particular, this was because one 'human institution' above all returned again and again to play havoc with economic development: international war.[18]

It is crucial to Smith's 'four stages' model that it begins with shipwrecked survivors on an uninhabited desert island. International relations are thus automatically removed from the picture: the nascent society gets on with improving its own lot without fear of external aggression. But as Smith knew, and highlighted repeatedly in both the *Lectures* and *WN*, in reality conflict was a staple of relations between different communities throughout human history. This was most especially true when it came to real-world shepherding peoples, most dramatically the 'Tartar' nations whom Smith claimed were responsible for 'more of the great revolutions in the world . . . than any other nation' (*LJ(A)* iv.53). Indeed, 'Nothing . . . can be more dreadful than a Tartar invasion has frequently been in Asia. The judgment of Thucydides, that both Europe and Asia could not resist the Scythians united, has been verified by the experience of all ages' (*WN* V.i.a.6). Whereas the shepherds of Smith's desert island would presumably be only minimally nomadic (because confined to an island) and did not come into contact with other groups (because the island was previously uninhabited), in the history of real-world Eurasia the shepherd peoples of the eastern steppe had spread out across vast territories so as to graze their large flocks, and to seek plunder. In the process they came into direct military competition with rival groups. War was the inevitable result, and over time the tribes that were conquered became assimilated by the victors, meaning shepherd clans rapidly grew to enormous sizes. According to Smith this is how Tamerlane and Genghis Kahn were able to amass bodies of over a million men, and in turn overrun the whole of Asia and encroach upon Europe, a model later followed by Omer, who, after the Arab tribes had been united by Mahomet on the same lines as the Mongol hordes, 'over ran the neighbouring countries, who could not resist their immense power' (*LJ(A)* iv.40).

18. Luban has noted that 'while the four stages theory may account for the emergence of trading slave societies such as Athens and Carthage, it is not clear that it can explain the emergence of fully fledged commercial society at all'. Indeed, but Smith was perfectly aware of this, hence why he expected the four stages model to do no such thing. We should, furthermore, take issue with Luban's locution of 'fully fledged' commercial society, with its teleological assumption that only modern European commercial society is the real deal. This, as we shall see below, is not right (Luban, 'Smith on Vanity', 293).

In the actual historical experiences of the vast majority of Eurasian peoples prior to the rise of the Mediterranean republics, most populations simply did not have the luxury of being left alone long enough to develop the sedentary agriculture of the third 'age', as they would on the imaginary desert island. Instead they either became nomadic shepherds and stayed that way, or were destroyed by rival shepherding clans.[19] The result was a widespread development trap. Smith made this point explicitly:

> Among neighbouring nations in a barbarous state there are perpetual wars, one continualy invading and plundering the other, and tho' private property be secured from the violence of neighbours, it is in danger from hostile invasions. In this manner it is next to impossible that any accumulation of stock can be made. It is observable that among savage nations there are always more violent convulsions than among those farther advanced in refinement. Among the Tartars and Arabs, great bands of barbarians are always roaming from one place to another in quest of plunder, and they pillage every country as they go along. Thus large tracts of country are often laid waste and all the effects carried away: Germany too was in the same condition about the fall of the Roman Empire. Nothing can be more an obstacle to the progress of opulence. (*LJ(B)* 288)

For much of Eurasian history, most peoples were stuck in the shepherd age because the shepherd age was one of near-constant international conquest periodically resetting the progress of civilization. Indeed, even when Europe first managed to get out of a shepherd-dominated international system through the fortuitous, geographically unique, and unexpected rise of the ancient Mediterranean republics, the progress of civilization was nonetheless dramatically reset one final time, as the last round of barbarian hordes overthrew the Roman Empire and imposed a millennium of backwardness in their wake.

We can now, however, see how Smith's 'four stages' model of economic development properly connects up with, but also gives way to, his account of real history. In real history, human societies initially more or less conformed to what would be predicted by economic theory: hunter societies came first, but then gave way to shepherding ones. Yet because shepherding peoples engaged so enthusiastically in the 'human institution' of war, and at which they

---

19. America was a different case: relative natural abundance and low population densities meant that shepherding technology never got going. Below I consider the case of China, which is an evident problem for Smith's historical account in the *Lectures*.

proved particularly adept, for thousands of years most of Eurasia remained stuck at this level of development. In order to move things forward particular accidents of history had needed to occur. The most significant of these was the decision by those shepherding peoples who settled in the naturally well-defended lands of Attica and collected their populations in walled cities as protection from seaborne raiders (*LJ(A)* iv.55–74; *LJ(B)* 30–36). This was the kernel of future European civilization, but as we shall see below, it was a process that took place entirely outside the predictions of the four stages model. For Smith, real human history simply did not follow the predictions of the four stages account—a fact that turns out to be absolutely central to his wider analysis, as we shall see momentarily.

When he first introduced the 'four stages' account into his 1762 lecture, Smith was happy to appeal to facts about the 'Tartars and Arabians' in illustrating his case. The historical facts that Smith possessed about those shepherding societies remained usefully illustrative precisely because the second-stage type societies of the theory could more or less be observed in historical practice. Similarly, when Smith dismissed the limited use of some agriculture by Native American tribes as not constituting progression to the third 'stage', this is consistent with his emphasis on the fact that a third agricultural stage as predicted by the model would consist in a level of development that made nomadic pasturage, and not just hunter-gathering, entirely redundant—something which had not come to pass (or so Smith thought) in North America prior to European colonial settlement (itself, it is worth noting, an immensely important geopolitical historical event outside the remit of the simple four stages model). In other words, these appeals to historical and contemporary examples are indications not that the four stages account is intended as a primarily historical picture, conjectural or otherwise, but rather that Smith is using relevant facts to illustrate his model of logical economic development. This is perfectly appropriate, not least given that he thinks that the first two stages of his model do indeed roughly approximate real-world development. But they do not make the four stages model any kind of history, conjectural or otherwise. Likewise, Smith illustrates the 'age of commerce' by pointing his audience towards obvious contemporary examples ('Thus we send to France our cloths, iron work, and other trinkets and get in exchange their wines. To Spain and Portugall we send our superfluous corn and bring from thence the Spanish and Portuguese wines' [*LJ(A)* i.31–32]). But again, using real-world examples to illustrate the model, and to help make its logic perspicuous, is not the same thing as claiming that model *is* the real world.

With this in mind, it is a striking fact about both sets of notes composing *LJ* that the only times that Smith makes explicit use of a *four* stages account come at the outset of his discussion of the origins of property, in the context of the rights of ownership that men have when considered as individuals, separate from the discussions of man considered as part of a family or society (*LJ(A)* i.27–35; *LJ(B)* 149–50). When it comes to the discussion of the actual historical development of different property orders, and hence to actual political regimes and forms of government, Smith only ever refers to societies from the *first two* stages, that is, hunters and shepherds. He never, however, discusses any of the subsequent regime forms as being in either 'agricultural' or 'commercial' stages, and instead analyses them consistently not in terms of their prevailing modes of economic subsistence, but with regard to their forms of government (*LJ(A)* iv.1–v.149; *LJ(B)* 18–99). To emphasize: the only times at which Smith invokes the four stages account are in sections of the lectures that are dealing not with the historical, but only with the juridical, nature of property ownership. (This makes sense, insofar as it is a general truth for Smith that conventions governing property rights necessarily supervene on given levels of economic development.) As soon as Smith moves into making *historical* claims, by contrast, the 'four stages' account is conspicuously absent, and we hear only of hunters and shepherds, before contingent and specific historical developments outside of the four stages model are brought into the analysis. And again, this makes sense. The 'four stages' is not primarily a historical account, but a model about anticipated economic development under idealized assumptions, and so Smith does not make use of it when advancing historical claims.[20]

WN, which constitutes Smith's more advanced and polished thoughts, presents a different case. After all, does Smith not clearly employ a four stages

---

20. For example, when Smith in the *Lectures* discusses the severity of punishment for different crimes in different epochs, he does not invoke the four stages theory—as might be expected on the standard interpretation—but speaks merely of 'the first stages of society, when government is very weak' contrasted with later points at which a society 'gathers greater strength', charting how collectively organised punishment starts out as practically nonexistent in the earliest periods, becomes very repressive and severe when government proper first emerges, and then becomes more restrained and moderate as increasingly sophisticated and advanced societies evolve. Smith clearly means these to be historical claims about the facts of organised punishment, and how they are dependent upon overall social and economic development—but in doing so he makes no use of the four stages theory to make the case. This is because when it comes to real history the four stages was simply inadequate to model reality, so Smith didn't use it (see *LJ(A)* ii.152–54).

model at the outset of Book V when discussing the duties of the sovereign with regards to both defence and the administration of justice? As we shall see below the answer is again no—but this will be easier to appreciate once we have examined the material from the *Lectures* in more detail. Before doing so, however, it is worth remarking that the lecture notes from 1762–63 and 1766 are likely to be marked by at least two things. First, they are records of lectures given to students, so may contain attempts at simplification of material to attempt to make some points more vivid to the audience. Imagining society as passing through distinct stages, so as to make supervening points about changing notions of property rights, has obvious advantages as a pedagogical tool, and this may help explain Smith's use of the four stages model at those specific points in his lecture course concerned with how property is acquired and respected. Second, and probably more importantly, Smith in the 1760s was still working out his own thoughts for himself. As anybody who has given a lecture course knows, trying out one's ideas on a live audience is a good way to see whether they can be made to work. Yet in time, one may decide that something that initially functioned as a helpful heuristic—a simplified model of economic development, for example—cannot do what is required when it comes to the hard work of putting fully developed ideas down on the page. Accordingly, in one's more well-developed writings—in an extended monograph treatment, for example— one might drop the earlier idea, or modify it in important ways. Below I will suggest that something like this happened with Smith's use of the four stages theory: imagining a smooth stadial economic development was a useful heuristic when Smith was developing his ideas, some of which would make it into *WN*, but many of which were (presumably) burned in the manuscript on law and government that Smith had destroyed shortly before his death, precisely because he did not believe them to be adequately worked out. At any rate, by the time he came to publish his thoughts on political economy in 1776, the four stages account did not retain a functional position in his magnum opus. What did remain was a residual appeal to the uses of a simplifying economic model, but notably Smith in 1776 referred to only *three* 'periods' or 'states' of development, and in doing so thereby made use of a three stages model which was a commonplace during the time he was writing, and would have been familiar to his readers as such.[21] We shall see the reasons for and significance of this in

21. Berry, *Idea of Commercial Society*, 38–40; Stein, 'Four Stage Theory', 400; Hont, 'Language of Sociability', 160, 179; Hont, 'Adam Smith and the Political Economy', 364–70; Meek, *Social Science*, 227–28.

due course. But first, we must consider in more detail the actual historical account that Smith supplied in the *Lectures*.

The Real History of Europe

If we turn to Smith's discussion of the rise of European economic development, and his account of the original breaking out of the shepherd-dominated international system that first took place in ancient Attica, we find that he does *not* think that this epochal moment in the development of human civilization followed the stadial model of the four stages theory. For a start, the focus of discussion in these sections of *LJ* is not on stages of economic development at all, but on forms of government, and the way that different legal and political regimes arose in different socioeconomic circumstances. Smith, for sure, begins his analysis with hunters and shepherds, and argues in turn that they are notable from the perspective of considering different forms of government because they are both fundamentally democratic (*LJ(A)* iv.1–13; *LJ(B)* 18–30).[22] And certainly, Smith makes this claim in conjunction with his wider assessment of how establishing property regimes, and the need to provide protection for the rich from the depredations of the poor, as well as the provision of judicial arbitration to settle disputes, means that as hunters have only limited use for and understanding of government, such an innovation really gets going only with shepherding peoples (*LJ(A)* iv.22). In this, he makes good on his general principle, originally stated when introducing the simplifying four stages model, that regarding property rights the 'regulations . . . concerning them must vary considerably according to the state or age society is in at that time' (*LJ(A)* i.27). Yet as we have already noted this is not evidence that Smith is, at this point, using the four stages model, because he takes it that the real histories of hunter and shepherd peoples roughly converge with the first two stages of the model. In these sections, Smith is just appealing to what he takes the real histories—and forms of government—of these sorts of peoples to be.

Yet we must again recall that Smith's main objective in these historical sections of *LJ* was to explain the rise of the ancient Mediterranean city-states, and thus the origin of European civilization with regards to the progress of law and government, as the necessary background to understanding how modern

22. For discussions of this notable feature of Smith's thought, see Richard Bourke, 'Enlightenment, Revolution and Democracy', *Constellations* 15, no. 1 (2008); Sagar, *Opinion of Mankind*, chap. 5.

Europe arose, albeit via the intermediary epochs of alodialism and feudalism. This meant, in particular, explaining 'in what manner those governments which were originally Tartarian ones or under chiefs in the same manner as the Tartars, came from thence to settle in towns and become republican' (*LJ(A)* iv.60). Smith's analysis in these sections of the *Lectures* is trained on how different forms of government—in particular republican democracies and aristocracies, and later monarchies, as well as the crucial innovation of legislative assemblies that were unknown to shepherd societies—first arose in the ancient world, before tracing their legacies down to the European present. Economic development certainly underpins the analysis, but these sections of the *Lectures* are primarily about understanding and tracing historical change in forms of government. As a result, the four stages theory makes no appearance, because it is not a historically useful heuristic at this point in Smith's analysis.

Particularly noteworthy in this regard, and indeed proof of the above, are the details of how Smith explains the rise of the Attican city-states, and the prosperity and freedom that they in turn gave rise to, in the ancient world. For the story Smith tells turns out, upon close inspection, to be at odds with what is predicted by the simplifications of the four stages theory, again indicating that Smith is not using the latter at this point in his analysis, and indeed is not offering any kind of stadial history at all. On Smith's account, the rise of the ancient city-states was the unexpected outcome of nomadic warrior shepherd peoples coming to settle permanently in the relatively fertile lands of Greece.[23] They did so in part because Attica was naturally well defended by mountainous terrain on the one hand and the sea on the other (both difficult to cross for horse-mounted shepherd aggressors from the eastern steppe). Although they for a time practiced the old ways of roving and pillaging—Smith cites the Trojan Wars and the information that can be gleaned from Homer as evidence—relative geographic security inclined these populations towards more sedentary forms of subsistence, taking advantage of the comparable fertility of Attica vis-à-vis the eastern steppe and Arabian deserts. Danger still came from the sea, however, in the form of pirate raids, and the response was to collect populations in walled cities. The result in turn was that mighty city-states arose. They did so because the rapid

23. On this see also Haakonssen, *Science of a Legislator*, 159–61; Hont, 'Smith's History', 157–60.

and intense concentration of populations in conditions of relative military security and an economically favourable environment led to rapid advancement. Agriculture certainly played an important role in this development, for as Smith says, 'The soil must be improveable, otherwise there can be nothing from whence they might draw that which they should work up and improve' (*LJ(A)* iv.61). But Smith does not present the rise of Hellenistic city-states as a stadial transition through the four stages model. On the contrary, he depicts the Attican economic (and by the same lights, political) revolution as happening not through the 'logical' development of agriculture, then internal commerce, then external trading, as predicted by the four stages model, but as occurring practically all of a piece:

> We may easily conceive that a people of this sort, settled in a country where they lived in pretty great ease and security and in a soil capable of yielding them good returns for cultivation, *would not only improve the earth but also make considerable advances in the severall arts and sciences and manufactures, providing they had an opportunity of exporting their sumptuous produce and fruits of their labour.* Both these circumstances are absolutely necessary to bring about this improvement in the arts of life amongst a people in this state. (*LJ(A)* iv.60–61, emphasis added)

As Smith explains, although a fertile territory 'must be the foundation of their labour and industry', nonetheless,

> it is no less necessary that they should have an easy method of transporting their sumptuous produce into foreign countries and neighbouring states. When they have an opportunity of this, then they will exert their utmost industry in their severall businesses; but if their be no such opportunity of commerce, and consequently no opportunity of increasing their wealth by industry in any considerable degree, there is little likelyhood that they should ever cultivate arts to any great degree, or produce more sumptuous produce than will be consumed within the country itself; and this will never be wrought up to such perfection as when there are greater spurs to industry. (*LJ(A)* iv.61–62)

This marked a crucial difference with the shepherd peoples who remained outside Attica. For those more easterly shepherds not only subsisted in hostile, infertile, environments, but 'neither have they any opportunity for commerce' (*LJ(A)* iv.62). It was the lack of *both* agriculture *and* commerce *simultaneously* that kept the 'Tartars' and 'Arabians' stuck in their shepherd conditions, whilst the cradle of European civilization turned out to be Greece.[24]

When it came to real-world economic and political history, on Smith's account the ancient republics that arose out of the wider international shepherd system did so by a series of events contingent on particular historical pressures, not predictable via any a priori model, and not in the neat stadial sequence imagined in the four stages account. Of particular importance to the actual historical process was the building of walled cities for defence, in a naturally hard to attack and fertile peninsula, next to easily navigable waterways, that allowed almost immediate trade with neighbouring groups, all of which was undertaken in the context of a violent and insecure international arena. The result is that there was not in practice—as the four stages model predicted in theory—a logical progression through discrete stages. On the contrary, the Ancient republics accelerated rapidly to engaging in activities that the four stages model predicted as being part only of the age of commerce whilst simultaneously developing the supposedly third stage practices of agriculture. In other words, although the process was less dramatic the first time around, the original progress of ancient European economic and political development was, like the later emergence of modern post-feudal Europe, unnatural and retrograde. The most developed of the ancient Attican republics—in particular Athens—which Smith analysed in terms of innovations in forms of government, were effectively in what the four stages model labelled the 'age of commerce' (and as we shall see below, they also qualified on Smith's analysis as commercial *societies*). But they did not get there in the manner predicted by the four stages model. Hence why Smith never invoked that model when explaining the actual historical rise of ancient Greek societies and the political regimes that emerged out of them.

Likewise, Smith in the *Lectures* moves abruptly to talking about the forms of rule employed in Rome, and the various revolutions that occurred there and their implications for later European history. But whilst Rome was in what the four stages model labelled the 'age of commerce', Smith never presented his discussion of Rome in terms of a stadial economic history, instead taking over Machiavelli's distinction between 'defensive' and 'conquering' republics, and

---

24. Hont presents Smith's discussion accurately in terms of the ancient republics becoming 'sophisticated agricultural and commercial states', but does not seem to notice that this is in fact incompatible with Smith's also being an adherent of a four stages model in historical reality: Hont, 'Smith's History', 156. See also Hont, 'Adam Smith and the Political Economy', 365–66.

offering Rome as a paradigmatic case of the latter $(LJ(A)$ iv.87–91).[25] And this makes perfect sense: the complex and varying history of what became the most formidable conquering republic on the planet could not plausibly be understood along the simplistic lines of the desert-island model, and so to explain that history Smith used a different analytic frame entirely.

It should now be evident that Smith did not think that real history for the most part conformed to the stadial scheme of the four stages model. This is especially true of the era of feudalism, which is on Smith's account a vitally important period in the development of modern European politics, being the gateway through which modern liberty was forced to pass. We must therefore reject the suggestion of Christopher J. Berry that feudalism is a 'third stage' agricultural society on Smith's view, as delineated by the four stages account, and which sequentially predates the 'fourth stage' of modern European commercial society.[26] That this is not so should to a large extent already be clear. Feudalism was on Smith's account a result of the destruction of the Roman Empire, which occurred when the remaining northern barbarian shepherd peoples were drawn to attack the ancient centres of opulence governed by Rome, but whose populations had been made militarily weak by the promulgation of

25. Niccolò Machiavelli, *Discourses on Livy*, ed. H. C. Mansfield and N. Tarcov (Chicago: University of Chicago Press, 1996), bk. II, chaps. 1–4. For discussion in relation to Smith, see J. G. A. Pocock, *Barbarism and Religion, Volume 3: The First Decline and Fall* (Cambridge: Cambridge University Press, 2003), 394–95; Hont 'Smith's History', 158–60.

26. Berry, *Idea of Commercial Society*, 32, 39. Berry discusses Smith's positions simultaneously and as of a piece with those of Kames and Millar, which is problematic as it prevents clear identification of where these thinkers differ. Kames and Millar may well have described feudalism as the third stage in a four stages model—but Smith most certainly did not. Skinner, 'Adam Smith', 158–60, also characterizes feudalism as a third-stage, agricultural, society on Smith's view. A better reading is Hont's, who writes, 'After the Gothic shepherds overran Europe, they settled in the ex-provinces of the Roman Empire, in large territorial units that later became the medieval kingdoms. The Germans represented the politics of shepherds. Once they settled down in Europe, they created feudalism, a mongrel kind of polity that consisted of the superimposition of shepherd military government over a nascent agricultural stage, based on the permanent settlement of the population within well-delineated tribal or national borders': Hont, 'Smith's History', 162. Whether or not it is quite right to describe feudalism as a 'nascent' agricultural society (I would argue that it is instead an extremely badly organised, economically backwards, and perversely governed form of *commercial* society, insofar as many individuals therein still live primarily from exchange), Hont's characterisation nonetheless helps make the correct point that whatever feudalism is, it simply does not fit into the four stages model. Salter, 'Adam Smith on Feudalism', 228, offers a similar critique of Skinner's identifying of feudalism with agrarianism, correctly noting that this is 'a confusion of the categories employed by Smith'.

luxury.[27] Indeed, it is worth noting that on Smith's account at this point of history the Germanic shepherding peoples themselves employed some level of agriculture, and had stable notions of property rights, indicating that they were not neatly classifiable in terms of the 'four stages' scheme, either (*LJ(A)* iv.114). In any case, emerging after a period of what Smith calls 'allodial' rule, feudalism was an economic and political monstrosity, unique to the peculiar conditions of post-Roman Europe (*LJ(A)* iv.115–51; *LJ(B)* 52–57). Certainly, a large agricultural base could be expected to exist in such societies: all populations need to eat, and nomadic shepherding was not a viable option by this point of European development.[28] But as Book III of *WN* explains, feudal society was centrally characterized by unique post-Roman contingencies, including especially the practice of primogeniture, the power of the barons, the advanced state of manufacturing trades in cities, and the existence of international trade with centres of southern European luxury that were several centuries ahead of the neighbouring feudal regimes in terms of economic development.[29] In no meaningful way could such a complex, and deeply historically specific, form of social, economic, and political organization be approximated to the desert-island simplification of the 'age of agriculture'. Feudalism is simply outside of the remit of the four stages model. In Smith's analysis, by the time we reach post-Roman Europe the four stages model lacks any meaningful explanatory power, and real historical facts are required instead. Furthermore, such real history will not turn out to be *stadial*, because 'human institutions' have by this point long upset any neat development that might be predicted by a stadial (let alone merely economic) account, in myriad and complex ways.

Book V of *The Wealth of Nations*

All that has been said so far may appear to be belied, however, by the existence of Book V of *WN*. Does Smith not there make use of the four stages theory when discussing the origins of the 'duties' of government?[30] Yet, once again, if we look carefully we see that the answer is no.

---

27. For detailed accounts, see Hont, 'Smith's History'; Sagar, *Opinion of Mankind*, chap. 5.

28. See Hont, 'Adam Smith and the Political Economy', 364–65, on agriculture as the necessary basis of commercial relations and hence of any 'fourth-stage' society as qualitatively different from hunting, shepherding, or husbanding, insofar as commerce is a 'secondary activity helping to improve the quality of human existence'.

29. Hont, 'Smith's History', 162–63.

30. That Smith uses the four stages theory in *WN* is a commonplace in the literature: see for example Meek, *Social Science*, 99; Winch, 'Adam Smith's "Enduring Particular Result"', 260;

It is highly significant that the opening discussion of Book V is centred on war, and the manner in which different forms of human community can defend themselves from external aggression. Given that Smith recognized international relations to be a key determinant of economic development, it made sense that the first duty of the sovereign to be analysed was the paramount one of providing military security. Yet Smith writes in Book V of only *three* 'different states of society, in the different periods of improvement': hunters, shepherds, and 'nations of husbandmen' (*WN* V.i.a.1; V.i.a.6). He does *not*, that is, write of a fourth, 'commercial', state when describing more economically developed conditions, but instead uses nonspecific terms such as 'a more advanced state of society' (*WN* V.i.a.80), or simply a 'civilized society' (*WN* V.i.a.11). What to make of this?

The best way to read Smith here is to see that he is not invoking a *four stages* model at all, whilst nonetheless making use of the benefits of a simplified economic framework so as to facilitate the primary aim of these sections of the book, namely explaining how different levels of economic development condition the provision of defence and justice. To do so, however, Smith employed not the experimental four stages model he had tried out on his audience in the *Lectures*, but a standard three stages model that was already widely familiar to readers of his time. Crucially, however, Smith once again did so with only limited application, and did not extend the simple model to any attempt at explaining the developments of real military and judicial history beyond relatively basic settings. To see this, consider the following.

According to Smith in *WN*, the first 'state' of society, that of hunters illustrated by the North American tribes, is not militarily formidable due to incapacity of numbers (no more than two or three hundred men could take the field at any one time) and inability to maintain subsistence for extended periods. By contrast, shepherd nations like the Tartars, Scythians, and Arabs are able to amass armies of many thousands, and as roving horseback nomads who rely on pastoral flocks, for most of history they posed enormous military threats to 'civilized' nations. Here Smith made the point, familiar from *LJ*, that shepherding nations were extremely dangerous to their neighbours: 'The inhabitants of the extensive, but defenceless plains of Scythia or Tartary, have been frequently united under the dominion of the chief of some conquering horde or clan; and the havock and devastation of Asia have always signalized

---

Bowles, 'Origin of Property', 207; Hont, 'Introduction', 101–2. Berry, *Idea of Commercial Society*, 42, 47, notes that Smith does not explicitly employ the four stages account in *WN* but implies that Smith is nonetheless drawing on it.

their union' (*WN* V.i.a.5). Unlike in the *Lectures*, however, Smith did in Book V go on to postulate a third agricultural stage as emerging more or less directly out of the second, shepherding, stage in real history. This was 'a yet more advanced state of society; among those nations of husbandmen who have little foreign commerce and no other manufactures, but those coarse and household ones which almost every private family prepares for its own use'. Amongst such a people, 'every man, in the same manner, either is a warrior, or easily becomes such', and their military capacities accordingly did not differ all that much from the shepherding peoples, at least at first (*WN* VI.a.6). Smith gave some examples of such 'husbanding' peoples (although they were notably thin on the ground in recorded history): the early Greeks before the Peloponnesian Wars, the pre-Republican Romans, and those land-tilling individuals forced to fight for baronial lords in the early periods of feudalism (*WN* VI.a.7).

What is going on here? Smith saw that the basic logic of a three stages model, one already familiar to his readership because it was widely used by other writers in the period, could help make perspicuous certain facts about the sovereign's ability to provide defence. In primitive hunter societies this duty was extremely limited, and also not particularly necessary, as war was a short-lived and relatively infrequent affair. By contrast, in shepherding and early 'husbanding' societies, the scope for military exploits—and hence the need for organized military defence—was much more pronounced, and required a greater level of sovereign involvement. Sedentary communities, in particular, were faced with the problem that men who went out to war could not work the fields, and this required centralized coordination by a governmental agent to ensure adequate balance between defence and subsistence:

> Agriculture, even in its rudest and lowest state, supposes a settlement; some sort of fixed habitation which cannot be abandoned without great loss. When a nation of mere husbandmen, therefore, goes to war, the whole people cannot take the field together. The old men, the women and children, at least, must remain at home to take care of the habitation. All the men of the military age, however, may take the field, and, in small nations of this kind, have frequently done so. In every nation the men of the military age are supposed to amount to about a fourth or fifth part of the whole body of the people. If the campaign too should begin after seed-time, and end before harvest, both the husbandman and his principal labourers can be spared from the farm without much loss. He trusts that the work which must be done in the mean time can be well enough executed by the

old men, the women and the children. He is not unwilling, therefore, to serve without pay during a short campaign, and it frequently costs the sovereign or commonwealth as little to maintain him in the field as to prepare him for it. (*WN* V.i.a.7)

A standard three stages model was thus perfectly adequate for explaining the more important supervening point that Smith was making in these passages: that matters of defence are conditioned by the subsistence methods prevalent in any form of human community. To make this apparent to his audience Smith did what he had done in the 1760s lectures and illustrated the basic economic model he was employing by appealing to relevant real-world examples, drawn mostly from the shepherd nations of the Tartars and Arabs, and the early Greeks and Romans.

However, Smith understood perfectly well that such a basic economic model was inadequate for making sense of the complexities of the real-world military developments that had actually taken place in Eurasia during, and then after, the long history of shepherd-dominated international affairs. Avoiding any language denoting a fourth 'state' of development, let alone one labelled 'commercial', Smith in Book V writes instead that 'in a more advanced state of society, two different causes contribute to render it altogether impossible that they, who take the field, should maintain themselves at their own expence. Those two causes are, the progress of manufactures, and the improvement in the art of war' (*WN* V.i.a.8). Smith accordingly went on to note the difficulties faced by having to deploy troops who needed to be maintained by the wider population, in terms of both soldier pay, or compensation for lost earnings, as well as ensuring the maintenance of wider economic functioning for the community as a whole.[31] Over time, Smith claimed, this led to the development of militias, and crucially, to centralized tax bases in the post-shepherding societies. For a long time, however, barbarian shepherd peoples represented a huge danger to these more 'civilized' nations, because the latter's wealth was a temptation to invasion, and as a direct result of their sedentary habitations and more specialized economic bases, they could put out only limited numbers of nonspecialist militia troops in response to attack, and who typically proved no match for battle-hardened nomadic aggressors. This explained the long and bloody history of barbarian invasions from shepherding peoples that accounted for the many revolutions in world politics that

---

31. Evensky, *Smith's Moral Philosophy*, 215–19.

punctuated Eurasian history, and periodically reset the progress of civilization (*WN* VI.a.15). Yet Smith insisted that the cycle had now been broken: the division of labour eventually led to the creation of specialist standing armies that, when possessed of the crucial innovation of militarized gunpowder, decisively turned the tables on the shepherding peoples.[32] These innovations finally allowed 'civilized' nations to break out of the pattern of shepherd-led international destruction that had existed for millennia, and hence led to the rise of barbarian-free European modernity (*WN* V.i.a.16–44).

None of this, however, could be explained through a stages model, because such a simplified rendering of human economic development could not explain (for example) the rise of manufactures, domestic and international trade, evolving tax bases, the division of labour, international war, the eventual transformation of militias into standing armies (and in some cases, like Rome, the degeneration back into ineffectual militias and reliance on mercenaries), the comparative abilities of shepherd militias versus those of advanced city-states, and the crucial incorporation of gunpowder by European militaries that Smith reminded his audience together characterized the development of real history, and hence the evolving 'duties of the sovereign'. By the same token, the *four* stages model of *LJ* could not do so, either. Hence Smith did not invoke the latter at all, and employed the former only to make the basic point that defence capacities are conditioned by prevailing levels of economic development. What the three stages model was not intended to do was explain the actual economic—or by the same lights, military and historical—development that really took place over the longue durée of Eurasian international relations. The only thing that could do that was real history, which is precisely what Smith therefore employed in the rest of his discussion, offering an overview that stretched from the Greek resistance to Xerxes, the conflict between Rome and

---

32. We must therefore reject Hanley's claim that Smith thought that the barbarian destruction of European civilisation remained a real possibility. On the contrary, he is clear that the barbarian threat has been permanently neutralised. See Hanley, 'Wisdom of the State', 378–81, and compare Smith, *WN* V.i.b.44, which explicitly states that 'in modern war the great expence of fire-arms gives an evident advantage to the nation which can best afford that expence; and consequently, to an opulent and civilized, over a poor and barbarous nation. In antient times the opulent and civilized found it difficult to defend themselves against the poor and barbarous nations. In modern times the poor and barbarous find it difficult to defend themselves against the opulent and civilized. The invention of fire-arms, an invention which at first sight appears to be so pernicious, is certainly favourable both to the permanency and to the extension of civilization'. See also Pocock, *Barbarism and Religion, Volume 3*, 397–99.

Carthage, the fall of the Western Empire, the continued shepherd barbarian threat to Western civilization, and the eventual rise of the standing armies of modern European states (*WN* V.i.a.28–40).

Exactly the same approach characterizes Smith's discussion of the provision of justice in the next section of Book V. The three stages model is again used to illustrate the basic truth that the administration of justice varies with the level of economic development. In a state of hunters virtually no government exists, because only very limited notions of property are in effect, and hence little third-party arbitration is required to settle disputes (*WN* V.i.b.2). In a state of shepherds, by contrast, inequality leads to the introduction of property rights and the need for the rich to be defended from the poor, and hence in turn the need for third-party arbitration in disputes over who owns what (*WN* V.i.b.12–15). In practice this led to enormous levels of corruption as judgements were predominantly based on who could bribe the sovereign most effectively. (In this period, Smith claims, sovereigns were possessed of the judicial functions due precisely to the lucrative trappings these made available, citing the practices of the Tartar warlords as proof.) Smith is, if anything, apparently reluctant to apply even the third stage of husbanding to his account of the rise of advanced duties of justice, but he does make some allowance for it, invoking as examples 'those nations of husbandmen who are but just come out of the shepherd state, and who are not much advanced beyond that state; such as the Greek tribes appear to have been about the time of the Trojan war, and our German and Scythian ancestors when they first settled upon the ruins of the western empire' (*WN* V.i.b.16). Yet even these peoples, he explains, had very corrupt notions of justice, as their sovereigns predominantly saw the administration of dispute arbitration as little more than a source of personal enrichment.

Yet once again, in order to understand the real historical development of justice as a duty of the sovereign, Smith moved beyond the confines of an illustrative stages model and drew instead on real history to make his case. In particular, he explained that the rise of modern notions of justice was necessarily intertwined with the progress of government in regard to the administration of military affairs, which for him did not follow the logic of any simple economic model:

> But when from different causes, chiefly from the continually increasing expence of defending the nation against the invasion of other nations, the private estate of the sovereign had become altogether insufficient for defraying the expence of the sovereignty; and when it had become necessary

that the people should, for their own security, contribute towards this expence by taxes of different kinds, it seems to have been very commonly stipulated that no present for the administration of justice should, under any pretence, be accepted either by the sovereign, or by his bailiffs and substitutes, the judges. Those presents, it seems to have been supposed, could more easily be abolished altogether, than effectually regulated and ascertained. Fixed salaries were appointed to the judges which were supposed to compensate to them the loss of whatever might have been their share of the antient emoluments of justice; as the taxes more than compensated to the sovereign the loss of his. (*WN* VI.b.17)

We shall consider Smith's account of the rise of justice in more detail in the next chapter, for it is central to his account of the rise of modern liberty. But for now we can simply note that the rest of Book V's discussion again proceeds without any appeal to any stages model (not the three stages model it began with, let alone a four stages one, which again remains entirely absent from these passages), and instead considers the real histories of the rise of courts and court fees, legislatures, independent judiciaries, the separation of powers, and so forth that characterized what Smith took to be the actual development of modern European states (*WN* VI.b.18–25).

Contrary to what is widely believed, therefore, in Book V of *WN* Smith made no use of the 'four stages' account found in *LJ*. Instead, he made limited use of a standard 'three stages' account, but only so as to make basic points about how governmental duties are conditioned by economic development. Following the approach of the *Lectures*, when it came to explaining the specifics of what such governmental duties actually consist of in the real world, Smith moved away from a simplifying economic model and made appeal instead to real historical factors that were outside of the model's remit. In other words, in Book V of *WN* we see Smith synthesizing techniques earlier developed in *LJ*: first, the use of a basic economic model (in this case a three, not four, stages schema) to make crucial points about how the level of development in a society conditions its legal and political affairs; second, splicing this economic model with appeals to real history so as to make its logic more perspicuous; third, moving beyond the model into real history, precisely because the economic model cannot by itself explain what has actually happened, and hence why things now are as they are—and indeed are frequently *not* as any purely economic model would predict. Real history is thus first used to elucidate the basic model, but then eventually takes over from the model entirely so as to complete the fully fledged analysis.

It is worth remarking, in the light of all this, that if the four stages model that Smith made limited use of in the 1760s has a legacy in the 1776 *Wealth of Nations*, it is not in Book V, but in Book III.[33] After all, Smith's *four* stages model predicts that agriculture will precede the rise of manufactures and commerce—but of course this is exactly what has not happened in modern Europe, because in historical reality the development of this part of the world was highly 'unnatural and retrograde' (*WN* III.i.9). Smith's working out of how real history diverged from the predictions of the four stages model probably helped him to construct the pivotal argument of Book III— that modern European economics and politics must be understood as shaped by unique and specific historical factors. Again, however, this shows the extent to which Smith *resisted* applying any simplified stadial model when it came to offering an adequate explanation of major political-economic events, and likewise how he maintained that real human history *did not* progress neatly and linearly through clearly defined, let alone prede-termined, stages.[34]

The Case of China

We are almost at the point of being able to properly understand Smith on the question of commercial society. Before finally returning to that matter, how-ever, an important further case is worth bringing into consideration: China.[35] As with feudalism, China has previously been described as a society in the 'third' stage of agricultural development on Smith's account, as for example by Ryan Patrick Hanley.[36] But as in the case of feudalism, this is incorrect.

33. Hont, 'Introduction', 102.

34. On which note it is worth pointing out that in the sixth and final 1790 edition of *TMS*, the newly added part VI made reference only to 'pastoral countries' (NB not 'shepherds') versus 'commercial countries' (*TMS* VI.ii.I.12–13), in reference to the security provided by the law and the corresponding social role of family, and *without* invoking a stadial theory of either three or four stages. This indicates that Smith was not committed to a four stages account in any meaning-ful way by the end of his life, as evidenced by the fact that he made no reference to it whatsoever in these late revisions at what would have been an otherwise entirely natural point to do so.

35. For detailed discussion of Smith's view of China, see especially Ashley Eva Millar, 'Re-visiting the Sinophilia/Sinophobia Dichotomy in the European Enlightenment through Adam Smith's "Duties of Government"', *Asian Journal of Social Science* 38, no. 5 (2010), and also Arrighi, *Smith in Beijing*, chap. 2.

36. Hanley, 'Wisdom of the State', 376.

Before seeing why, it is worth noting that China presents a fairly serious problem for Smith's historical analysis in *LJ*. China's economically advanced status—for several millennia far ahead of Europe, with China described in the 'Early Draft' of *WN* as being possessed of 'immense opulence' (*ED* 34)—was well known to Smith. Yet the existence of this enormous outpost of economic advancement is hard to square with the ravages supposedly inflicted by the shepherd nomads of the eastern steppe, as suggested by Smith's central historical account in the *Lectures*. China was evidently *not* locked into the development trap perpetuated by shepherding peoples across much of Eurasia that Smith identified. Similarly, Smith was aware that the Mongol hordes not only frequently attacked the Chinese throughout their history, but had eventually conquered the Chinese state and imposed themselves as the ruling emperors under the leadership of Kublai Khan. Similarly, the Manchu invasion by the Aisin-Gioro clan that overthrew the Ming dynasty and established the Qing in the seventeenth century was part of Mongol heritage.[37] As Smith noted in the *Lectures*, 'The present Sultans, Grand Seignors, Mogulls, and Emperors of China are all of Tartarian descent' (*LJ(A)* iv.108). The Chinese, however, had managed to attain a level of advanced economic and social development far outstripping that of the steppe nomads, in spite of the activities of those fearsome raiders over thousands of years. When the Mongol Khans became the emperors of China in the thirteenth century they were taking over a very advanced society indeed. Smith's history of Eurasia as primarily the history of the steppe nomads, at least prior to the emergence of the Mediterranean republics who found a path out of the wider developmental trap, is conspicuously incomplete insofar as the place of China in all of this is simply not explained. (We might speculate that problems such as this go some way to explaining why Smith had his unfinished work on history and politics burned before his death.)[38] Nonetheless, if we put such matters aside and concentrate

---

37. Hanley, 'Wisdom of the State', 372; Millar, 'Revisiting the Sinophilia/Sinophobia Dichotomy', 724–25.

38. These are not the only notable gaps and problems in Smith's history. As Pocock points out, 'This Clydeside view of world history is excessively focussed on nomads and blue water. Caravan routes play no part in it, and if the Jordan and the Yenisei lead nowhere in particular, what of the Nile and the Euphrates? The romanticism of the desert has already begun to play a part in confusing Western understanding of Arab history, but there must be other reasons for the extraordinary importance which nomadism assumed in Scottish theory. However, we are now in a Mediterranean and archipelagic setting, and the history of the *polis* and *res publica* has begun, in a scarcely mediated emergence from heroic barbarism': Pocock, *Barbarism and*

on what Smith does explicitly say about China in *WN*, we see that it cannot plausibly be understood by him as a 'third stage' society on the lines of the four stages model.

In the course of Book I Smith repeatedly draws upon the example of China when discussing the extent of the division of labour and the relative levels of economic development found in different nations. He is explicit, however, not only that China is a 'much richer country than any part of Europe' (*WN* I.xi.e; see also I.xi.n.1 and I.viii.24), but that it exhibits advanced levels of both agriculture *and* manufacturing, the latter of which are at least comparable to those of Europe: 'in manufacturing art and industry, China and Indostan, though inferior, seem not to be much inferior to any part of Europe' (*WN* I.xi.g.28; cf. II.v22). Indeed, Smith claims that China has a healthier balance between its manufacturing and agricultural sectors than most of Europe, where nefarious mercantile interests have more effectively distorted prices and markets: 'the rank and the wages of country labourers [in China] are said to be superior to those of the greater part of artificers and manufacturers. They would probably be so every where, if corporation laws and the corporation spirit did not prevent it' (*WN* I.x.c.24).

The existence of widespread agricultural *and* manufacturing sectors ought, by itself, to dispel the idea that China is in a third stage 'age of agriculture', as described by the simplistic four stages model of the *Lectures*. But there is more. For China does not neatly fit into the *fourth* stage, either. This is because, according to the four stages schema as deployed by Smith in the 1762 *Lecture*, the 'age of commerce' is characterized first by internal domestic exchange, and then by international trade: 'exchange of commodities extends in time not only betwixt the individualls of the same society but betwixt those of different nations' (*LJ(A)* i.31–32). Yet what Smith's analysis in *WN* emphasizes with regards to China, as well as other important Eastern nations such as 'Indostan' and ancient Egypt, is that they have largely *not* engaged in foreign trade, and instead confined exchange to within their domestic territories due to the presence of navigable waterways.

Being situated along the deltas and great river systems of enormous inland waterways such as the Yangtze, the Nile, and the Ganges, nations like China, ancient Egypt, and 'Indostan' did not follow the expected (the economically 'natural') path of trading with foreign nations. Instead, 'It is remarkable that

---

Religion, Volume 3, 391. On the limits of Smith's history, see also Harkin, 'Smith's Missing History', 331–33.

neither the antient Egyptians, nor the Indians, nor the Chinese, encouraged foreign commerce, but seem all to have derived their great opulence from this inland navigation' (*WN* I.iii.7). The result, however, was that on Smith's estimation China became economically *stationary*:

> China has been long one of the richest, that is, one of the most fertile, best cultivated, most industrious, and most populous countries in the world. It seems, however, to have been long stationary. Marco Polo, who visited it more than five hundred years ago, describes its cultivation, industry, and populousness, almost in the same terms in which they are described by travellers in the present times. It had perhaps, even long before his time, acquired that full complement of riches which the nature of its laws and institutions permits it to acquire. (*WN* I.viii.24; see also *WN* I.viii.40)

The silver lining to this situation was that China at least did not seem to go 'backwards': 'Its towns are no-where deserted by their inhabitants. The lands which had once been cultivated are no-where neglected', and in turn its population levels stayed relatively stable (*WN* I.viii.25). However this was a less than optimal situation. And the source of the ill was easily identifiable in the form of China's long refusal to open its economy to foreign trade:

> China seems to have been long stationary, and had probably long ago acquired that full complement of riches which is consistent with the nature of its laws and institutions. But this complement may be much inferior to what, with other laws and institutions, the nature of its soil, climate, and situation might admit of. A country which neglects or despises foreign commerce, and which admits the vessels of foreign nations into one or two of its ports only, cannot transact the same quantity of business which it might do with different laws and institutions. (*WN* I.ix.15)

Although China's troubles were also exacerbated by the corruption of petty officials, making it easy prey for the predations of unscrupulous merchants, Smith claims that what is holding China back in its overall economic development is its refusal to expand beyond domestic commerce into international trade, whilst relying upon foreign merchants for what little cross-border trade it does permit. As he put it later on in Book III, the 'wealth of antient Egypt, that of China and Indostan, sufficiently demonstrate that a nation may attain a very high degree of opulence, though the greater part of its exportation trade be carried on by foreigners' (*WN* III.i.7). The implication was plain: if China conducted the foreign trade for itself, its wealth would become vastly greater as a result.[39]

This exploration of the case of China has been undertaken for two reasons. The first is to show—once more—that when it comes to real economic cases, and hence the analysis not just of historical but also of present-day regimes, Smith does not use the 'four stages' model in his explanatory matrix. China is a stand-out example: it is manifestly not a third stage 'agricultural' society, because it possesses extensive manufactures and internal commerce. But its refusal to engage in external commerce—and its rendering its own development 'stationary' as a result—is outside the predictions made for the 'fourth stage' by the model. Again, a specific economic and political outcome is for Smith always conditioned by actual geographical and historical circumstances. In the case of China, the fertility yielded by extensive rivers and their deltas, and the opportunities for inland navigation they afforded, combined with xenophobic political measures purposefully preventing foreign trade, were crucial determinants.[40] These factors combined to mean that the apparently economically logical next step of moving to extensive international trade was never properly taken by China.

The second reason Smith's analysis of China is worth considering in detail is that we are now finally ready to gain a proper appreciation of Smith's use of the term 'commercial society'. For as should now be clear, we can identify *at least three* different kinds of commercial society on Smith's wider analysis: the ancient Mediterranean republics (in particular Athens and Rome); China in the 'stationary' condition it has occupied for hundreds, if not thousands, of years (the reasons for this will be expanded upon below); and what most commentators usually have in mind when they speak of 'commercial society' in relation to Smith: modern, post-feudal western Europe. Yet the *politics* of such societies are very different indeed, the implications of which we shall consider next.

Commercial Society Reconsidered

We are now in a position to properly understand Smith's use of the technical term 'commercial society'. We begin by comparing the final stage of economic development predicted in the 'four stages' account as found in *LJ* with Smith's

39. Evensky, *Smith's Moral Philosophy*, 74–75.

40. On obstacles to foreign trade being the product of political decision making, see *WN* IV.iii.c.11; IV.ix.40; Hanley, 'Wisdom of the State', 375.

technical definition of commercial society in Book I of *WN*. As noted above, in the 1762 lecture notes Smith indicates that the 'age of commerce' in fact progresses in two parts: first, members of a society begin exchanging with each other, and later they exchange with members of other, neighbouring, societies. Smith is here working with an early picture of the consequences of the division of labour. As he puts it:

> As society was farther improved, the severall arts, which at first would be exercised by each individual as far as was necessary for his welfare, would be seperated; some persons would cultivate one and others others, as they severally inclined. They would exchange with one an other what they produced more than was necessary for their support, and get in exchange for them the commodities they stood in need of and did not produce themselves. This exchange of commodities extends in time not only betwixt the individualls of the same society but betwixt those of different nations. (*LJ(A)* i.31)

By contrast, when Smith comes to offer his technical definition of a commercial society in *WN* no mention of external or foreign trade is made. We are simply told that following widespread advent of the division of labour 'every man thus lives by exchanging, or becomes in some measure a merchant' (*WN* I.iv.1). This distinction—between a commercial *society* and a commercial *nation*—is subtle, but important.

To see why we must notice that although Smith uses the compound term 'commercial *society*' on only two occasions—and in both cases in reference to the effects of the division of labour—in *WN* he uses the terms 'commercial nation' and 'commercial country' many times, as well as, on occasion, 'commercial state', whilst also making reference to what he calls the 'commercial world', a term denoting the web of international trading networks that characterizes the global economy of his day.[41] Yet when using the terms 'commercial country', 'commercial nation', and 'commercial state', Smith does so when explicitly discussing *international trade*.[42] This distinction—between commercial

---

41. For example, *WN* I.xi.c.4; *WN* I.xi.c.5; *WN* I.xi.d.2; I.xi.m.4, 7, 18, 20–21; *WN* I.xi.n.1, 3; *WN* II.ii.105; *WN* IV.v.a.16.

42. See for example at *WN* I.iv.5 and I.v.23 when discussing the use of metals as media of exchange for use in trade; *WN* I.xi.c.4 when explaining that 'the present commercial state of the world' means that even the *barbarous* nations are often now inducted into some 'foreign commerce'; *WN* I.xi.e.38 when discussing how 'very rich and commercial countries' like the

society versus commercial *nation* (or *state* or *country*; Smith treats these terms as synonymous)—is important, and indeed one that we should not be surprised to find Smith making broad use of. This is because the term 'society' properly denotes the *internal* relations of a given community. As a participant in the long-running Enlightenment debate over the basis of human sociability—inherited from Hobbes and transmitted to Smith via the works of Hume, Mandeville, and Rousseau, as well as the writings of Pufendorf, which were a central feature of the jurisprudence syllabus Smith inherited at Glasgow—Smith would have been alert to using a term like 'society' precisely,

---

Netherlands and Genoa need to import corn so as to feed their artisan populations; *WN* I.xi.o.14 on the fine manufactures made for export in Flanders; *WN* III.iv.16 on how commercial nations exposed to foreign trade very rarely have very old families possessed of great estates because the scions of family fortunes fritter their wealth away on imported baubles and trinkets; *WN* III.iv.21 on how 'France seems to have had a considerable share of foreign commerce near a century before England was distinguished as a commercial country'; *WN* IV.i.10 on the mercantile system's distortion of the imperatives of foreign and domestic trade in not just England but 'all other commercial countries'; *WN* IV.i.28 on how 'there is in all great commercial countries a good deal of bullion alternately imported and exported for the purposes of foreign trade'; *WN* IV.i.30–31 on how sovereigns of advanced commercial nations relate to the benefits of foreign trade; *WN* IV.iii.c.11 on how 'a nation that would enrich itself by foreign trade is certainly most likely to do so when its neighbours are all rich, industrious, and commercial nations'; *WN* IV.iii.c.14 on how the modern commercial countries of Europe are subject to the spurious doctrine of the 'balance of trade'; *WN* IV.vi.3 on commercial countries and the issuing of monopolies over foreign trade; *WN* V.i.e.4 on merchant organizations accruing to themselves the authority to run schemes designed to promote foreign trade in commercial 'nations', which Smith also refers to here interchangeably as 'states'; *WN* V.iii.3 on how sovereigns of commercial countries spend on luxury that is imported from overseas.

An interesting case comes at *WN* V.iii.5 when Smith writes—in relation to the innovation of war finance and sovereign debt—of 'the same commercial state of society which, by the operation of moral causes, brings government in this manner into the necessity of borrowing, produces in the subjects both an ability and an inclination to lend. If it commonly brings along with it the necessity of borrowing, it likewise brings along with it the facility of doing so'. Smith is here indicating that sovereign debt is a reaction to the external imperative of war finance, but that the willingness and ability of subjects to themselves finance such debts makes sense only when we consider the *internal* state of such *society* as being commercial—i.e., a web of interdependence founded in market relationships via the division of labour, in other words, a commercial society. In the next two paragraphs (*WN* V.iii.6–7) he explains that the ability of a 'commercial state' to lend is ultimately rooted in the presence of manufacturers and merchants who are willing to advance capital on loan—groups who are, however, engaged in cross-border trade relationships (directly or indirectly) in their pursuit of private wealth.

and in turn in a way distinct from 'nation', 'country', or 'state'.[43] In Smith's usage, 'nation', 'country', and 'state' denote a community in regards to its *external* relations, that is, when coming into contact with other human groupings, in particular in the arenas of military and economic competition, which by the late eighteenth century had become indelibly fused.[44] Whilst in the nineteenth century 'nation' and 'state' would take on importantly different meanings as theories of nationalism emerged in the wake of the French Revolution, writing prior to this historical development Smith uses these terms interchangeably in *WN*.[45] But what we can nonetheless see is that the specific conjunction 'commercial society' was thus reserved by Smith in *WN* for explaining how a community was *internally* characterized with regards to advanced economic development, and specifically where the division of labour meant that people must live from exchange.[46] By contrast, the conjunctions 'commercial nation', 'commercial country', and 'commercial state' were employed by Smith when considering the outward-facing economic and especially trading relationships between different human communities.

Why does this matter? In the first place, because Smith's technical delineation of 'commercial society' occurs only in *WN*, by which point (as I have argued above) he did not employ the four stages model, and hence it is not technically accurate to describe 'commercial society' as the final stage of the four stages model, which itself anyway belongs only to *LJ*. The correct term for the fourth stage of the four stages model is 'the of age commerce', not 'commercial society'. Similarly, although commercial societies abound on Smith's picture, both in recorded history and in the world of his day, their origins lie *not* in a sequential, stadial process of development as predicted by the four stages model, but in the complexities of real history. Furthermore, whilst the fourth stage of the four stages model is properly not commercial *society*, but the 'age of commerce', we can see that by 1776 Smith makes an analytic

43. Sagar, *Opinion of Mankind*, chaps. 1 and 2; Hont, 'Introduction' and 'The Permanent Crisis of a Divided Mankind', in *Jealousy of Trade*. On Smith's use of the term 'society', see also Schliesser, *Adam Smith*, chap. 6.

44. On this see Hont, 'Introduction', 5–37.

45. Hont, 'Introduction', 123–24.

46. In Book V of *WN* Smith refers to hunter, shepherding, and husbanding 'societies'—i.e., when indicating their internal relations as regards economic development. For further evidence that Smith used the term 'society' to refer to internal relations of composition, see the famous discussion in *TMS* where he explicitly contrasts two models of society, wherein 'different members . . . are bound together' either by benevolence or utility: *TMS* II.ii.2.1–2.

distinction that was absent in the 1762 lecture: between the domestic relations of exchange that constitute commercial *society*, and the international trading relations that characterize a commercial *nation*, *state*, or *country*. But what this means in turn is that it is possible to separate these things: a community could be a commercial *society* (characterized internally by high levels of the division of labour, where every man is in some measure a merchant) yet simultaneously not a commercial *nation*, because not engaging in extensive foreign trade. Indeed, this is apparently Smith's view of China: a commercial *society* that is nonetheless not a commercial *nation*. Possessing advanced manufactures and extensive domestic commerce, China is on Smith's account a commercial *society*, insofar as its inhabitants live from exchange.[47] But its refusal to engage in extensive foreign trade means that it is not properly a commercial *nation*. To be sure, China is likely to be something of an anomaly: most commercial societies will likely also be commercial nations, because the division of labour and in turn the incentive to exchange goods and services usually seeks to transcend political borders in the pursuit of profit. China didn't go this way because of its vast size and the opportunities afforded by its internally navigable waterways (something Smith thinks was also the case in India and ancient Egypt). Nonetheless, these are distinct categories of analysis, and hence they can—and sometimes, as in the case of China, do—come apart.

This matters because it should be clear in turn that the precise label 'commercial society' is for Smith radically underdeterminate in terms of what it tells us about the *politics* of any particular community, and in turn of its normative status. Due to the fact that commercial society is a technical term relating to how the division of labour conditions the ways that individuals secure subsistence, it cannot by itself tell us *anything* about wider social, economic, and political realities. On Smith's analysis, advanced and powerful ancient city-states like Athens, and later Rome, qualify as commercial societies in terms of how the

---

47. Or at least many of its inhabitants experience it as such. It is worth pointing out that there is nothing preventing Smith from granting that in an enormous country like China, some sections of the population may be engaged in direct subsistence agriculture whilst others (e.g., those subsisting in towns) live by exchange. The latter are in the state of commercial society, but not the former—and it is simply a fact of life that within one large political entity different forms of society may exist. Indeed, something like this seems to have been the case in early European feudalism. There should be no obstacle to allowing such a possibility to be part of Smith's overall schema, once we abandon the erroneous reading of him as committed to a linear, discrete, country-specific, stages theory of economic development in real-world cases.

division of labour determines that most members of such economically advanced communities live by some sort of exchange.[48] The same is likewise true of China (a commercial society but not a commercial nation), and of the modern European post-feudal commercial *nations* (that are also commercial *societies*) of Smith's day. But the politics of such human groupings are very different indeed. The early republican experiments with democracy and aristocracy in Athens, later crushed by the Macedonian kings, were different from the kind of republicanism practiced in Rome for a much longer duration, a response to different geographical and historical circumstances, and which in turn eventually gave way to what Smith calls 'military monarchy' after Caesar overthrew the Republic (*LJ(A)* iv.95–99, 104–9; *LJ(B)* 43–46). Smith does not explicitly discuss the politics of China, another commercial society on his framework, but he cannot possibly have thought that the rule of different imperial dynasties over several millennia looked anything like the governments of ancient Mediterranean city-states like Sparta and Athens, that themselves became differing sorts of empires. Likewise Smith—following Montesquieu and Hume—thought that modern European commercial societies took their political lead not from the collapsed southern republics of the ancient world, but from the northern Germanic shepherd peoples, a 'Tartarian species of government' who inherited the post-Roman rubble and eventually rose to constitute the great monarchies of modern Europe (*LJ(A)* iv.114). Modern European commercial societies had forms of politics all of their own, that could be understood only by examining the real histories of how they actually came about.

It is thus imperative that we do not attempt to discuss Smith's political thought in reference to 'commercial society' *simpliciter*. On the contrary, we must always ask *what kind* of commercial society is under discussion. In turn, it will simply be false to suppose that for Smith commercial society is (for example) incompatible with (say) republican political organization. On the contrary, the ancient commercial societies of the Mediterranean were originally republican, notably so (on Smith's analysis) in the case of Athens, and

---

48. For example, that Rome was a commercial society is made plain in Book V of *WN*, where Smith writes that 'the fall of the western empire is the third great revolution in the affairs of mankind, of which ancient history has preserved any distinct or circumstantial account. It was brought about by the irresistible superiority which the militia of a barbarous, has over that of a civilized nation; which the militia of a nation of shepherds, has over that of a nation of husbanders, artificers, and manufacturers' (*WN* V.i.a.36).

also in pre-Imperial Rome, the two most important European civilizations of the ancient world.[49] China has obviously never been republican (a uniquely Western phenomenon), and modern Europe, Smith thinks, cannot and should not aspire to be republican, at least not in anything like the classical sense. This is not because of any inherent incompatibility between republicanism and commercial society (the ancient world puts paid to that idea), but because of the very different historical conditions modern commercial societies in Europe have emerged from, and the political challenges that they thus find themselves faced with. Evaluating modern post-feudal commercial societies thus means evaluating post-feudal *modernity*. To focus on 'commercial society', as has been so common in recent Smith scholarship, is to seriously misidentify what is most important in his analysis.

If we want to understand Smith's assessment of the politics of—and, in turn, the value and the future prospects of—modern Europe, we cannot operate in reference only to the underspecified term 'commercial society' (which, it is again worth noting, is a term Smith himself only ever used twice in his entire published corpus: a telling indication that it was not for him the privileged locus of analysis that recent commentary has taken it to be). What we must do instead is speak of *modern European* commercial society (which will often also be instances of commercial *nations*), and where the analytically most important components of that conjunction are the first two words. What this means is that just as it is vacuous to speak of Smith's analysis of the politics of commercial society without specifying *which kind* of commercial society is under discussion, so it is a mistake to speak of Smith's normative attitude towards commercial society per se. In fact, Smith's assessment of the normative status of commercial societies again depends upon the concrete realities of whichever kind of commercial society is under discussion—which is why Smith dedicates so much more substantive discussion to varying concrete circumstances in specific historical locales, and only twice employs the label of 'commercial society' when speaking in the abstract about a general mode of subsistence. And this ought not to be surprising: the label 'commercial society'

---

49. For an insightful discussion, keenly aware that Smith saw the ancient republics as commercial societies, and of the importance of colonialism to his views of politics both ancient and modern, see Barry Stocker, 'Smith on the Colonialism and Republicanism of the Ancients Compared with That of the Moderns', in *Adam Smith Review*, vol. 9, ed. F. Forman (London: Routledge, 2017). That for Smith commercial societies existed in the ancient world is also noted by Salter, 'Adam Smith on Feudalism', 227.

is, in and of itself, too underspecified from Smith's perspective to provide an adequate starting point for a meaningful normative assessment. In turn, and as I will argue at greater length in chapter 4 and the conclusion, it is a crucial mistake of recent scholarship to read Smith as offering a 'defence' of 'commercial society'. Doing so fundamentally mischaracterizes his position, because for Smith *there is no alternative* to commercial society, at least for those who wish to persist in anything recognizable as a civilized standard of living. (Smith is assuming, plausibly enough, that nobody seriously wants to go back to a state of barbarism or savagery, that is, pre-commercial forms of political and economic organization.) What matters to Smith is how the specific politics of specific commercial societies are organized, not whether or not one lives in a commercial society simply in and of itself.

To understand Smith's political thought, therefore, we need to understand his assessment of the precise politics of modern Europe, which means leaving behind the economic modelling device of the four stages theory, and engaging with Smith's account of the real history of how post-feudal European politics emerged, what is distinctive about it, and hence where its true strengths and weaknesses lie. Talking loosely about Smith and 'commercial society'—as so much of the literature at present is content to do—hinders rather than helps this task. The next chapter seeks to make progress in light of the above reconfigurations. It does so by paying particular attention to what Smith meant by the rise of modern liberty in post-feudal European conditions. I argue that what is centrally important to Smith about the politics of modern European states is that they have—unexpectedly, without design, and yet with consequences that are overwhelmingly to be applauded—managed to install political regimes that massively reduce the prevalence of domination for their subject populations. Smith, in an important sense, is a theorist of nondomination. Yet he is no part of a 'republican', or 'neo-Roman', tradition focused on a particular philosophical understanding of freedom as the absence of arbitrary interference.[50] On the contrary, he is engaged in the project shared by Hume and Montesquieu: of explaining the politics of modern Europe not as the

---

50. As has most famously been argued for by Philip Pettit and Quentin Skinner. See, for example, Philip Pettit, *Republicanism: A Theory of Freedom and Government* (Oxford: Oxford University Press, 1997); Quentin Skinner, *Liberty Before Liberalism* (Cambridge: Cambridge University Press, 1998). For Smith-inspired scepticism about the viability of republicanism in a modern world of markets, see Paul Sagar, 'Liberty, Nondomination, Markets', *Review of Politics* 81, no. 3 (2019).

outgrowth of ancient southern European republican politics, but as the legacy of the gothic peoples of the north.[51] On this account, liberty is secured not by active citizen participation on the model of the ancient republics, but via the elimination of slavery and other forms of political and economic oppression, aided in particular by the unexpected and historically unique emergence of the rule of law.

51. Pocock, *Barbarism and Religion, Volume 3*, 372–75; Hont, 'Smith's History', 156–57, 162, 166; Hont, 'Introduction', 92; Hont, *Politics in Commercial Society*, 70–75; Michael Sonenscher, *Before the Deluge: Public Debt, Inequality, and the Intellectual Origins of the French Revolution* (Princeton: Princeton University Press, 2008), chap. 2; Paul Sagar, 'Istvan Hont and Political Theory', *European Journal of Political Theory* 17, no. 4 (2018): 484–94.

2

Domination, Liberty, and the Rule of Law

Modern Liberty?

It is widely recognised that in political matters Smith was both a theorist and a proponent of modern liberty. But what *is* liberty, according to Smith, and what is distinctive about its *modern* instantiation? Readers of Smith's corpus will search in vain for any equivalent of (say) chapter XXI of Hobbes's *Leviathan*, wherein a clear and precise definition of freedom is set forth and we are told, in unambiguous philosophical terms, what correct understanding should take it to be.[1] This of course may simply be a function of the fact that none of Smith's published works are primarily about politics. If his great unfinished book on history and law had been preserved, things might have been otherwise. After all, whilst *TMS* is stylistically a very different work from *Leviathan*, and does not offer definitions in anything like a Hobbesian style, Smith there had no problem offering sustained philosophical analysis of complex normative phenomena: 'sympathy', 'propriety', 'virtue', 'justice', etcetera, if not *defined* in strict and specific terms, are nonetheless subjected to sustained

---

1. According to Hobbes, 'Liberty, or Freedom, signifieth (properly) the absence of Opposition (by Opposition, I mean externall Impediments of motion;) and may be applied no lesse to Irrationall, and Inanimate creatures, than to Rationall', meaning in turn that '*A FREE-MAN, is he, that in those things, which by his strength and wit he is able to do, is not hindered to doe what he has a will to do*': Thomas Hobbes, *Leviathan*, ed. N. Malcolm, (Oxford: Oxford University Press, 2012), 324. Of course Hobbes himself ran into considerable difficulties when attempting to account for the more specific idea of 'the *Liberty of Subjects*' (328)—but regardless, what we find in *Leviathan* is a clear attempt to demarcate, via pure philosophical analysis, the precise nature of liberty.

philosophical interrogation with the aim of facilitating clear understanding.[2] There is, however, no equivalent for liberty in Smith's corpus.[3]

Despite Smith's published works never explicitly stating what he takes liberty to be, it is nonetheless possible to reconstruct his position from the materials that we do have. Yet even if Smith had gone on to offer a close analysis of the nature of liberty in a dedicated work on politics, we should not expect his treatment to have consisted primarily in the offering of a definition. This is because Smith's understanding of freedom was inherently and irreducibly historicised, dependent on prevailing contextually conditioned political and legal realities the complexities of which could never be captured by a definition, but had instead to be drawn out through detailed historical analysis. What precisely I mean by this will become clearer by the end of the chapter. But one thing that I do mean to claim, and which it is worth being explicit about from the start, is that from Smith's perspective whilst liberty may be subject to fruitful philosophical interrogation, any such philosophical interrogation has to take history, political circumstance, and socioeconomic context not just seriously, but as preconditions for meaningful understanding. From Smith's perspective, hoping to settle the question of what freedom is by casting it primarily in terms of a philosophical definition—in particular one conceived of as applying prior to, or independent of, specific contextual and historical situations—is going to be deeply misguided *as a political-theoretic enterprise*, whilst simultaneously constituting a failure to grasp the nature of the phenomenon under discussion.[4] But as a result, when it comes to freedom, Smith's

2. This method of proceeding is deliberate on Smith's behalf. As he put it in *LRBL*, regarding efforts to provide definitions it 'is very difficult in all things of a very generall nature and cannot be applied on many occasions. The best way of defining generally is to enumerate the severall qualities of the thing to be defined' (*LRBL* ii.205).

3. Hence one commentator has bluntly stated that 'Adam Smith did not present readers with a theory of freedom per se', whilst acknowledging that Smith nonetheless offered a range of considerations about things that might promote or hinder freedom in practical experience: David Schmidtz, 'Adam Smith on Freedom', in *Adam Smith: His Life, Thought, and Legacy*, ed. R. P. Hanley (Princeton: Princeton University Press, 2016), 208. It is true that Smith did not offer a *theory*, if by that one means a primarily philosophical analysis of the idea of political freedom. But as I hope to show below, that is not the only way to try to understand what freedom is—as indeed is exemplified by Smith's own works.

4. This distinctive feature of Smith's thought has attracted surprisingly little attention. Duncan Forbes some time ago noted that Smith uses the word 'liberty' in different senses at different points, when referring to both different social phenomena and different modes of economic dependence, but sustained investigation of what Smith means by liberty has tended not to take

thought cannot be assimilated to mainstream approaches in contemporary political theory today. He is doing something different, as we shall see by the end of the chapter.

That Smith never defines liberty—and, I suggest, would not have expected a definition to do any serious work even if he had offered one—did not mean that he wasn't deeply preoccupied with trying to understand it, most especially in terms of its relationship to politics, history, and the interplay between the two. On the contrary, the *Lectures* are to a significant extent given over to precisely this task, whilst the argument and ambitions of *WN* are fundamentally (although of course not exclusively) structured by it. To some degree this feature of Smith's work has long been recognised, in particular his famous claim—first made in *LJ*, later immortalised in Book III of *WN*—that the medieval barons traded their wealth and power for baubles and trinkets, meaning that the luxury that originally brought down the Roman Empire and ushered in the

---

precedence in the scholarship, with work instead focusing on his macro-narrative of how 'modern' liberty is supposed to have emerged, rather than what it specifically is. See Forbes, 'Sceptical Whiggism, Commerce and Liberty', in *Essays on Adam Smith*, ed. A. S. Skinner and T. Wilson (Oxford: Oxford University Press, 1976), 186–87. Forbes's discussion on this score is helpfully highlighted by John Salter, 'Adam Smith on Feudalism, Commerce and Slavery', *History of Political Thought* 13, no. 1 (1992): 238–39, who is more attuned than most to the complexities embedded in Smith's understanding of political liberty. An important recent exception is Christopher J. Berry, 'Adam Smith on Liberty "in Our Present Sense of the Word"', in *Essays on Hume, Smith and the Scottish Enlightenment* (Edinburgh: Edinburgh University Press, 2018), which I return to in more detail below. Edward J. Harpman, 'The Problem of Liberty in the Thought of Adam Smith', *Journal of the History of Economic Thought* 22, no. 2 (2000), has attempted to substantiate Smith's account of liberty, but as I will argue below, his approach is misguided. I do not here consider those accounts of Smith's views of liberty as constructed through interpretations grounded primarily in his moral psychology, but focus instead on the overtly political writings, which in this dimension can be recovered with only minimal reference to *TMS*—see in those regards especially Samuel Fleischacker, *A Third Concept of Liberty: Judgement and Freedom in Kant and Adam Smith* (Princeton: Princeton University Press, 1999) and Duncan Kelly, *The Propriety of Liberty: Persons, Passions and Judgement in Modern Political Thought* (Princeton: Princeton University Press, 2010), chap. 3. One important exception is Eric Schliesser, who has argued that Smith conceives of liberty as 'the sense of security that is a consequence of living under the impartial rule of law, and this liberty involves a kind of self-ownership that allows one to exercise one's judgement in order to make meaningful choices': *Adam Smith: Systematic Philosopher and Public Thinker* (Oxford: Oxford University Press, 2017), 220. As will be seen in what follows I roughly agree with Schliesser, but I suggest that his treatment is too brief, and based too narrowly on Book I of *WN*, to be convincing as it stands. To deliver substantive conclusions about Smith's understanding of freedom we need a wholesale integration of *LJ* with distinct aspects of *WN*, as I attempt below.

monstrosity of feudalism in time came to re-inaugurate liberty for the moderns by breaking the power of the great lords. As István Hont has put it, Smith's grand narrative is one of 'liberty gained, lost, and re-gained'.[5] This aspect of Smith's thought is already very well known.[6] But it is also, I claim in this chapter, only a part of Smith's fully fledged account—and not even its most important part at that. Furthermore, it is a part that by itself cannot explain what liberty *is* on Smith's view. After all, that the barons traded away their power, unintentionally destroying feudalism through self-undermining luxury consumption, is a purely historical claim about various causal processes—and by itself that does not, indeed cannot, explain what liberty is supposed to be. We need therefore to go further than merely pointing, once again, to Smith's famous story about the unintended consequences of the rise of opulence.

What then needs to be recognised in Smith's account, and how does recognising it help us to understand what he thinks liberty is? Smith's understanding is constituted by necessary reference to two other central aspects of his enormously ambitious history of law and government: the massive prevalence of domination in most societies throughout history, and the emergence of the rule of law as a historically unique check to domination that happened to emerge (for contingent, largely unintended, and surprising reasons) in western Europe—and especially Britain—during the long historical transition out of feudalism. For Smith, liberty is deliverance from the spectre of domination, understood in terms of lack of security over both possessions and physical safety, and which are standardly the hallmarks of conditions of hierarchy,

---

5. István Hont, 'Adam Smith's History of Law and Government as Political Theory', in *Political Judgement: Essays for John Dunn*, ed. R. Bourke and R. Geuss (Cambridge: Cambridge University Press, 2009), 165.

6. Donald Winch, *Adam Smith's Politics: An Essay in Historiographic Revision* (Cambridge: Cambridge University Press, 1978), chap. 4; Christopher J. Berry, *The Idea of Luxury: A Conceptual and Historical Investigation* (Cambridge: Cambridge University Press, 1994), 152–73; Berry, *The Idea of Commercial Society in the Scottish Enlightenment* (Edinburgh: Edinburgh University Press, 2013), chaps. 4 and 5; Hont, 'Smith's History', 165–68; Hont, 'Adam Smith on the Political Economy of the "Unnatural and Retrograde" Order', in *Jealousy of Trade: International Competition and the Nation-State in Historical Perspective* (Cambridge, MA: Belknap, 2005); Hont, 'Introduction', in *Jealousy of Trade*, 106–11; Daniel Luban, 'Adam Smith on Vanity, Domination and History', *Modern Intellectual History* 9, no. 2 (2012); A. S. Skinner, 'Adam Smith: An Economic Interpretation of History', in *Essays on Adam Smith*; Forbes, 'Sceptical Whiggism'; Salter, 'Adam Smith on Feudalism'; Dennis C. Rasmussen, *The Problems and Promise of Commercial Society: Adam Smith's Response to Rousseau* (University Park: Pennsylvania State University Press, 2008), chap. 4.

where social and economic superiors use their power to exploit weaker parties. The only way deliverance from such domination could be reliably instituted and maintained on a large scale, Smith thought, was via the rule of law.[7] In turn, because the rule of law was an exclusively modern (and western European) phenomenon, modern liberty was qualitatively different from its historical predecessors, because it operated specifically through such recent and local innovations. It was also, Smith thought, superior, being both more robust and more extensively applied to all members of society than any other known mode of attempting to secure nondomination in conditions of unequal power and wealth.[8]

In this regard Smith had a clear historical forerunner. In *The Spirit of the Laws*, Montesquieu declared,

> Political liberty in a citizen is that tranquillity of spirit which comes from the opinion each one has of his security, and in order for him to have this liberty the government must be such that one citizen cannot fear another citizen. When legislative power is united with executive power in a single person or in a single body of the magistracy, there is no liberty, because one can fear that the same monarch or senate that makes tyrannical laws will execute them tyrannically.[9]

7. Salter, 'Adam Smith on Feudalism', points towards something like the account I give here, although his engagement is only in passing as part of his examination of the extent to which Smith's economic and political thought can be understood as materialist; likewise Luban, 'Smith on Vanity'. Forbes, 'Sceptical Whiggism', Knud Haakonssen, *The Science of a Legislator: The Natural Jurisprudence of David Hume and Adam Smith* (Cambridge: Cambridge University Press, 1981), Berry, *Idea of Luxury* and *Idea of Commercial Society*, and Winch, *Smith's Politics*, all make reference to the importance of the rule of law to Smith's historical account of the rise of liberty, but they do not examine this feature of Smith's political thought in detail, nor do they explain how it is integral to his understanding of what exactly freedom is. I take up both tasks in what follows. For a discussion of the general connection between law and liberty, and as regards Scottish thought in the eighteenth century more generally, see Christopher J. Berry, *The Idea of Commercial Society in the Scottish Enlightenment* (Edinburgh: Edinburgh University Press, 2013), chap. 4. For a helpful overview of Smith's treatment of justice, law, and rights in *LJ*, see David Lieberman, 'Adam Smith on Justice, Rights, and Law', in *The Cambridge Companion to Adam Smith*, ed. K. Haakonssen (Cambridge: Cambridge University Press, 2006), and to a lesser extent Fabrizio Simon, 'Adam Smith and the Law', in *The Oxford Handbook of Adam Smith*, ed. C. J. Berry, M. P. Paganelli, and C. Smith (Oxford: Oxford University Press, 2013).

8. Berry, 'Smith on Liberty', 386.

9. Montesquieu, *The Spirit of the Laws*, ed. A. M. Cohler, B. C. Miller, and H. S. Stone (Cambridge: Cambridge University Press, 1989), 157. Smith did not explicitly employ Montesquieu's distinction between the liberty of the constitution and the liberty of the subject, but it is clear

Smith knew Montesquieu's work, referring to it on several occasions, and indeed his own history of law and government is in many ways a response to *The Spirit of the Laws*, attempting to work out more satisfactory answers to what he took to have been at least many of the right starting questions about possible forms of constitution, the historically conditioned nature of modern European politics, and the nature and role of freedom that resulted from the two.[10] Although Smith did not explicitly follow Montesquieu's emphasis on 'tranquillity of spirit' as a core indicator of freedom, he agreed with Montesquieu on the need to protect individuals from living in fear due to the threat posed by those who desired to dominate them. That threat came most especially from economic and political superiors who were liable to oppress those within their power. Although Smith famously claimed that law was originally an invention of the rich to secure themselves against the depredations of the poor, he also thought that once society grew to any size, it was the poor who had most to fear from the rich, who unless they were subject to control inevitably used their position of advantage to exploit and subjugate the less powerful. Like Montesquieu, Smith believed that laws were key to containing that threat, a fact which was to some extent paradoxical, in that laws were originally

---

that he likewise saw both as important, and if anything held them to be even more interdependent than Montesquieu had originally suggested. Fair criminal trials and restraints on governing powers were an important facet of liberty for the individual, according to Smith, and a separation of powers and the rule of law constraining the forces of government guaranteed the liberty of the constitution. Yet on Smith's analysis these things grew up together and mutually reinforced each other over time (most notably in Britain), as I show below. On this see also Robin Douglass, 'Montesquieu and Modern Republicanism', *Political Studies* 60, no. 3 (2012): 708–11; as will be seen, my reconstruction of Smith's account of 'modern liberty' exhibits strong similarities to Montesquieu's idea of the liberty of the subject as presented by Douglass, in particular due to its emphasis on rule of law and the separation of powers. For Smith as working in broadly the same vein as Montesquieu regarding freedom, see also Forbes, 'Sceptical Whiggism'. On Montesquieu as offering an avowedly anti-republican conception of freedom (which, I argue below, is also true of Smith), see Annelien de Dijn, '*On Political Liberty*: Montesquieu's Missing Manuscript', *Political Theory* 39, no. 2 (2011).

10. For further substantiation of this claim, see Paul Sagar, *The Opinion of Mankind: Sociability and the Theory of the State from Hobbes to Smith* (Princeton: Princeton University Press, 2018), 182–92; Hont, 'Introduction', 106–7. In his obituary for Smith, Dugald Stewart explicitly placed Smith in reference to Montesquieu's political project, something also done by Smith's pupil John Millar, both in a contribution to Stewart's obituary and in his later published remark that Montesquieu 'was the Lord Bacon of his branch of philosophy. Dr. Smith is the Newton' (*EPS* 293–95); John Millar, *An Historical View of the English Government, from the Settlements of the Saxons in Britain to the Revolution in 1688* (London, 1818), 429–30.

a source of domination, not freedom. As a result, he came to emphasise the importance not just of laws, but the rule of law, and what has come to be known as the doctrine of the separation of powers, as the mechanisms via which law was transformed from an instrument of oppression into one of liberation.[11]

There is no 'smoking gun' where Smith explicitly affirms this Montesquieuean vision of liberty (although he comes pretty close).[12] Nonetheless, a careful reconstruction of *LJ*, before turning to *WN* in the light of that reconstruction, brings out this aspect of his political thought. The result is that Smith can fairly be characterised as a theorist of liberty as nondomination. Yet he is not a republican, in his understanding either of what liberty is, or of the institutional structures required to maintain and promote it. Given recent attention paid to nondomination, liberty, and republicanism, not just in the history of political thought but in contemporary political theory, examining Smith's account of the rise and nature of modern liberty ought to be of interest beyond specialist scholarship on his work. Not just for what he can help us to see about the potential connections between liberty and nondomination, but about how to think about liberty tout court.

Slavery and the Love of Domination

Smith's declining to define or explicitly specify what he means by liberty can be frustrating, not least because he obviously believed that there *is* something qualitatively different—and superior—about the liberty experienced by modern Europeans. Probably the most obvious point of frustration comes in Book III of *WN*, where in the process of discussing the increasing rights and privileges of the burgher classes in the transition out of feudalism, Smith writes that 'the principal attributes of villenage and slavery being thus taken away from them, they now, at least, became really free in our present sense

---

11. For further elaboration of Smith's understanding of liberty and law as in part a response to Montesquieu (and also Hume), see Paul Sagar, 'On the Liberty of the English: Adam Smith's Reply to Montesquieu and Hume', *Political Theory* (forthcoming), which serves as a companion piece to this chapter.

12. Most notably in *WN*, when he writes that 'upon the impartial administration of justice depends the liberty of every individual, the sense which he has of his own security. In order to make every individual feel himself perfectly secure in the possession of every right which belongs to him, it is not only necessary that the judicial should be separated from the executive power, but that it should be rendered as much as possible independent of that power' (*WN* V.i.c.25). We shall return to this passage below, once we are ready to place it in its proper wider context.

of the word Freedom' (*WN* III.5). Here, the reader might not unreasonably expect Smith to stop and tell us what exactly is meant by 'our present sense of the word'. But instead the remark apparently features merely as an aside, with Smith instead continuing his historical account of the unnatural and retrograde founding of the modern European economic and political system.[13] I will argue below that appearances here are deceptive: Smith *does* go on to tell the reader what he thinks liberty, in our present sense of the word, consists in. Yet we will be able to appreciate that this is so only once a good deal of wider interpretative reconstruction has been undertaken, and to which we now turn.

As frustrating as Smith's apparent omission to explain himself may initially seem, there is actually a very large clue offered as to what he had in mind when making this remark. This comes from the fact that the notion of a 'present sense' of freedom is introduced with direct and specific reference to the historical throwing off of the conditions of 'villanage and slavery'. If we want to get a firmer grip on Smith's understanding of liberty, it is to his thoughts on slavery that we must first look.

Unlike thinkers such as Hobbes and Mandeville, Smith did not foreground or emphasise a love of domination, nor the need to satisfy desires for positional superiority via efforts at publicly recognised status seeking, in his published moral psychology. On the contrary, *TMS* opened by affirming something like the opposite: 'How selfish soever man may be supposed, there are evidently some principles in his nature, which interest him in the fortune of others, and render their happiness necessary to him, though he derives nothing from it except the pleasure of seeing it' (*TMS* I.i.1.1). Yet whilst Smith emphasised the capacity for sympathy (in the technical sense of literally entering into each other's sentiments) in his published moral psychology, this did not mean that he was sanguine about, or inattentive to, the human propensity to dominate and oppress. On the contrary, and as Daniel Luban has shown, a recognition of the widespread desire to dominate others, itself founded in the love of vanity (i.e., seeking approval in the opinions of others), was an integral feature of Smith's thought, underlying not just his moral philosophy but his

---

13. Berry, 'Smith on Liberty', 385–91, has noticed this striking passage and made it central to an initial attempt to tease out what Smith means by modern liberty. I turn to Berry's analysis below, but before doing so we must systematically make clear the wider superstructure of Smith's thought, which helps us not only to clarify the issues Berry has raised but also to build upon them in turn.

wider account of the intertwined economic and political progress of all known civilizations.[14]

Smith's attentiveness to the love of domination is especially evident in his discussion of slavery.[15] Smith insisted that slavery was not only an ethical abomination but also a piece of economic stupidity that made the slaveholders, as well as the wider society they operated in, worse off than they would be if free labour were employed instead (*LJ(A)* iii.111–17; *WN* III.ii.9). Yet as he put it in *WN*, repeating what he had earlier taught his Glasgow students in the 1760s, 'The pride of man makes him love to domineer, and nothing mortifies him so much as to be obliged to condescend to persuade his inferiors. Wherever the law allows it, and the nature of the work can afford it, therefore, he will generally prefer the service of slaves to freemen' (*WN* III.ii.10; cf. *LJ(A)* iii.114). Slavery was, furthermore, the *normal* condition of human economic relations beyond the most primitive condition of hunter-gathering: the earliest shepherding societies were all slave-based, and almost all of them retained the institution in some form or another as they developed into more advanced economic conditions. Smith insisted that the abolition of slavery in western Europe was not the norm but a surprising and historically unlikely event, the fortunate confluence of the ambitions of European monarchs and the Catholic Church, who by chance united in a combined effort to undermine the power of the baronial lords by supporting indentured villeins and serfs in opposition to their masters (*WN* III.ii.12). As a result, however, western Europeans were 'apt to

14. Luban, 'Smith on Vanity', passim. As Donald Winch has noted, on Smith's view 'compared with the persistent desire for vanity, social status and love of domination, man's purely material wants are easily satisfied': 'Adam Smith's "Enduring and Particular Result": A Political and Cosmopolitan Perspective', in *Wealth and Virtue: The Shaping of Political Economy in the Scottish Enlightenment*, ed. I. Hont and M. Ignatieff (Cambridge: Cambridge University Press, 1983), 259. See also Rasmussen, *Problems and Promise*, chap. 4, on Smith's views of earlier human societies as characterised by extensive dependence, insecurity, and unfreedom.

15. For discussions of Smith and slavery, see John Salter, 'Adam Smith on Slavery', *History of Economic Ideas* 4, no. 1/2 (1996), and 'Adam Smith on Feudalism'; Luban, 'Smith on Vanity'; Spencer J. Pack, 'Slavery, Adam Smith's Economic Vision, and the Invisible Hand', *History of Economic Ideas* 4, no. 1/2 (1996); Thomas Wells, 'Adam Smith's Real Views on Slavery: A Reply to Marvin Brown', *Real-World Economics Review* 53 (2010); Haakonssen, *Science of a Legislator*, 140–41, 175–77, 180–81; Thomas J. Lewis, 'Persuasion, Domination and Exchange: Adam Smith in the Political Consequences of Markets', *Canadian Journal of Political Science* 33, no. 2 (2000): 273–89. Lisa Hill, *Adam Smith's Pragmatic Liberalism: The Science of Welfare* (Cham: Palgrave Macmillan, 2019), 204–8, discusses Smith's notable omission of any discussion of abolition of the slave trade of his day, given his stated condemnation for the practice in general.

imagine that slavery is entirely abolished at this time, without considering that this is the case in only a small part of Europe; not remembering that all over Moscovy and all the eastern parts of Europe, and the whole of Asia . . . all over Africa, and the greatest part of America, it is still in use' (*LJ(A)* iii.101–2; *WN* III.ii.8). Acknowledging the vast scale of slavery in the contemporary world, as well as historically, Smith was in turn pessimistic that it would ever be abolished from more than just one 'corner' of western Europe, precisely because it was the love of domination that encouraged those who held slaves to continue to hold them even against their own economic self-interest: 'Slavery therefore has been universall in the beginnings of society, and the love of dominion and authority over others will probably make it perpetuall' (*LJ(A)* iii.117).

Whilst the broad contours of Smith's assessment of slavery are well known, still underappreciated are its wider implications. To begin to see these it is helpful to focus on the precise wording of the set of student lecture notes from 1766, where Smith is recorded as saying, 'It is to be observed that slavery takes place in all societies at their beginning, and proceeds from that tyranic disposition which may almost be said to be natural to mankind' (*LJ(B)*134). Yet why is this tyranic disposition only *almost* natural? Although we cannot be sure that these were Smith's exact words, they are nonetheless apt, even if only attributed to him by the student note taker. For consider: in *TMS* Smith had shown that sympathetic sharing of sentiments was the baseline of all human moral psychology, from which all subsequent normative practices grew. A desire to dominate, therefore, could to that extent only *almost* be said to be natural, because what was properly natural in the first instance was sentimental reciprocity via sympathy. Nonetheless, the reason this tyranic disposition could indeed 'almost be said to be natural' lay in its sheer prevalence, as exemplified by the widespread existence and persistence of institutionalised slavery in particular. (When something happens *that* much, calling it natural is hardly a stretch.) But how to reconcile a baseline sympathetic psychology with this 'tyranic disposition'? How can we be both fundamentally disposed towards fellow feeling with each other, and yet so liable to oppress and dominate others when we get the chance, as Smith thought we evidently are? Although Smith does not make the point explicitly, one answer suggested in *LJ* is that the love of domination typically comes to predominate when people find themselves in conditions of material and social inequality.[16]

16. This is not Smith's only answer: again see Luban, 'Smith on Vanity', who explores the role of the love of domination as it appears, albeit in more submerged fashion, in *TMS*, alongside

Whilst Smith postulates that slavery is universal in the beginnings of all societies, he also insists that slaves are treated best in the 'poor and barbarous', and worst in the 'rich and polished', nations (*LJ(A)* iii.105). This is because in less economically developed eras there is typically not much difference in the living and working conditions of the slave and the master, who spend a great deal of time in each other's company, and hence where bonds of sympathy encourage humane treatment. By contrast as the masters grow richer they separate themselves from the position of the slaves, ceasing to live and work alongside them, they find it harder to sympathise with their situation, and instead come to view them less like fellow humans and more like animals that it is acceptable to brutalise whilst exercising power over (*LJ(A)* iii.105–11).[17] Such a situation becomes particularly severe, Smith thinks, in opulent and especially republican states, where citizen freemen use their wealth to acquire large numbers of slaves, but then live in constant fear of mass slave uprisings, and respond by enacting vicious repressive measures designed to terrorise enormous slave populations into submission. This led to an irony: arbitrary monarchies were more likely to treat slaves well than republican regimes, because it was not in the king's interest to brutalise the slaves of his nobles

and bound up with the importance of sympathy. At any rate, it is important not to invoke an overly stylised and neat opposition between sympathy on the one hand and the love of domination on the other. As Luban makes clear, love of domination is for Smith founded in vanity, which is itself founded in the desire to be thought well of by others, but which is possible only because of our underlying capacity for sympathy.

17. Haakonssen, *Science of a Legislator*, 141; Jennifer Pitts, *A Turn to Empire: The Rise of Imperial Liberalism in Britain and France* (Princeton: Princeton University Press, 2005), 30–31. Smith may here seem to contradict himself, given that he also writes in *WN* that 'the second period of society, that of shepherds, admits of very great inequalities of fortune, and there is no period in which the superiority of fortune gives so great authority to those who possess it. There is no period accordingly in which authority and subordination are more perfectly established' (*WN* V.i.b.7). In fact, there is no contradiction in Smith's account: although it is true that individual shepherd warlords stand in conditions of vast material inequality vis-à-vis their subject populations, within that wider population there is relative homogeneity and hence more amicable master-slave relations than in more opulent societies where significant distinctions of wealth emerge between individuals, and not just between individual rulers and their subordinated subjects. On Smith's claim that economic inequality disrupts the proper functioning of sympathy, see especially Denis Rasmussen, 'Adam Smith on What Is Wrong with Economic Inequality', *American Political Science Review* 110, no. 2 (2016): 347–51 (although this does not consider Smith's discussion of slavery, focusing on the issue of morality instead—to which we return in the following chapter).

and retainers, and indeed he was more likely to enact humane laws to protect the slaves in the face of the power of their masters (who were typically also the monarch's rivals). By contrast, in aristocratic and especially democratic republics, because political power was directly in the hands of the slaveholders who ruled as a collective class, this ensured the severe repression of the slaves.

This assessment led to a striking statement from Smith, which attests to the depth of his disgust at the institution of slavery, and the extent to which he cared for the well-being of the most oppressed and exploited of all human beings. On the one hand, Smith claimed, 'Opulence and freedom' are 'the two greatest blessings that men can possess'. But on the other, it was precisely in conditions of opulence and freedom that slaves were treated worst (*LJ(A)* iii.110–11). Yet it was also the case that opulent and free societies based on slavery typically maintained—because of their very opulence—vast numbers of slaves. In other words, throughout most of history opulence and freedom were synonymous with the violent mass subjugation of huge numbers of people, something Smith illustrated by pointing to the appalling practices of the later Romans (*LJ(A)* iii.90–99, 103–5; *WN* IV.vii.b.55).[18] In response to this, Smith told his Glasgow students in no uncertain terms that 'a humane man would wish therefore if slavery has to be generally established that these greatest blessing[s], being incompatible with the happiness of the greatest part of mankind, were never to take place' (*LJ(A)* iii.111). That is, the man who would go on to write a foundational tract on how to best promote the wealth of nations explicitly taught his own students that if slavery was a necessary condition of opulence, it was better to wish that the whole world be poor.

What we can detect here are two submerged, but important and connected, egalitarian impulses in Smith's thought.[19] First, that with regards to slavery the well-being, dignity, and liberty of some could not legitimately be sacrificed for

18. Smith in similar fashion argued (erroneously, one suspects, but that is another matter) that the slaves of mainland North America in his day were better treated than those on the sugar plantations of the Caribbean, principally because the masters in the former case were substantially poorer than the latter (*LJ(A)* iii.107–8).

19. On Smith's egalitarianism, see also Elizabeth Anderson, *Private Government: How Employers Rule Our Lives (And Why We Don't Talk about It)* (Princeton: Princeton University Press, 2017), 17–22; Anderson, 'Adam Smith on Equality', in *Life, Thought and Legacy*; Stephen Darwall, 'Equal Dignity in Adam Smith', in *The Adam Smith Review*, vol. 1, ed. V. Brown (London: Routledge, 2004); Samuel Fleischacker, *On Adam Smith's Wealth of Nations: A Philosophical Companion* (Princeton: Princeton University Press, 2004), 72–80.

the benefit of others, even in the service of the creation of civilization itself. Slavery delegitimated any form of politics that supervened upon it: the 'humane' perspective Smith urged was that *all* people mattered, no matter how lowly, downtrodden, and oppressed ill fortune happened to have rendered them. There is never even a hint in Smith's oeuvre of anything like an Aristotelian argument that some people might by nature be more suited to slavery than others. Similarly his condemnation of the contemporary slave trade of his own day is unambiguous, whilst notably absent from his work is the sort of unthinking racism that on occasion mars the writings of Hume, Rousseau, and Kant.[20] Second, Smith's discussion of the 'almost' natural love of domination was grounded in his observation that the love of domination arises, or at the very least becomes especially manifest and prevalent, when human beings find themselves in positions of inequality. Insofar as people enter into social relations on a more or less equal standing, the mechanism of sympathy will tend to regulate their conduct and encourage (for the most part) respectable and humane treatment, as evidenced by the earliest master-slave relations as compared with the brutality of later and more 'refined' societies.[21] Yet danger emerges as soon as people face each other on unequal terms, for then mutual sympathy is liable to be over-ridden by the 'pride' which makes man 'love to domineer'. Insofar as Smith's 'humane' perspective insists that all persons matter, he therefore suggests that we have reason to try to avoid, mitigate, or control situations of domination, and therefore to avoid situations in which individuals find themselves on unequal terms, given what we know about how that is likely to play.[22] Insofar as domination is bad—Smith's logic

20. For example, Hume's notorious racist footnote with regard to Black Africans (*Essays Moral, Political, and Literary*, ed. E. F. Miller (Indianapolis: Liberty Fund, 1985) 208 n.10); Rousseau's pronouncement that Black people sell their beds in the morning forgetting that they will need them in the evening (*The Discourses and Other Early Political Writings*, ed. V. Gourevitch [Cambridge: Cambridge University Press, 1997], 143), and Kant's open declarations of the inferiority of nonwhite races (e.g., Immanuel Kant, *Anthropology, History, and Education*, ed. G. Zöller and R. B. Louden [Cambridge: Cambridge University Press, 2007], 82–98, 143–60). For discussion, see Schliesser, *Adam Smith*, 164–69.

21. On this see also Luban, 'Smith on Vanity', 296–300, on the importance of properly commercial relations as freeing individuals from domination by rendering members of society interdependent upon many others for their subsistence, rather than dependent on a dominator and forced into relations of subjection.

22. The capriciousness, and sheer meanness, of the spirit of domination is noted by Smith in his observation that the rich and powerful assert property over the wild beasts of the forest, and the fish of the sea and rivers, despite it making no sense to claim property over living

suggests—we have good reason to be suspicious of inequality, because the latter precipitates the former.

Yet this confluence of considerations generated, Smith also saw, a massive problem. On the one hand, a 'tyranic disposition' tends to take precedence in many people's behaviour when they find themselves in positions of superiority over others. Yet on the other hand, politics is *by necessity* hierarchical: the few always command, and the many always obey, typically based on psychological processes of deference to collectively recognised signifiers (which are frequently also generators) of authority, such as age, wisdom, and, in particular, wealth (*WN* V.i.b.3–12; *TMS* I.iii.2.1–12; VI.ii.1.20).[23] Smith's grim conclusion is that the normal condition of politics is not likely to be equality based on the mutual recognition of the equal worth of each person (as would be acknowledged by Smith's 'humane' observer, governed by the proper functioning of sympathy) but the tyranic domination of the many by those few who have managed to get them under their power.

What Smith's sobering assessment of human psychology taught the studious observer to expect was not just, as Luban puts it, that Smith's 'view of human nature suggests that the natural and stable endpoint of the drive for approbation is a slave society based on relations of domination', but that the normal condition of politics tout court, for almost all of human history, will be the existence of more or less formally institutionalised systems of domination.[24] Indeed, turning next to Smith's history of the actual progress of politics amongst known human societies, we find him confirming that what was predicted by theory was indeed what occurred in practice—albeit with one remarkable, and extremely important, exception. Once this legacy of domination is appreciated, however, we will then be in a position to properly make sense of Smith's understanding of freedom.

---

creatures that move around beyond human control. It is not because the rich have any good economic reason to do so, but rather from their great 'inclination they have to screw all they can out of their [the poor's] hands' and to encroach on the natural rights of the 'lower people', taking away from them things that ought properly to be held in common (*LJ(A)* i.56). See also Smith's detailing of the capricious and oppressive treatment that the nobles inflicted upon their vassal during the feudal era, rooted in a love of domination for its own sake (*LJ(A)* i.115–31).

23. Regarding authority and the psychological mechanisms of opinion upon which it is founded in Smith's thought, see Sagar, *Opinion of Mankind*, 192–94.

24. Luban, 'Smith on Vanity', 292.

Histories of Domination

Smith sees the history of politics in most of human experience as essentially synonymous with domination. In the earliest periods of human society politics was largely absent, and so therefore was domination. In mankind's most primitive condition, that of small groups whose subsistence is based on hunting, due to the fact that property extends only over immediate possession and disputes between parties are in turn relatively few, there is 'very little government of any sort' (*LJ(A)* iv.4; cf. *LJ(B)* 25–26). Insofar as there are political relationships at all, these consist of particular leaders whose authority stems from their individual prowess and skill, but is not transmitted much beyond that. Resolutions to disputes between aggrieved parties may have been directed by leaders, but were typically dealt with on a communal basis through collective sanction 'by the community as one body' (*LJ(A)* iv.4). In particular the idea of third-party judges, let alone independent arbiters enforcing an established code, had not yet emerged. (Smith insists that laws are invented *after* judges, as a way of bringing the judges themselves under control [*LJ(A)* v.110–11].) In this earliest of human conditions, then, material and relative status equality—and the corresponding near absence of government—meant that the earliest social experiences were in large part free from domination.

This situation, however, did not last. As soon as groups developed pasturage, they in turn developed notions of property extending beyond immediate possession, covering things that belonged to some but not others even when not under immediate personal control (livestock being the likely originator of this change, but the concept rapidly expanding outwards to other material possessions). Alongside huge increases in population facilitated by the superior subsistence generated by herding animals, property disputes required resolution not on the ad hoc basis enacted spontaneously by the assembled community (which was no longer possible), but by recognised and agreed-upon third-party arbiters. The obvious choice for this role were those already preeminent in political leadership, and who would to that extent also be wealthy vis-à-vis the rest of the population. These individuals in time assumed governmental functions, which were intimately bound up with the initial administration of justice via arbitration over property disputes.[25] This led in turn

25. The precise nature of justice is most extensively analysed by Smith in *TMS*, where he insists that its administration—which following Hume he identifies closely with resolution of property disputes—is the 'main pillar' that upholds society (*TMS* II.ii.3.4). As Donald Winch

to an explosion in inequality of property holdings as government facilitated prosperity—and in turn the extensive domination of the many by the few.

The reasons for this extensive domination were multiple. In the first place, when the rich were originally appealed to in order to settle disputes they did not conceive of themselves as neutral arbiters administering an impartial standard (this was far too complex an idea for them to have yet developed). Instead they saw—and enthusiastically grasped—an opportunity for profit. As a result, justice was administered largely in terms of gifts, which were required to 'open' the ears of judges (*LJ(A)* iv.16). Whichever party was able to most effectively bribe the arbiter was most likely to win. Inequality in turn increased as the rich cemented and expanded their position via the system of now institutionalised dispute arbitration. In turn, they used their wealth as Smith believed wealthy individuals throughout history typically did: by acquiring retainers over whom they exercised extensive dominating control, for 'in this manner every wealthy man comes to have a considerable number of the poorer sort depending and attending on him. And in this period of society the inequality of fortune makes a greater odds in the power and influence of the rich over the poor than in any other' (*LJ(A)* iv.8). Rising inequality, however, was a direct threat to the rich insofar as they became subject to the jealous depredations of the poor. This led to the introduction of laws, whose original intention was to enable the wealthy few to continue in positions of dominating superiority over the far greater numbers of poor: 'Laws and government may be considered in this and indeed in every case as a combination of the rich to oppress the poor, and preserve to themselves the inequality of the goods which would otherwise soon be destroyed by the attacks of the poor' (*LJ(A)* iv.22–23).[26]

---

has put it, Smith held 'the belief, shared with Hume, that enforcement of the rules of commutative justice, protecting "the perfect rights" associated with injuries to person and property, was the foundation of social existence': Winch, *Riches and Poverty: An Intellectual History of Political Economy in Britain, 1750–1834* (Cambridge: Cambridge University Press, 1996), 97. I discuss the technicalities of Smith's account of justice in Sagar, *Opinion of Mankind*, 168–73; see also Berry, *Idea of Luxury*, 161; Berry, *Idea of Commercial Society*, 101–8.

26. The same argument is made in *WN*: 'For one very rich man, there must be at least five hundred poor, and the affluence of the few supposes the indigence of the many. The affluence of the rich excites the inclination of the poor, who are often both driven by want, and prompted by envy, to invade his possessions. It is only under the shelter of the civil magistrate that the owner of that valuable property, which is acquired by the labour of many years, or perhaps of many successive generations, can sleep a single night in security' (*WN* V.i.b.2). See also Winch, *Smith's Politics*, 93–95.

Important to note here is Smith's observation both that in such periods although government existed it was weak, and that the laws it enacted were by no means instruments for the protection of ordinary individuals, but usually the opposite (*LJ(A)* iv.29–40).[27] These points are importantly interconnected. Government was weak to the extent that it largely failed to restrain behaviour other than through retrospective punishment applied unreliably via crooked justice in the application of loosely defined and orally transmitted codes. By contrast, 'Written and formall laws are a very great refinement of government, and such as we never meet with but in the latest periods of it' (*LJ(A)* iv.35), not least because written laws postdated the innovation of legislative assemblies, something entirely unknown to shepherding peoples (*LJ(A)* iv.14, 34–36, v.108). Crucially, however, Smith claimed that 'it is a sign of great authority in the government to be able to make regulations which bind themselves, posterity and even persons who are unwilling' (*LJ(A)* iv.35). Shepherding societies entirely lacked this advanced concept of law, and anyway could not have enforced it even if they had managed to conceive of it, due to the weakness of government at the time. But as we shall see in more detail below, Smith thinks that it is the hallmark of advanced, and in particular modern European, societies that they are able to pass laws that meaningfully bind rulers themselves, as well as future generations, and even those who disagree with the content of a particular law but obey it nonetheless. Indeed, in many ways *this* is precisely what enables and constitutes liberty under modern conditions, for it is in this self-regulating manner that government is in turn able to reliably advance the security of ordinary people. But this necessarily requires strong and centralised administrations, which are known only to very economically advanced societies, and that emerged only in particular geographical locales at specific points in history. By contrast, in earlier and less developed periods of human society laws were instruments of oppression, and hence the judges who administered them would 'appear very terrible' to the common people. By contrast—and the central importance of this point to Smith will become clear below—for modern peoples 'a judge is now rather a comfortable than a terrible sight as he is the source of our liberty, our independence, and our security' (*LJ(A)* v.109). How human beings transitioned from seeing a judge as a 'comforting' rather than a 'terrible' sight is critical to Smith's wider story about liberty, and we will return to this point. In the meantime, however, we must

27. On the importance of early government being always weak in Smith's account, see Haakonssen, *Science of a Legislator*, 140–41.

stress that for Smith law by itself is not enough to secure people from domination—indeed usually quite the opposite. In order for law to become an instrument of security rather than exploitation, a great deal of evolution in both the application, and crucially also the conceptualisation, of law was required.

This evolution however did not take place in shepherd societies, but in other forms of sociopolitical organisation, and the significance of this fact for Smith extends far beyond a purely historical claim about early forms of society. This is because his designation of 'shepherds' not only covers the condition of most human beings in Eurasia throughout most of human history, but also includes the Arabs and Tartars of his own day (*LJ(A)* iv.56–57), whilst the governments 'in the eastern countries, were all established by Tartarian or Arabian chiefs. The present Sultans, Grand Seignors, Mogulls, and Emperors of China are all of Tartarian descent' (*LJ(A)* iv.108). Shepherd politics for Smith is inherently a system of material and social inequality married to a politics of domination, in which law is an instrument of exploitation. Yet shepherd politics, or at least a politics directly derived from it without much improvement, was both the historical and contemporary norm in most of the world.

Yet outside of that norm the trajectory of the non-shepherd societies that had happened to emerge were in many ways, Smith thought, no improvement for the vast majority of subject peoples. Whilst Smith recognised that the free citizens of the Attican republics that first broke out from the long cycle of shepherd conquest enjoyed both material prosperity and the liberty to engage in political self-rule, this was possible only because the free citizens were liberated from toil by the presence of vast slave populations. These slaves—the epitome of dominated peoples—were the true price of the liberty of the ancients: a minority of citizens freed themselves from domination under an even smaller minority by uniting with that smaller minority to dominate vast numbers in turn (*LJ(A)* iv.68–71; *LJ(B)* 34–36). In renouncing slavery, the republics of modern Europe (located especially in Italy and the Swiss cantons) had by contrast given up the capacity for ordinary citizens to rule themselves, insofar as working for personal subsistence took necessary precedence, and so politics was delegated to a permanent aristocratic ruling class.[28] As a result, Smith thought, democracy was a form of politics known only to the ancient world. But given that democracy in either its shepherding or ancient republican forms was intimately bound up with huge levels of domination, as well as

28. Hont, 'Smith's History', 164.

internecine violence both within and between political communities, Smith intimated that this was no bad thing.[29]

Yet the ancient republics—being economically and politically advanced societies—did represent an important advance over the condition of shepherds in at least one crucial respect: not only was judicial power typically separated from that of the executive in these states, but they also developed the innovation of the legislature as a source of laws to some degree independent of the other two. An innovation in government entirely unknown in shepherd societies, the processes of developing legislatures occurred in different ways in Athens and Rome (Smith's key examples), but in both cases marked an important evolution in the development of both the understanding and application of law. This is because once legislative assemblies were established, the source of law could be located outside of the whims and dictates of individual leaders, and be taken to stand for the will of the wider community as a whole, to some extent free of any particular interest in the moment, and even being used to constrain the rapacious tendencies of those judges who previously posed a 'terrible' prospect to most who came under their purview (LJ(A) v.108–10). This innovation of legislative power, and hence of law as more than simply an instrument to protect the rich from the poor, was a crucial step in the development of more advanced sociolegal relations. It would, however, take many centuries for the potential of nonarbitrary law to come to full maturity, long after the ancient republics who began the process had been wiped from the map.[30]

If ancient republicanism was for the privileged minority a politics of freedom, but for huge numbers one of systematic institutionalised domination, then somewhat ironically the 'military monarchies' that came to succeed the ancient republics—which were either conquered by external aggressors and ruled as puppet states, or conquered by their own wayward generals and turned into new regime forms accordingly—represented an *improvement* in terms of reduction of domination for the majority of people in Smith's assessment. Caesar's conquest of the Roman Republic, and the eventual instalment of the emperors following Augustus, was the prime example of the form of politics that came to preponderance in the late classical period. Yet Smith here

29. On Smith's understanding of democracy, see Richard Bourke, 'Enlightenment, Revolution and Democracy', *Constellations* 15, no. 1 (2008): 21–23; Sagar *Opinion of Mankind*, 195–200.

30. Hont, 'Smith's History', 157–58.

skipped forward in his narrative to include Cromwell's rule over England following the Civil War as another evident case in point (*LJ(A)* iv.89–100; *LJ(B)*
41–43). Crucial in both instances was that the 'military monarchs' retained
many of the laws that were in place under the previous regime form because
it was not in their interests to throw society into chaos by attempting to impose
entirely new modes of administration, and on the contrary they had an interest
in maintaining 'the course of justice betwixt man and man as before, and indeed made several improvements' (*LJ(A)* iv.97). In the case of the Romans
this led to a reduction in the level of domination suffered by ordinary people,
who had previously been subject to rapacious tendencies of regional gover-
nors under the republic, but whom the emperors brought more effectively to
heel. Whilst it remained evidently the case that 'no body can indeed have a fair
trial where the emperor is immediately concerned', nonetheless 'where he is
in no way interested, it is his interest to adhere to the ancient laws' (*LJ(B)* 45).
Thus although machinations in the capital were often spectacularly bloody,
and the rule of the emperors was capricious and arbitrary with regards to affairs of state and their own personal conduct, for many ordinary people the
centralisation and concentration of imperial power meant that they were more
likely to be left alone, relatively undominated, than under earlier republican
arrangements.[31] What separated Western 'military monarchies' from apparently similar regimes in 'Turky and the east' was precisely the fact that 'a system of laws had been introduced beforehand. This it was not his [the military
monarch's] interest to alter' (*LJ(A)* iv.97–98). The Western military monarchies were to a significant degree (albeit imperfectly) administered according
to law, and for this reason were much less oppressive forms of politics than
their Eastern neighbours, who being of Tartarian descent and without regular
administration of justice according to established law, constituted the most
'miserable and oppressive government' that could be 'imagined' (*LJ(B)* 46).

Yet the mighty ancient military monarchy inaugurated by Caesar and his
immediate successors failed after 'the barbarous nations of the north overran
the Roman Empire, and settled in the western parts of Europe' (*LJ(A)* i.116).
With origins firmly in shepherd politics—and thus in forms of institutionalised
domination—there first came the era of allodialism, which was eventually
succeeded by that of feudalism, wherein the last vestige of popular participation
in local courts was extinguished by the power of the barons (*LJ(A)* iv.137–39,

---

31. Hume had earlier made this same point in his essay 'That Politics May Be Reduced to a
Science', citing Tacitus as his source (Hume, *Essays Moral, Political, and Literary*, 20).

149; *LJ(B)* 55–56). In effect reverting the nations of Europe to the condition of preclassical shepherd dependency, but with a large agricultural subsistence base replacing the migration of large herds, the local lords possessed sufficient independence from the nominal king of the nation to take over the administration of justice in local affairs, becoming de facto rulers in their lands and 'in all respects to be considered as little princes in the kingdom' (*LJ(A)* i.129; cf. *WN* III.iv.7). Collapsing for all practical purposes the separation of executive, judiciary, and legislature that had to some degree been retained under the Roman military monarchs as part of their republican legal inheritance, 'these lords therefore had great jurisdictions independent of all the courts, whose order was thereby intirely destroyed' (*LJ(A)* iv.126; cf. *LJ(A)* i.129–30). The feudal barons in turn promptly behaved as any good shepherd warlord did: using outsize wealth to employ retainers, binding them into dependency, and dominating and exploiting all who came within the orbit of their power.[32] Domination once again became the norm in the politics of western Europe— just as it was everywhere else.

Such was Smith's history of government from prehistoric times down to the long night of feudal darkness that had existed until only recently in western Europe, and which continued very much to exist in the east. (Germany, Smith claimed, remained in the condition of feudalism due to its vast size and where luxury had not sufficiently undermined local baronial power, whilst nations such as Poland, Greece, Bohemia, Moravia, and Russia were all unambiguously slave states [*LJ(A)* iii.121–22; *LJ(A)* v.50; *WN* III.ii.8].) In the course of his narrative Smith explicitly took himself to have covered 'all the forms of government which have existed in the world, as far as we have any account' (*LJ(A)* iv.113). Given that almost all known governments had been, and indeed still were, either geographical variants on shepherd exploitation, or forms of post-shepherding society based not on the elimination of domination but on its reconfiguration in terms of either urban slave populations or the instigation of indentured agricultural labour, this meant that the history of government was, overwhelmingly, the history of domination. As Forbes has put it, for Smith 'opulence without freedom is the norm rather than the exception'.[33] Any exception ought thus to be both surprising, and in need of special explanation.

---

32. Berry, *Idea of Luxury*, 157.

33. Forbes, 'Sceptical Whiggism', 201; see also Winch, *Smith's Politics*, 86. Forbes's remark should however be somewhat qualified, in that opulence may exist in many conditions without freedom, but is then typically restricted to a small dominating class—only modern European

Modern Europe and the English Example

As noted in the previous section, the rise (and fall) of independent legislatures in advanced societies, and the gradual development of law as more than simply an instrument of exploitation, was a key thread running through Smith's history of government as the history of domination. It is vital to recognise this because in doing so we come in turn to see that his famous account of how the feudal barons unwittingly traded away their power for 'trinkets and baubles' (*WN* III.iv.15) only fully makes sense in the wider context of the importance of different systems of law to the administration of varying forms of politics.

Although it is true that without self-regarding luxury consumption facilitated by the rising burgher classes—who had previously kept them in states of villeinage bordering upon the condition of slaves (*LJ(A)* iv.142–48)—the barons would have held on to their dependent retainers, and thus their real political power, it is nonetheless the case that their simply trading away this power was not sufficient for ensuring the emergence of either prosperity or modern liberty in western Europe. As Smith remarked in Book I of *WN*, 'the feudal system has been abolished in both Spain and Portugal' but 'it has not been succeeded by a much better' (*WN* I.xi.n.1). Whilst the abolition of baronial power might be a necessary, it certainly wasn't a sufficient condition for the rise of modern liberty. Getting rid of the barons, by itself, guaranteed nothing.[34]

What else was required? Central to Smith's story about those nations that were 'succeeded by a much better' condition than feudalism is that they were all characterised by the possession of underlying systems of laws, which already organised their background constitutional structures in the period when the barons lost power. These systems of laws had typically originated at some point during the long period of feudalism, and whilst not able to effectively check the power of the barons until they traded away their political influence for trinkets and baubles, they were nonetheless already in place, ready to be taken over and developed in important ways by the absolute monarchs who

---

societies have achieved *widespread* opulence for the population at large, and this is umbilically connected to the rise of liberty. For further discussion, see Rasmussen, *Problems and Promise*, 151–53.

34. The developmental trajectories of Spain and Portugal were, of course, heavily disrupted by their exploits in South America, and the disastrous effects that the discovery of gold there had upon their domestic economic and political affairs, something Smith noted at length in *WN*.

stepped in to fill the post-feudal power vacuum. Particularly important in this regard were the ecclesiastical courts, which whilst highly imperfect, nonetheless initially enabled the clergy to act as 'the chief support of the peoples rights' at a time when the civil law was mostly used to exploit and oppress the general population (*LJ(A)* ii.50–51).[35] In time religious courts were replaced by properly functioning civil ones—which was good, insofar as the Catholic Church itself morphed into a leading source of domination during the Middle Ages—and nowhere was this process more fully developed than in Britain, which boasted the most well-developed form of constitutional government ever seen, and was by that measure the nation in which political domination was most effectively brought under control. The story of how this happened, however, was complex, and Smith spent a considerable portion of the *Lectures* explaining how such an unusual state of affairs had come to pass.

Following the initial collapse of the barons, Smith explained to his students, England was as much an arbitrary and absolutist monarchy as any other nation of western Europe: 'The Tudors . . . were absolute. They imprisoned any one at will; which liberty destroys the freedom of the people altogether, as imprisonment will compel one to agree to anything' (*LJ(A)* iv.160). Yet history again repeated itself. Whilst the Tudors were despots who oppressed all those they came into contact with, in a large country like England that also meant that they left most subjects in peace. Absolutist Tudor rule was for most individuals a marked improvement compared to previous oppressions inflicted by the local lords: 'In an absolute government, as that of the Tudors, the greatest part of the nation, who were in the remote parts of the kingdom, had nothing to fear, nor were in any great danger of being appressed by the sovereign, who was terrible to those only who were near at hand to the seat of his court' (*LJ(A)* iv.165–66). In this regard England exactly resembled other European monarchies in the immediate post-feudal era. But its unique geographical circumstances led it down a different subsequent path.

---

35. As Smith remarks, the clergy under feudalism were the 'only obstacle that stood in the way of the nobles; the only thing which made them keep some tollerable decency and moderation to their inferiors. The people saw this; they saw that if that body of men were oppressed, the would be oppressed at the same time. They were therefore as jealous of their liberties as of their own, and with reason paid them a very high degree of veneration. Thus an ecclesiastical court, which in a country where the regulations of the civill government are arrivd to a considerable perfection is one of the greatest nuisances imaginable, may be of very great benefit in a state where the civil government is baddly regulated' (*LJ(A)* ii.51).

Being an island, and following the unification of the crowns of Scotland and England under James I/VI in 1603, there was no serious threat of invasion, and hence no need to develop a standing army as was done in the neighbouring commercial nations of the European mainland. The British crown thus lacked a principal means of oppressing the people and of enforcing absolutist rule in the style of continental kings. Instead, the fiscal mismanagement of the Tudors eventually bequeathed to Charles I a financial crisis, that metastasised into a constitutional crisis, which ultimately led to civil war, restoration, and eventually the settlement of 1688. Parliament emerged by the end of the seventeenth century as the dominant political force, with the House of Commons in particular holding the upper hand. This culminated in a constitutional order wherein the monarchy was purposefully restrained, leading Smith to declare, 'Liberty thus established has been since confirmed by many Acts of Parliament and clauses of Acts. The system of government now supposes a system of liberty as a foundation. Every one would be shocked at any attempt to alter this system, and such a change would be attended with the greatest of difficulties' (*LJ(A)* v.5).

Yet why would an attempt to change the British constitutional settlement be attended with 'the greatest of difficulties'? Crucial to Smith's story is that alongside particular constitutional innovations which served to check the power of the monarch—such as the power to impeach Crown officials, the establishment of habeas corpus, and the frequency of elections to the Commons (*LJ(A)* v.5–10; *LJ(B)* 61–64)—by the late seventeenth century the administration of justice in Britain was characterised by the entrenchment of the common law, administered by judges who 'hold their offices for life and are intirely independent of the king' (*LJ(A)* v.5).

Smith's narrative in this section of the *Lectures* is particularly dense and at times difficult to follow, being interspersed with frequent historical digressions into the origins of the various courts and offices that constituted the British legal system. But central to his account is the role of independent judges acting under the common law. The origins of this practice were ironic and unintended. Edward I, fearing the power of the judiciary in his own time, abolished the previous system of courts and instigated a new one, selecting as judges individuals of low status, often initially drawn from the clergy, who would not dare to make their own rules or interpretations, and instead acted loyally in accord with royal demands (*LJ(A)* v.21–26; *LJ(B)* 64–67). But over time the position of a judge became one of prestige and standing, and those who held it became personally identified with the legal decisions that they made. This

incentivised them to take responsibility for official judgements, being inclined
to issue rulings precisely and with care, out of both personal interest as well as
respect for what had become a hallowed public office. Law as based in custom
and precedent emerged as the norm, but because of the 'little power of the
judges in explaining, altering, or extending or correcting the meaning of the
laws, and the great exactness with which they must be observed according to
the literall meaning of the words', this massively circumscribed the discretionary power of individuals (*LJ(A)* v.15). Due to the fact that judges were bound
by precedent and had little leeway for personal interpretation or innovation,
their decisions were ever more regular and predictable. This ensured that the
laws of the land were applied uniformly, and in ways that curtailed the ability
of power holders to abuse the judicial system by wielding it as an instrument
of personal self-aggrandisement at the expense of weaker parties. Hence 'the
liberty of the subjects was secured in England by the great accuracy and precision of the law and decisions given upon it'. When coupled with the retention
(unique at that time, Smith claimed, in all of Europe) of the system of trial by
jury in criminal cases, justice in Britain generated 'a great security of the liberty
of the subject' (*LJ(A)* v.36). For

> one is tried here by a judge who holds his office for life and is therefore in-
> dependent and not under the influence of the king, a man of great integrity
> and knowledge who has been bred to the law, is often one of the first men
> in the kingdom, who is also tied down to the strict observance of the law;
> and the point of fact also determined by a jury of peers of the person to be
> tried, who are chosen from your neighbourhood, according to the nature
> of the suit, all of whom to 13 you have the power of challenging. (*LJ(A)*
> v.36–37)

This system of judicial independence and of ruling on cases according to common law generated a historically unparalleled level of individual security, and
hence a striking exception to the historical norm of institutionalised
domination.

The achievement was not, however, confined to the individual level, very
considerable though that was. This is because the post-1688 settlement's effective separation of powers between Crown, Parliament, and the judiciary
thereby also introduced the innovation of the rule of law into government—
that advanced state of affairs wherein a strong and centralised government can
'make regulations which shall bind themselves, their posterity, and even persons who are unwilling' (*LJ(A)* iv.35). Whereas the kings of England had once

been 'considered as the fountain of justice, and had originally the power of erecting courts by his own authority as he did the 4 great courts of Westminster, yet this is now taken away. . . . He can not now however create any court without the consent of the Parliament; nor can he judge by himself in any cause but must allow the common course of justice to be followed' (*LJ(A)* v.41–42). But it was not only the king who was brought to heel: 'There seems to be no country in which the courts are more under regulation and the authority of the judged more restricted' (*LJ(A)* v.42). What had unintentionally emerged in Britain—originally a result of monarchs discharging the tedious administration of justice to delegated magistrates who over time grew into a separate body of institutional power, coupled with the constitutional settlement that succeeded the revolutions of the seventeenth century—was the advent of a condition wherein those who held political power were themselves meaningfully subject to law in a cross-checking system of balancing control. In Britain, 'the power of making laws and regulations, of trying causes or appointing judges, and of making peace or war' were not 'all vested in one person', and not even in one branch of government (*LJ(A)* iv.1). Likewise, if either 'Parliament or king should act in the legislative way without the consent of the other' the system of separated powers allowed the other branch of government to intervene in response (*LJ(A)* v.141). This ensured that arbitrary government was blocked from returning in Britain, and that the entire constitution could truly be said to be geared towards the general protection, rather than the purposeful domination and exploitation, of ordinary people. As a result, 'a rational system of liberty has been introduced into Brittain' (*LJ(B)* 63).[36] As Smith put it with especial clarity in *LRBL*, the advent of the common law and the independent judiciary 'may be looked on as one of the most happy parts of the British Constitution tho introduced merely by chance and to ease the men in power that this Office of Judging causes is committed into the hands of a few persons whose sole employment it is to determine them' (*LRBL* ii.203). Combined with the abolishing of villeinage following the collapse of feudalism, and thus the elimination of what was effectively slavery as the basis of economic production, what Britain had achieved was of world-historic significance in terms of the unprecedented scale in the reduction of domination thus facilitated. It was in Britain that a politics explicitly and genuinely geared towards freedom rather than oppression had for the first time most fully come into being.

36. Hill, *Smith's Pragmatic Liberalism*, 45–46.

Yet although Britain was the most advanced instance, and certainly to be celebrated, it was by no means entirely unique in this regard.[37] The mainland monarchies of western Europe that succeeded feudalism were also law-governed administrations. Even if the monarchs themselves were not meaningfully subject to the rule of law, nonetheless the regular administration of justice in civil affairs took place to the unambiguous benefit of subject populations. Hume famously wrote in the essay 'Of Civil Liberty' that 'it may now be affirmed of civilized monarchies, what was formerly said in praise of republics alone, *that they are a government of Laws, not of Men*'.[38] Hume plainly had France in mind, and Smith seemed to agree that the Bourbon kings, as well as other legally ordered continental monarchies, were no despots—although they remained inferior to British arrangements as regards liberty.[39] In the first place, European states lacked a tradition of common law with their courts having been erected after the discovery of the Justinian codex, which alongside canon law formed the basis of their legal codes. Smith, however, maintained that the common law was less arbitrary, and because of its spontaneous evolution closer to the 'naturall sentiments of mankind', than the civil laws developed in Europe—with the implication that the latter were usually inferior, whilst it was the common law that was 'more deserving of the attention of a speculative man' (*LJ(A)* ii.74–75).[40] Furthermore, the relative newness of many European court systems was itself a drawback: 'New courts and new laws are . . . great evills. Every court is bound only by its own practise. It takes time and repeated practise to ascertain the precise meaning of a law or to have precedents enough to determine the practise of a court. Its proceedings will be altogether loose and inaccurate' (*LJ(A)* v.43). Nonetheless, the existence of regular mechanisms of justice in western Europe, while less perfect than in Britain—not least due to the persistence of arbitrary power wielded by

37. Winch, *Smith's Politics*, 39–40; Forbes, 'Sceptical Whiggism', 182–83, 185–87, 192; Haakonssen, *Science of a Legislator*, 132; Skinner, 'Adam Smith', 177–78.

38. Hume, *Essays Moral, Political, and Literary*, 94.

39. Hill, *Smith's Pragmatic Liberalism*, 50. Smith's remarks on the continental monarchies are, however, frustratingly brief. Compared to the long and detailed consideration of English liberty, we get only passing generalisations about other European monarchies. Indeed, it is at times unclear whether Smith simply has France in mind when he speaks of continental monarchies that facilitate liberty, given that he apparently ruled out Spain and Portugal on grounds of their having failed to achieve conditions of modern liberty, that he viewed Russia and other Eastern nations as despotisms, and that most of his other remarks were about republics.

40. For discussion, see Haakonssen, *Science of a Legislator*, 151–53.

monarchs not themselves meaningfully subject to the rule of law—was still a major historical achievement, outside of the course of ordinary societal development across the rest of the globe.[41] As for those small states in Europe that had remained republican—such as the independent city-states found in Italy and parts of Germany, the United Provinces of the Netherlands, and the cantons of Switzerland (LJ(A) v.46–51)—whilst all had given up any potential for the democratic involvement of ordinary people when they renounced slavery, and become by necessity varying species of aristocracy, insofar as they were administered according to law they were likewise a massive historical improvement in terms of the reduction of domination. Furthermore, because the modern monarchies of Smith's day were 'the prevailing government; they set the fashion and give the tone to the custom' of all the states of Europe (LJ(A) v.57). Whilst Smith made this point specifically to explain why the legitimacy of tyrannicide had gone firmly out of favour, the point can be generalised: the 'fashion' and 'tone' of modern European politics was the employment of law not as an instrument of exploitation by immediate local superiors, but to facilitate the regular administration of justice throughout the land largely to the benefit of ordinary peoples. In this, the small modern republics followed the lead of the large modern monarchies.

Smith judged that by his day the states of Europe had managed—without any conscious design or intention on the part of individuals—to solve a complex political problem. As already noted, Smith claimed that for a 'savage' the sight of a judge was terrible. This was not just because judges were in the first instance usually extractive oppressors, but also because the very idea of a rule that might bind one's future actions, and indeed threaten one's very bodily integrity, was inherently a thing to be feared. Every person could envisage themselves breaking the law (or having serious motivation to do so), and so the idea of setting up a power that would inflict severe harm in response to any future breakage was, to the 'savage', a most unappealing prospect. This fact remained so *even though* law was evidently on balance to the benefit of all in any society of notable size, that is, where property relations needed to be effectively regulated on a more than piecemeal basis. Adding to this the fact that

---

41. Lisa Hill's recent claim that Smith 'believed that liberal commercialism was natural and historically inevitable' must therefore be rejected once we restore Smith's assessment of modern Europe to the properly global context under which he himself viewed it (Hill, *Smith's Pragmatic Liberalism*, 95). Luban, 'Smith on Vanity', and Forbes, 'Sceptical Whiggism', are better guides in these regards.

early judges were not simply impartial arbiters, but typically social superiors on the take, the result was that in early human conditions 'the judge is necessary and yet is of all things the most terrible' (*LJ(A)* v.110). Explaining how the systematic institutionalisation of both laws and judges could not only have come about historically, but more fundamentally have come to be widely accepted by those living under both as not only an entirely normal, but also a deeply desirable, state of affairs, required special explanation. The account that Smith supplied on this score was, unsurprisingly, thoroughly historical.[42] Whilst judges were originally appealed to in order to settle individual property disputes—a necessary solution to increasing incidences of conflict in communities that were growing in wealth and size—over time the realisation that the judges themselves needed to be controlled saw the development of legislative power as the source of laws that could check the rapacious tendencies of the judges: 'This was the case at Athens, Sparta, and other places where the people demanded laws to regulate the conduct of the judge for when it is known in what manner he is to proceed the terror will be in a great measure removed' (*LJ(A)* v.110). This meant that the idea of laws was posterior to the idea of judges in terms of historical sequencing, but crucially also that 'were laws to be established in the beginnings of society prior to the judges, they would then be a restraint upon liberty, but when established after them they extent [*sic*] and secure it, as they do not ascertain or restrain the actions of private persons so much as the power and conduct of the judge over the people' (*LJ(A)* v.110).[43] Law could thus be transformed from an instrument of domination into one of liberation, coming to be viewed by more advanced populations not as an instrument of the 'terrible' judge, but as a restraint upon the judge's dominating tendencies.

Yet what modern European societies had achieved was a considerable step beyond what the ancient societies had managed when they first erected legislative power as a way of checking judicial discretion. As Smith put it in *LRBL*, no longer confining his analysis to Britain alone, 'This Separation of the province of distributing Justice between man and man from that of conducting publick affairs and leading Armies is the great advantage which modern times

---

42. Smith rejected contractualist suppositions for how such a state of affairs could have been engendered as evident fantasy, in turn possessed of no meaningful explanatory power, either historically or normatively: *LJ(A)* v.114–19, 127–29; *LJ(B)* 15–18; Hont, 'Smith's History', 138–50.

43. Hont, 'Smith's History', 148–49; Sagar, *Opinion of Mankind*, 152.

have over antient, and the foundation of that greater Security which we now enjoy both with regard to Liberty, property and Life' (*LRBL* ii.203).[44] The modern monarchies and law-governed aristocratic republics of contemporary Europe used law not just to control judges, but to regulate and control government itself, in part by instituting a separation of powers between its branches. This led directly to the security of their populations, who were able to reap the benefits of the most mature phase of the millennia-long revolution which had eventually transformed law from an instrument of oppression into one of security.

Freedom in 'Our Present Sense of the Word'

Having considered Smith's wider conceptualisation of the history of politics, the persistent prevalence of domination, and the evolution of the use and idea of law into the fully fledged implementation of the rule of law, we are now in a position to properly appreciate his understanding of liberty. This is best brought out by paying careful attention to what Smith says at key moments in *WN* in the context of his wider historical framework as explored above. We begin, however, by first considering the analysis offered by Christopher J. Berry.

One of the few commentators to pay attention to not just the 'destination' of modern liberty in Smith's thought, but the 'route' to it, Berry emphasises the importance of how the expanding privileges of the burgher classes—whose supply of luxury goods unintentionally facilitated the destruction of baronial power—was key to enabling modern freedom.[45] Central is the fact that for Smith modern freedom goes hand in hand with opulence, and is thus markedly different from liberty as understood in an older republican, or civic humanist, conception, which can be traced back through its Renaissance revival to the ancient city-states (most especially Rome). As Berry points out, Smith's 'modern liberty' is friendly to luxury consumption (and hence opulence) rather than hostile to it, and this yields three distinct features. First, sumptuary laws regulating consumption are done away with, and luxury is embraced as an engine of welcome opulence rather than a corrupting threat to the moral and political integrity of the polity. This in turn yields an increased level of freedom for individuals: 'It is not the wanting to choose one's clothing (or diet or furnishings) that is modern but that its expression in pre-modern eras is regulated'. As a result, 'modern liberty [confines] law to matters of justice, not personal choice/preference/taste'.[46] Second, the republican insistence that liberty can be maintained and safeguarded only by active citizen participation—both in terms of domestic political engagement, and also especially through military virtue honed in an active militia—is obsolete in modern conditions, where large standing armies prove far more effective in terms of national defence, and hence where old worries that luxury and opulence would undermine the martial spirit of the citizenry can be left behind.[47] Third, justice becomes a matter of administering affairs through regular institutional channels, which can be appealed to as predictable, nonarbitrary mechanisms facilitating social cohesion and coordination, making obsolete the need to rely on individual virtues like courage and self-sacrifice.[48] Again, this has the effect of altering the status of opulence: instead of being perceived as a threat to liberty (because of luxury's allegedly deleterious effects upon civic virtue), liberty and opulence now go hand in hand insofar as liberty—itself reconfigured so as to be understood as individual market freedom, rather than active civic participation in the polis—becomes the companion rather than the antagonist of opulence.

Berry is right in all these regards. Yet his analysis is in danger of making Smith appear to be what his more superficial critics have long alleged: a narrow theorist of bourgeois self-interest, for whom freedom is simply being left alone in the market to pursue personal consumption, with the implication that because society as a whole becomes richer in the process, the liberty that enables it do so is valuable only to that extent. To ensure that we avoid this inaccurate conclusion we need to recognise that Berry's analysis covers only a part of Smith's overall account, and that the aspects that Berry identifies supervene on a set of more fundamental contentions about the nature and structure of liberty in modern conditions.

To some extent this should already be clear from what has been said above, where we have seen that Smith frequently uses the term 'liberty' as synonymous with securing conditions of nondomination, understood especially in terms of safeguards against the powers of social and economic superiors who

46. Berry, 'Smith on Liberty', 390; see also Berry, *Idea of Luxury*, 158–60; Berry, *Idea of Commercial Society*, 125–29.

47. Berry, 'Smith on Liberty', 391–94.

48. Berry, 'Smith on Liberty', 394–97.

are a threat to weaker parties' persons and possessions. At the most basic level, liberty for Smith simply means not being dominated. Yet as his claim that there is a 'present sense' of the word indicates, the *form* that such nondomination takes can and does vary, in that the means of securing nondomination change across different times and places. But in turn, the way that liberty is itself conceptualised will be different in differing contexts and historical settings: the 'sense' of the 'word Freedom' will itself be subject to change. This is because for Smith how we conceptualise freedom is conditioned by the way freedom is realised in a given social setting: 'modern liberty', for example, requires the rule of law and the separation of powers, and once those are in place an understanding of freedom—a 'sense of the word'—emerges that is qualitatively and conceptually distinct from understandings that predated the emergence of these domination-reducing innovations, and hence could not conceive of freedom in the same way. For these reasons, on Smith's outlook ascertaining the precise meaning of liberty in any specific time or place requires understanding how domination—which is for Smith the *normal* condition of politics—has been mitigated and brought under control. In its modern instantiation—that experienced in western Europe in the post-feudal era—liberty is secured specifically through the rule of law and the separation of powers, whereby the regular and impartial administration of justice introduces a level of predictability and equal standing into the affairs of ordinary life. This is what modern liberty *is* for Smith—not just a reconfiguration of the conditions via which nondomination can be secured, but in turn a qualitative change in what nondomination *means*, insofar as new possibilities for configuring the conditions alter the relevant conceptualisations. This will become evident by considering the following.

When discussing the nature of property under conditions of feudalism, and how this contrasts with the experience of modern peoples, Smith in *LJ* makes the following claim:

> In this state [that of dependence on the feudal lords] a small property must be very insecure, as it could not defend itself, and must be entirely dependent on the assistance of some of the neighbouring great men. Nowadays the smallest property is as secure as the greatest; a single acre is as securely possessed by its owner as 1000, and as the law takes the defence of property under its protection there could not in this condition be any hazard in dividing an immoveable subject into as many parts as one inclined. (*LJ(A)* i.131)

This equal security of property was a result of regular legal administration, which in modern European states tended to ensure that all property was secure even in the face of encroachment by those of greater political and economic power. In a condition where all property is equally sacred—whoever it is held by, and no matter how small the holding—what emerges is the possibility of meaningful independence for those individuals who hold small amounts of property vis-à-vis those who traditionally dominated them through their possession of greater holdings. Insofar as the feudal barons traded away their outsize political influence for baubles and trinkets, whilst rising opulence simultaneously led to the diffusion of wealth amongst the lower strata of western European societies, once this was coupled with the regular and predictable administration of justice, to that extent liberty as a form of security from domination was meaningfully inaugurated for the population at large. Crucial to understand here, however, is that the liberty of the individual was itself both enabled *and also constituted by* security through the rule of law and the protection of property, precisely because the protection of property meant the protection of individuals from the threats posed by those of greater wealth. We can thus expand Berry's analysis in an important way: Smith's modern liberty is not simply the freedom to enjoy liberalised market exchanges in a society relaxed about the generation of opulence via luxury consumption, it is the great blessing of being protected from domination by those who traditionally used highly monopolised and concentrated wealth to exploit and oppress others. The crucial mechanism by which this security was enabled is not freer market exchange in and of itself, but rather the undergirding rule of law and the system of courts that generate a stability in property that not only enables opulence-generating free consumption, but more fundamentally entails a security for ordinary individuals on a scale unknown and unrivalled outside of modern Europe.

Turning now to *WN*, in chapter 2 of Book III Smith twice reiterates that security of property is a key aspect of modernity. Whilst condemning the practice of entails, he notes that although such an institution might once of have served to protect individuals from the rapaciousness of local lords, it has become 'completely absurd' in an age 'when small as well as great estates derive their security from the laws of their country' (*WN* III.ii.6). Similarly, one of the most remarkable developments in England—a key cause of its prosperity compared to other European nations, whose agricultural development had been more extensively stifled—is that 'the security of the tenant is equal to that of the proprietor'. The result was that the yeomanry developed their lands at a far more effective rate than the insecure tenant farmers of the continent, which 'perhaps contributed more to the present grandeur of England than all their boasted regulations of commerce taken together' (*WN* III.ii.14). But establishing security of property had been no easy or quick task, given the extensive oppressive restrictions imposed by dominating feudal lords. So how had it come about?

Smith claims that the phenomenon of security in property—that is, when property holdings are backed meaningfully by the rule of law—first emerged not in the countryside, but in the cities. Whereas the population of the countryside long laboured under the oppression of local barons, and whilst the burghers of the towns were initially 'a very poor, mean set of people' (*WN* III. iii.2), the latter 'arrived at liberty and independency much earlier than the occupiers of land in the country' (*WN* III.iii.3). The reason for this was that the burghers manged to establish themselves as the principal collectors of taxation paid to the Crown in their respective towns, and in doing so were granted dispensation from the monarch to regulate their own affairs, 'being thus altogether freed from the insolence of the king's officers' (*WN* III.iii.3). This was an arrangement that was in the self-interest of both the monarch and the merchants. Managing their own affairs allowed the townsmen to specialise in long-distance trade, getting rich as a result. Paying higher taxes to the king was a tolerable price for the right to be independent of the barons, increasing their overall wealth in turn. On the other side, the monarch received a higher and more consistent overall tax take, whilst weakening the position of rival sources of power, insofar as the feudal lords were deliberately cut out. Initially royal exemptions and privileges were allotted on a personal and individual basis, but these were eventually institutionalised and passed on to successive generations of burgher families as a matter of birthright, eventually leading to the towns becoming de facto 'independent republics' within the wider nation (*WN* III.iii.7).[49] Yet it is precisely in the context of the rise of the burgher classes that Smith claims that 'the principal attributes of villanage and slavery being thus taken away from them, they now, at least, became really free in our present sense of the word Freedom' (*WN* III.iii.5). What we are now in a position to see—having identified Smith's wider understanding of modern liberty as deliverance from domination via the rule of law—is that his immediately

---

49. Winch, *Smith's Politics*, 76–7; Forbes, 'Sceptical Whiggism', 199–200; Hont, 'Smith's History', 162–63; Hont, 'Introduction', 107–8.

succeeding paragraph is, after all, a most revealing indication of what he takes modern liberty to be:

> Nor was this all. They were generally at the same time erected into a commonality or corporation, *with the privilege of having magistrates and a town-council of their own, of making bye-laws for their own government*, of building walls for their own defence, and of reducing all their inhabitants under a sort of military discipline, by obliging them to watch and ward; that is, as antiently understood, to guard and defend those walls against all attacks and surprises by night as well as by day. In England they were generally exempted from suit to the hundred and county courts; and all such pleas as should arise among them, the pleas of the crown excepted, *were left to the decision of their own magistrates. In other countries much greater and more extensive jurisdictions were frequently granted to them.* (*WN* III.iii.6, emphasis added)[50]

The significance of Smith's emphasising the role of making laws, of appointing magistrates, and of having 'extensive jurisdictions' granted to the burgher towns—something that happened alongside the provision of military self-defence, hence enabling the cities to resist the encroachment of local warlords—should now be evident in a way that it is not until we have restored the framing intellectual context of Smith's wider historical picture recoverable from the *Lectures*. For in being granted these privileges by the monarch, the burghers proceeded to erect for themselves conditions of law-governed administration, that is, not just the hallmarks, but the essential constituting features, of modern liberty.

This very liberty, however, put the burghers on a long-term collision course with the barons. The local lords hated the newly acquired independence of the burghers, and feared them as political rivals given the growing wealth of the cities, hence whenever they got the chance they 'plundered' the cities 'upon every occasion without mercy or remorse'. Yet whilst the monarch of a feudal nation 'might despise' the early burgher classes, he 'had no reason either to hate or fear' them (*WN* III.iii.8). The burghers, of course, both hated and feared the baronial lords. So naturally the monarchs joined forces with the burghers: the privileges and protections of the towns were constantly expanded by the king as a way of undermining the more dangerous threat posed by rival barons. In this way the most prosperous locales in all the nations of

50. Skinner, 'Adam Smith', 162–64.

Europe were, paradoxically, turned into de facto 'independent republics' within the lands of the very kings who simultaneously aspired to be absolute rulers. In the process of colluding with the burghers against the barons, the kings freely gave to the cities the means by which modern liberty—freedom from domination thanks to the effective presence of the rule of law—could be brought into effect:

> By granting them magistrates of their own, the privilege of making bye-laws for their own government, that of building walls for their own defence, and that of reducing all their inhabitants under a sort of military discipline, he [the monarch] gave them all the means of security and independency of the barons which it was in his power to bestow. Without the establishment of some regular government of this kind, without some authority to compel their inhabitants to act according to some certain plan or system, no voluntary league of mutual defence could either have afforded them any permanent security, or have enabled them to give the king any considerable support. By granting them the farm of their town in fee, he took away from those whom he wished to have for his friends, and, if one may say so, for his allies, all ground of jealousy and suspicion that he was ever afterwards to oppress them, either by raising the farm rent of their town, or by granting it to some other farmer. (WN III.iii.8)

In some places—Switzerland and Italy were prime examples—this process eventually saw the richest and most successful cities break away entirely, becoming sovereign entities in their own right. In the larger nations of western Europe, the cities remained part of the monarch's territory, but the burgher classes everywhere secured 'representation ... in the states general of all the great monarchies in Europe' (WN III.iii.11), reflecting their increasing importance and power.

It is vital to recognise, therefore, that for Smith the emergence of modern liberty *predates* the great revolution unleashed by the advent of luxury in modern Europe and which eventually brought down the feudal lords. Indeed, the burgher classes who supplied the luxury consumption goods to the barons were able to do so only because they had *already* secured modern liberty in their independent cities, and in which the manufacturing of consumption goods could then take place free from the rapacious intervention of the barons, who instead become the dupes that freely purchased the burghers' baubles and trinkets and in turn gave away their power. 'Order and good government, and along with them the liberty and security of individuals, were, in this manner, established in cities, at a time when the occupiers of land in the country were exposed to every sort of violence' (*WN* III.iii.12).[51] Liberty and the security of individuals as a function of good government would eventually come to the countryside as well, but that development took several centuries more, and first required the great lords to give up the power of holding dependent retainers in favour of purchasing diamond buckles and other childish gewgaws.[52]

Crucially, however, we find Smith again emphasising the rule of law as a necessary factor in enabling modern liberty to arise for rural populations once the power of the barons did finally collapse. Whilst the following passage is already well celebrated, what has tended to be noticed is only Smith's story about luxury destroying baronial power. What should also be appreciated is Smith's emphasising the importance of justice coming to be administered in a regular manner through the rule of law as what enabled liberty to flourish once the barons left the scene:

> The tenants having in this manner become independent, and the retainers being dismissed, the great proprietors were *no longer capable of interrupting the regular execution of justice,* or of disturbing the peace of the country. Having sold their birth-right, not like Esau for a mess of pottage in time of hunger and necessity, but in the wantonness of plenty, for trinkets and baubles, fitter to be the play-things of children than the serious pursuits of men, they became as insignificant as any substantial burgher or tradesman in a city. *A regular government was established in the country as well as in the city, nobody having sufficient power to disturb its operations in the one, any more than in the other.* (*WN* III.iv.15, emphasis added)

Thus, whilst Smith is never fully explicit in *WN* about his understanding of liberty, when placed in the context of the story told in *LJ* his position becomes much more perspicuous: liberty in general is deliverance from the spectre of domination, and *modern* liberty—our 'present sense of the word Freedom'—is such deliverance as enabled by the rule of law, which in its most highly evolved condition includes the separation of powers under a legally framed constitution.[53]

---

51. Smith repeats the connection between order and good government on the one hand, liberty and individual security on the other, at *WN* III.iv.4.

52. Skinner, 'Adam Smith', 166–68.

53. Winch, *Smith's Politics*, 95; Skinner, 'Adam Smith', 176.

We see Smith employing this understanding at several subsequent points in *WN*. In his discussion of the American colonists, for example, he insists that the Americans are as free as the British in all matters (with the important exception of whom they may trade internationally with) precisely because their liberty, like that of the British, is secured 'by an assembly of the representatives of the people, who claim the sole right of imposing taxes for the support of the colony government'. Crucially there is in America an established separation of powers, that is, a rule-of-law-based system: 'The authority of this assembly over-awes the executive power, and neither the meanest nor the most obnoxious colonist, as long as he obeys the law, has any thing to fear from the resentment, either of the governor, or of any other civil or military officer in the province' (*WN* IV.vii.b.51). By contrast the colonists of France, Spain, and Portugal suffer under the discretionary powers wielded by officers of arbitrary monarchs, meaning affairs are 'naturally exercised there with more than ordinary violence' (*WN* IV.vii.b.52). They are, accordingly, a great deal less free.[54]

Similarly, standing armies in modern rule-governed monarchies are not a threat to liberty but a support to it, precisely because when the king is possessed of a standing army he feels secure in his position, and hence is more likely to refrain from oppressive interference with the lives of subjects, whilst the centralisation of military power prevents the rise of petty local lords who are the most likely to attempt to dominate the populations of the provinces (*WN* V.i.a.41). Likewise, bringing the clergy to heel has been a great achievement of modern European states, because in the medieval past—when the church grew powerful in its own right and ceased to act as a check to the king and lords in defence of the ordinary populace, and instead turned to exploit it—the lack of ecclesiastical subordination to temporal law was a surefire recipe for domination. From the tenth century to the thirteenth, 'the constitution of the church of Rome may be considered as the most formidable combination that ever was formed against the authority and security of civil government as well as against the liberty, reason, and happiness of mankind, which can flourish only where civil government is able to protect them' (*WN* V.i.g.24). Finally, in the context of discussing the expenses that the sovereign must incur in the provision of justice as a core requirement of successful government, Smith states his position unambiguously:

54. Forbes, 'Sceptical Whiggism', 190.

When the judicial is united to the executive power, it is scarce possible that justice should not frequently be sacrificed to, what is vulgarly called, politics. The persons entrusted with the great interests of the state may, even without any corrupt views, sometimes imagine it necessary to sacrifice to those interests the rights of a private man. But upon the impartial administration of justice depends the liberty of every individual, the sense which he has of his own security. In order to make every individual feel himself perfectly secure in the possession of every right which belongs to him, it is not only necessary that the judicial should be separated from the executive power, but that it should be rendered as much as possible independent of that power. The judge should not be liable to be removed from his office according to the caprice of that power. The regular payment of his salary should not depend upon the good-will, or even upon the good œconomy of that power. (*WN* V.i.b.25)[55]

The impartial administration of justice, if it is to be most perfectly realised, necessarily requires the rule of law and the separation of powers.[56] If these are secured then domination is most extensively brought under control. Freedom in 'our present sense of the word' is the result.

Smith's understanding of modern liberty is thus complex. As Berry emphasises, to an important extent it relates to independence in economic terms: not only being free from oppressive market regulations such as sumptuary laws and restrictions on individual commercial activity, but being able to secure subsistence (and indeed more than subsistence in the form of luxury consumables) independent of the whims of dominating retainers possessed of vastly superior holdings. Being secured in the possession of individual property—and thus freed from the need either to rely on retainers for subsistence, or being at their mercy when securing ongoing economic survival—is a major plank of Smith's understanding of modern liberty, insofar as it is a major aspect of how nondomination is secured.

This economic dimension, however, itself supervenes upon a wider structure of established law and the regular administration of justice, such that at the individual level property is rendered secure, and so in turn are persons,

55. For related discussion, see Haakonssen, *Science of a Legislator*, 140–41, Winch, *Smith's Politics*, 95–96.

56. It will not, however, be sufficient: see Barry Weingast, 'Adam Smith's Constitutional Theory', *SSRN Electronic Journal* (2017), on the wider structure of incentives Smith believes will be required to make institutions function effectively and successfully over the long term.

across society. Furthermore, arbitrary interference from political superiors is checked by a system of separated and balancing powers, itself the most highly evolved embodiment of the rule of law. Modern liberty is the historically unique configuration arrived at for securing people from social, economic, and political domination in western Europe, evolved over hundreds of years, and erected on the ruins of the ancient states that existed prior to the barbarian collapse. Crucial to Smith's picture is that the economic, social, and political dimensions of modern liberty are thus not free-standing or self-perpetuating, but actualised only in a historically specific context in which law meaningfully controls the predations of the powerful upon the weak. Absent this wider context, the benefits of modern liberty could not be realised—indeed, modern liberty simply could not exist or even be coherently conceptualised.[57]

Yet precisely because modern liberty is so contextually conditioned, for Smith it can be fully and adequately understood only via reference to the specific historical circumstances of the moderns. Whilst for Smith liberty in general means not being dominated, taken by itself this formulation is too underdescriptive to be meaningful or informative. In order to make it meaningful and informative, one must understand whom the likely dominators are and have been, what mechanisms might exist for controlling them, and which mechanisms do in fact prevail (and with what degree of success) in any given time and place. Insofar as the answers to all those questions vary, the meaning

57. In this sense, Smith is anything but an adherent to the idea now often associated with so-called Classical Liberalism, proponents of which sometimes claim Smith as an inspiration, and according to which liberty is something that exists prior to the institutions of the state, and respect for which properly imposes restraints upon what the state may rightfully do. On Smith's view there can be no modern liberty without the institutions of the state, because it is only through the complexity of the rule of law, and the long-evolved checks to various forms of dominating power, that modern liberty is not only possible, but even conceptually coherent. And prior to the emergence of the rule-of-law-governed modern state, there was no meaningful individual freedom, only extensive domination. Whatever the merits of Smith's view versus those of many of his supposed later acolytes as regards a plausible conception of liberty and its relation to the state, at the very least we must see that Smith does not provide the kind of pedigree or authority that many who appeal to him on these questions have long claimed. (I say 'so-called' Classical Liberalism because as Rosenblatt has shown there was no unified vision of liberalism in the nineteenth century, any more than in the twentieth, and the idea of there being a 'classical' liberalism [typically meaning some form of state-minimalist, pro-market politics] as the alleged true heir to an original form of nineteenth-century progenitor, later deviated away from by twentieth-century theorists, is a partisan ideological constriction: Helena Rosenblatt, *The Lost History of Liberalism* [Princeton: Princeton University Press, 2018], chap. 7.)

of liberty—the 'sense of the word'—will vary also, because our conceptualisations of liberty are themselves downstream of, and made in reference to, the
actual ways that conditions of nondomination are secured in lived historical
experience: from social superiors, from political actors, from the economically
more powerful, and so forth. As a result, any meaningful understanding of
liberty on Smith's picture is necessarily and profoundly historicised, because
what forms domination takes, and what mechanisms have been deployed to
control it, are themselves historically variable phenomena. Yet the ways in
which liberty is itself conceived will in turn be thoroughly historically conditioned. Modern liberty, for example, required first the evolution of the rule of
law and the separation of powers to have been developed in order for the idea
of nondomination as being secured via these to be possible. But once those
institutional mechanisms had indeed been established, then not only the conditions of liberty as nondomination, but the very concept of liberty itself, underwent major transformation.

The ancient republics hit upon different ways to secure nondomination
than the moderns, and hence their 'sense' of freedom was different. The ancient mechanisms for attempting to prevent domination centred upon varying
levels of citizen participation in the affairs of state, designed in part to avoid
domination by would-be oppressor kings or rival aristocratic factions, enabled
by the presence of vast slave populations, coupled with the emergence of the
legislature (itself of more or less popular bent in different times and places) as
a way of checking judicial and executive power, all in the context of an extremely hostile international arena in which defence of the state was a key
public consideration leading to the centrality of military virtues amongst an
active citizenry $(LJ(A)$ iv.60–74).[58] Modern liberty, by contrast, is structured
differently because forged in response to different historical pressures. Not the
internal political machinations of slave-owning citizens freed from personal
toil in the wider context of intense Mediterranean warfare, but the centuries-
long backdrop of the quasi-shepherdic politics of warlord feudalism in large
northern European territories, and the complex judicial mechanisms developed over time for neutralising baronial domination and in turn subjecting
government itself to the rule of law. The nature of the threat of domination and

---

58. For discussion of Smith on ancient liberty, in the context of varying practices of colonialism, see Barry Stocker, 'Smith on the Colonialism and Republicanism of the Ancients Compared with That of the Moderns', in *The Adam Smith Review*, vol. 9, ed. F. Forman (London:
Routledge, 2017); Berry, *Idea of Luxury*, 160–62.

the nature of the laws and legislative institutions developed in response were different in conditions of modernity than in the ancient world, and hence the 'sense' of freedom was different in turn.[59]

Why, though, is modern liberty on Smith's outlook *superior* to that held by the ancients? Not simply because modern liberty enables individuals to engage in wide processes of market exchange, generating levels of opulence that by the eighteenth century meant that the prosperity of the modern European monarchies outstripped even the considerable achievements of an ancient city-state empire like Rome. Although this consideration is by no means unimportant—opulence is, after all, for Smith one of the two greatest 'blessings' that humans can enjoy—it is not the only one. For although Smith does not state his reasons explicitly, his preference for modern liberty over ancient is, in light of the above, not difficult to explain. In the first place, the ancient cities secured liberty for a narrow section of the total population by ruthlessly exploiting vast numbers of slaves. It was the enforced free labour of the enslaved that generated the economic independence that enabled citizens to engage in the running of the state as a means of checking the power of would-be monarchical dominators or rival aristocratic factions.[60] Furthermore, as Forbes notes, 'for Smith all the republics of the ancient world were nations of oppressed debtors'.[61] Lacking security in property, and being exposed to the rapacious tendencies of the rich, even those who were not directly enslaved lived for the most part under conditions of extensive domination. Modern liberty by contrast does away with slavery, and inaugurates (at least in theory) security in property for all. It thus promises to extend conditions of nondomination to the majority of the population, something greatly enhanced by the effective presence of the rule of law, all of which is a great improvement in the lot of the vast majority of ordinary individuals. This is an unambiguous advantage from Smith's perspective, not least given the egalitarian impulses in his political thought noted above. Closely connectedly, insofar as ancient liberty

59. There is, it can therefore now be noted, more than a passing resemblance between Smith's view and that more famously put forward by Benjamin Constant in 'The Liberty of the Ancients Compared with That of the Moderns', in *Political Writings*, ed. B. Fontana (Cambridge: Cambridge University Press, 1988); Berry, *Idea of Commercial Society*, 125–26. This is another point at which Smith resembles Montesquieu: Douglass, 'Montesquieu and Modern Republicanism', 716–17.

60. Berry, *Idea of Luxury*, 161; Berry, 'Adam Smith: Commerce, Liberty and Modernity', in *Essays on Hume*, 334–36.

61. Forbes, 'Sceptical Whiggism', 197.

was founded in direct participation in the political affairs of the state, it was to that extent highly unstable, because political actors constantly conspired with and against each other in attempts to either dominate others or avoid being dominated themselves. (Smith notes the frequency of constitutional revolutions in the Mediterranean republics, as unstable coalitions between different ranks of society saw an endless cycling between pseudo-monarchical aristocracies and various levels of democratic involvement from the wider population [*LJ(A)* iv.66–74].) Yet such constitutional strife tends towards periodic bloodshed and general insecurity for the individual, and is vastly less preferable than the stability of a settled constitution based on a separation of powers under the rule of law. Hence, again, the importance of Smith's remark in *LRBL* that the separation of powers 'is the great advantage which modern times have over antient'. Ancient liberty, like that of the moderns, was concerned with securing conditions of nondomination. But insofar as the moderns had found a more inclusive *and* more effective means of doing so, it was unambiguously the modern version that was superior.

Nondomination Without Republicanism

Smith is a theorist of liberty as nondomination. Yet in recent scholarship in both political theory and the history of political thought, the claim that liberty is a matter of nondomination is widely identified with the 'republican' understanding influentially put forward by Philip Pettit and Quentin Skinner, whereby one is free only to the extent that one is reliably secured from arbitrary interference.[62] Furthermore, Pettit and Skinner have urged that we look to a wider tradition of republican political thought, itself centred on understanding freedom as nondomination, as a superior alternative to thinking about political organisation vis-à-vis the liberal states that have come to

---

62. See especially Philip Pettit, 'Freedom as Antipower', *Ethics* 106, no. 3 (1996); Pettit, *Republicanism: A Theory of Freedom and Government* (Oxford: Oxford University Press, 1997); Pettit, 'Keeping Republican Freedom Simple: On a Difference with Quentin Skinner', *Political Theory* 30, no. 3 (2002); Pettit, 'Republican Liberty: Three Axioms, Four Theorems', in *Republicanism and Political Theory*, ed. C. Laborde and J. Manor (Oxford: Oxford University Press, 2008); Pettit, *On the People's Terms: A Republican Theory and Model of Democracy* (Cambridge: Cambridge University Press, 2012); and Quentin Skinner, *Liberty Before Liberalism* (Cambridge: Cambridge University Press, 1998); Skinner, 'A Third Concept of Liberty', *Proceedings of the British Academy* 117 (2003); Skinner, 'Freedom as the Absence of Arbitrary Power', in Laborde and Manor, *Republicanism and Political Theory*.

predominate in the West since the end of the eighteenth century. Hence an obvious question: is Smith a republican, either in his conception of freedom specifically, or in his politics more generally?

Despite Pettit suggesting that Smith might be considered a theorist of republican freedom,[63] it would be a severe mistake to assimilate his thought to the wider early modern republican tradition that Pettit and Skinner claim to identify.[64] For Smith is most certainly not a republican in his wider political theory: on the contrary, the republican states that continued to exist in eighteenth century Europe were in his view either lucky survivors of the barbarian holocaust that destroyed Rome, or unique configurations that emerged from the chance confluence of fragmented Swiss and Italian international political rivalries at a time when independent city-states were boosted by the historical aberration of enormous wealth flowing through their jurisdictions due to the unique phenomenon of the Crusades (*LJ(A)* iv.109–14; v.45–50; *WN* III.iii.10–14).[65] Whilst such small, politically anomalous entities might look backwards to ancient models of politics for inspiration, this was inappropriate for the large law-governed modern monarchies of northern Europe which had an entirely different provenance. Furthermore, like Hume and Montesquieu, Smith saw the direction of European politics as being set by the modern monarchies: the small southern republics had already had their day— the future belonged to the large states of northern Europe. Yet as Hont has noted, the modern monarchies of the eighteenth century would evolve to

63. Philip Pettit, 'Freedom in the Market', *Politics, Philosophy and Economics* 5, no. 1 (2006): 142.

64. That there *is* such a distinct tradition in the history of political thought, organised in particular around a way of understanding freedom, is not uncontroversial. For doubts, see Clifford Ando, 'A Dwelling beyond Violence: On the Uses and Disadvantages of History for Contemporary Republicans', *History of Political Thought* 31, no. 2 (2010); Douglass, 'Montesquieu and Modern Republicanism'; Charles Larmore, 'A Critique of Philip Pettit's Republicanism', *Philosophical Issues* 11, no. 1 (2001); Eric Nelson, *The Greek Tradition in Republican Thought* (Cambridge: Cambridge University Press, 2004); John McCormick, 'Machiavelli against Republicanism: On the Cambridge School's "Guicciardian Moments"', *Political Theory* 31, no. 5 (2003); Eric Ghosh, 'From Republican to Liberal Liberty', *History of Political Thought* 29, no. 1 (2008); Horatio Spector, 'Four Conceptions of Freedom', *Political Theory* 38, no. 6 (2010).

65. Forbes, 'Sceptical Whiggism', 197; Hont, 'Smith's History', 163. This stands regardless of whether there is a republican inheritance in some aspects of Smith's political thought, as argued by Leonidas Montes, *Adam Smith in Context: A Critical Reassessment of Some Central Components of His Thought* (London: Palgrave Macmillan, 2004), chap. 3, and to which I reply further in chapter 4 below.

become the developed commercial polities operating principles of popular sovereignty as organised through the rule of law, that is, 'the modern representative republic, our modern state form'.[66] In other words, Smith was an early theorist of what would become *liberalism*, and he is to that extent not part of any predecessor republican tradition rooted in sixteenth- and seventeenth-century civic humanist thought, and especially not one conceived of as an alternative, or challenge, to the now dominant liberal state.[67]

Of course, Smith might nonetheless be a theorist of republican *freedom*, even if his overall political thought points in the direction of what has come to be called liberalism.[68] However, and despite his central emphasis on

66. Hont, 'Introduction', 21, 106–8. See also Hont, 'Smith's History', 162; Hont, *Politics in Commercial Society: Jean-Jacques Rousseau and Adam Smith*, ed. B. Kapossy and M. Sonenscher (Cambridge, MA: Harvard University Press, 2015), 70–75. On this see also Paul Sagar, 'Istvan Hont and Political Theory', *European Journal of Political Theory* 17, no. 4 (2018): 484–91; Fleischacker, *On Adam Smith's* Wealth of Nations, 246–49.

67. In this regard Smith is not altogether dissimilar from Locke, another major figure in the history of political thought who is preoccupied with liberty, domination, law, and the relationships between all three, but who is generally read as a precursor theorist to an emergent liberal tradition, and who belies any neat classification of liberals versus republicans as determined by respective understandings of freedom. On this see especially Larmore, 'Critique of Philip Pettit's Republicanism', and Spector, 'Four Conceptions of Freedom'. On Smith's standing outside the republican, or civic humanist, tradition in the history of political thought, see also Winch, *Smith's Politics*, chap. 2. On the complexities of reliably identifying even a liberal tradition within the history of political thought, see Duncan Bell, 'What Is Liberalism?', *Political Theory* 42, no. 6 (2014). Part of the problem here is that Skinner and Pettit's framing of republicanism is focused on an understanding that predates many of the important conceptual innovations within republican political thought that began in the later part of the eighteenth century, and which allowed later republican and liberal thought to converge (to varying degrees) in places like the United States and France. To these later understandings of modern republicanism, Smith's thought is not explicitly hostile, but this underlines the extent to which any neat classification of 'liberals' versus 'republicans' is problematised by the actual historical complexity of these terms. On the later trajectory of republican thought and its relationship to emergent forms of liberalism, see for example Richard Dagger, *Civic Virtues: Rights, Citizenship and Republican Liberalism* (Oxford: Oxford University Press 1997) and Andreas Kalyvas and Ira Katznelson, *Liberal Beginnings: Making a Republic for the Moderns* (Cambridge: Cambridge University Press, 2008). At any rate, even if Smith's thought is more compatible with later republican idioms that postdate his writings than with earlier forms of republicanism, the point still stands that he cannot accurately be assimilated to the Skinner-Pettit understanding of republicanism as focused on securing freedom as nondomination.

68. Although if so it would make Smith very difficult to place in any grand narrative of a tradition of republican theorists championing liberty as the absence of arbitrary interference,

nondomination, Smith is not appropriately thought of as theorist of republican liberty, either.

For although Smith identifies security from domination as constitutive of freedom, his preferred mechanism for how to bring this about does not conform to republican understandings of freedom as requiring the active participation, or at least the residual political control, of the engaged citizenry. The essential logic of republican freedom, seminally articulated by Machiavelli in the sixteenth century—and from whom Pettit, and especially Skinner, take inspiration—is that insofar as one is to avoid being dominated by others, one must rule oneself, and that involves some level of direct participation in, or at the very least control over, the governing process.[69] Whilst Machiavelli indicated that popular tumults in response to oppressive measures by dominating noble classes might be sufficient to act as a check on the use of arbitrary power, a more regular and institutionalised form of attempting to secure nondomination in the republican tradition looks to the creation of popularly supervised law as the required instrument for securing freedom. Insofar as law is enacted as a means by which to control potential dominators, and thus acts to prevent arbitrary interference, it is to that extent the instrument of freedom. However,

---

but who were subsequently displaced by a liberal hegemony centred on 'negative' freedom as mere absence of interference *simpliciter*, precisely because given Smith's rejection of republican politics he would cut directly across any such dichotomy in the history of political thought. In this regard Smith presents as much of a problem for the Skinner-Pettit genealogy of republicanism as does Montesquieu, on which see Douglass, 'Montesquieu and Modern Republicanism', 715–16—something that ought to be unsurprising given the proximity between Smith and Montesquieu's understandings of freedom. Again, this is compatible with Smith's proto-liberal thought being much less hostile to later, eighteenth- and nineteenth-century, developments within republican thought, in the context of both traditions having to reckon with the emergence of liberalism and the new challenges faced by large-territory, constitutionally-ordered, law-governed states.

69. Niccolò Machiavelli, *Discourses on Livy*, ed. H. C. Mansfield and N. Tarcov (Chicago: University of Chicago Press, 1996), bk. I, chaps. 4–7. Pettit's 1997 book *Republicanism* is notable in that it does *not* privilege this essential logic of the republican position, giving little attention over to the way in which laws themselves must be subject to the control of those who live under them. However, his 2012 *On the People's Terms* is much more attuned to this crucial aspect of republican thought, and the extent to which control of the laws themselves is a logical requirement of any republicanism that seeks to secure nondomination via the use of law. However, Pettit tends to put his faith in processes of judicial review whereby empowered courts can strike down democratically enacted legislation, and yet this does not dominate the electorate because their decisions are in the end 'likely to be the ones that the people . . . would make or approve if they had all the relevant information or expertise' (237).

on this view *the law itself* must be under the control of those who live under it, or else it would be not an instrument of freedom, but itself a source of alien interference, and hence domination. The logic of such thinking is taken to its full end point most consistently (and famously) by Rousseau, in his declaration that in order for a population to be free it must be itself the author of the fundamental laws that it lives under. In his parlance, that the 'General Will' revealed by the assembled citizenry is of necessity sovereign in a free state—and hence in turn that individuals can be *forced* to be free, that is, by being forced to obey those laws that they have given to themselves, which is itself the mechanism by which freedom as nondomination is more fundamentally achieved.[70]

Whilst Smith shares with this republican way of thinking an emphasis on the importance of law as a means of preventing domination, he rejects the republican insistence that in order to be free one must exercise control over the laws that one lives under, either via direct citizen participation in creating the laws themselves (Rousseau's General Will, at one end of the spectrum), or via residual supervision over the implementation of the laws if one is not in a position to author them directly (Machiavellian tumults, at the other). On the contrary—and as we have seen above—Smith heralds the common law as the best safeguard against arbitrary interference when it comes to the security of individuals within a state. Yet the crucial point about the common law—and indeed, one of the main reasons Smith thinks it works so well—is that it is *not* directly authored or controlled by the populace, or indeed any living individuals, at all, but is the cumulative inheritance of several centuries of precedent

---

70. Jean-Jacques Rousseau, *The Social Contract and Other Later Political Writings*, ed. V. Gourevitch (Cambridge: Cambridge University Press), 49–53, 57–69, 82–86. Pettit is notable in having consistently and deliberately excluded Rousseau from his construction of the republican tradition on the basis that (like Hobbes) he refuses to accept the possibility of divided sovereignty, which is a central feature of the Atlantic republican tradition that Pettit has sought to draw upon. See in particular his 'Two Republican Traditions', in *Republican Democracy: Liberty, Law and Politics*, ed. A. Niederberger and P. Schink (Edinburgh: Edinburgh University Press, 2013). That, however, means that the general will and that kind of idea of collective self-rule cannot be a part of Pettit's republicanism. What this reveals is that Pettit's construal of republicanism is *itself* in deep tension with central tenets of major strands of republican thinking—which further problematizes his appeal to a supposed history of republican thought centred on liberty as nondomination, but also shows that Smith's emphasis on nondomination alone cannot be enough to determine whether or not he is a republican. Republicanism, it turns out, is just too complicated for such simple classifications. I am grateful to Rob Jubb for discussion on this point.

and custom. Nor is its operation curtailed by the potential resistance of the population at large, but proceeds instead by regular and predictable administration under the wider principle of the rule of law. It is the very fact that the common law is *beyond* the control of present individuals—be they specific judges, or the active citizenry—that has made it, Smith thinks, such an effective check on domination. The common law is a wonder of nondomination because it made the administration of justice regular by *breaking* any linkage between day-to-day politics (and hence whoever should happen to hold the power to make laws) and the functioning of the courts and judiciary.

Smith has no doubt that law can be the instrument of liberty as a block to domination, but he is highly sceptical that law will do this job effectively if placed in the hands of those embroiled in immediate political contestation, remaking laws anew with every turn of the wheel (let alone resisting them out on the street), and thus leaving judicial interpretation to the whim of whichever new arbiters happen to be in office. Rather than enshrining, Smith seeks to sever, the central republican linkage between law, political participation, and nondomination. In place of the republican linkage, Smith elevates the cumulative benefits of 'security and liberty' that have accrued not through purposeful design by an assembly of self-legislating citizens, or the effects of popular direct resistance to the activities of the socially privileged and powerful, but via the unintended consequences of centuries of complex legal and political processes that have by chance produced a historically unique—and uniquely effective—check on the tendency of political relations towards domination. In other words, simply because Smith cares about domination, and sees liberty as itself the securing of nondomination, that does not therefore make him a proponent of republican liberty. His example reminds us in turn that republicanism has no monopoly on concerns about domination, nor any claim to exclusivity as regards how to deal with this spectre.

There is, however, an even more fundamental reason to resist assimilating Smith to Pettit and Skinner's understanding of republican freedom. This is due to the fact that Smith is engaged in a qualitatively different enterprise when it comes to the nature of how to think about freedom. Despite their taking inspiration from what they take to be a vibrant and distinct republican tradition in the history of political thought, Pettit and Skinner are nonetheless firmly within the mainstream as regards contemporary Anglo-analytic approaches. This is because they see understanding freedom as primarily a *philosophical* matter, one that can be settled via abstract argument and the supply of independent conceptual criteria, which if correctly enumerated will demarcate what counts as freedom in the eyes of any rational and impartial enquirer, regardless of any particular historical and contextual factors. Hence republican freedom, according to Pettit, maintains that (e.g.) liberty *just is* the absence of arbitrary interference, and that this can be secured only if any interference an agent experiences is forced to reliably track their avowed interests, whilst interference that the agent authorizes is to that extent not freedom-restricting—and this is so in all times, and all places.[71] It is indeed revealing that Skinner and Pettit present their republican understanding as a 'third concept' of liberty, alongside Isaiah Berlin's famous dichotomy between 'negative' and 'positive' freedom.[72] That is, they do not seek to understand freedom in a fundamentally different way to the dichotomy suggested by a division between 'positive' and 'negative', but merely insist that this is neither the only, nor best, way to cut up the available logical space. In this sense, and despite a stated opposition (most especially from Skinner)[73] to Hobbes's extreme version of 'negative' liberty as consisting in the mere absence of physical restraint, Skinner and Pettit nonetheless share with Hobbes a more fundamental agreement: that liberty is something that can be defined and understood primarily as an abstract conceptual matter, achieved first and foremost via philosophical

71. For the details of Pettit's conceptualisation of republican liberty, see especially *Republicanism*, chap. 2, but also the refinements offered in 'Republican Liberty' and *On the People's Terms*, chap. 1.

72. For example, Skinner, 'Third Concept of Liberty'; Pettit, *Republicanism*, 17–19; cf. Douglass, 'Montesquieu and Modern Republicanism', 716–17. Interestingly, Berlin himself in his seminal 'Two Concepts of Liberty' shows a great deal of sensitivity to the extent to which notions of liberty will likely be dependent on other relevant political and contextual considerations, as experienced in different ways by different agents. Although unambiguously hostile to what he views as an arch-rationalist version of 'positive' liberty that he thinks leads to totalitarian forms of politics, Berlin is also clear that not only will many 'positive' understandings appear to have a good claim on us alongside the need to secure 'negative' freedom as noninterference, but this will be more pressingly so for some groups than others—for example the poor, or those throwing off external (and in particular colonial) oppression, and for whom the texture of what counts as liberty will appear to differ, given where they are starting from. It is an irony that an essay that emphasises the shifting complexity of how freedom has been and will continue to be understood tends now to be remembered only for a stylised distinction that its author himself sought to show was likely to often be hard to sustain in practice. Isaiah Berlin, 'Two Concepts of Liberty', in *Four Essays on Liberty* (Oxford: Oxford University Press, 1969).

73. Skinner, *Liberty Before Liberalism*, and especially Skinner, *Hobbes and Republican Liberty* (Cambridge: Cambridge University Press, 2008), but also Pettit, 'Keeping Republican Freedom Simple', 340, 345–46.

analysis, operating largely independent of and prior to thickly historicised or contextual concerns.

Smith is a different sort of thinker, hence in significant part why even if he had offered a definition of liberty we shouldn't expect him to have held that it could do much useful work by itself. For Smith, although it is true that at its core freedom essentially consists of not being dominated, this fact alone is not enough to tell us what freedom *is*, in any meaningful or interesting way, at least not in the situations where we might actually care about what is at stake. In order to get to something meaningful and interesting, Smith holds that a great deal of further contextual information must be supplied in terms of the complex interrelationships between prevailing facts about human psychology, political circumstance, historical inheritance, levels of economic development, social stratification, and so forth, all of which are in practice thoroughly historicised. As a result, from Smith's perspective thinking that one can ascertain the meaning of liberty—let alone how and why it can rightfully be understood to have different 'senses'—via primarily philosophical reflection is a fundamental mistake. Political theory may well employ the tools of philosophy to make progress (as Smith's frequently does), but regarding freedom, unless we turn seriously to history and the contextually conditioned nature of our 'present sense' of what freedom means, we will fail to adequately understand the phenomenon under investigation, and our intellectual efforts will be hobbled accordingly. As a result, Smith cannot appropriately be thought of as a 'republican' theorist of freedom in the terms urged by Pettit and Skinner because he is engaged in a different way of thinking: not just about how best to secure freedom as a form of nondomination, but regarding how to think about it at all.[74]

In his later work Bernard Williams insisted that 'various conceptions and understandings of freedom, including the ones we immediately need for ourselves, involve a complex historical deposit, and we will not understand them unless we grasp something of that deposit, of what the idea of freedom, in

---

74. The same can be said of Harpman, 'Problem of Liberty', one of the few studies that has attempted to establish what exactly Smith takes liberty to consist in. For whilst Harpman correctly rejects a republican reading of Smith on liberty, his own proposal—that Smith in *WN* puts forward a vision of 'negative liberty' and in *TMS* a complementary one of 'positive liberty'—is misguided for the same more fundamental reason: that Smith is not engaged in that kind of project. Hill, *Smith's Pragmatic Liberalism*, errs for the same reason when she asserts that Smith is preoccupied with promoting both 'negative' and 'positive' freedom in his pursuit of (as she puts it) a science of welfare (e.g., 28–29, 200–201, 203, 208–9).

these various connections, has become.[75] Indeed, Williams advised that if we hope to understand what freedom means, and why it is a value for us in any given time and place, then the most that a definition can hope to do is set up the barebones structure of a concept, which must then be fleshed out with historical, psychological, political, and other relevant factors. Smith would have strongly agreed with Williams—indeed, his corpus is one of the most serious efforts to attempt to do precisely what Williams claimed needs to be done that we possess. Smith is likewise a forerunner to the recent suggestion by Matthew Longo and Bernardo Zacka that taking an ethnographic perspective into account when doing political theory 'casts doubt on the prospect of defining freedom as an *objective property* of the *present structure* of our relationship to others, which is essential to most philosophical definitions of the term. If freedom is instead conditioned on past experiences, it may resist objective, time- and space-independent characterization.[76] Smith used history, not ethnography, in his efforts to understand freedom. But for those sympathetic to Longo and Zacka's suggestion about the limitations of a political theory dominated by the tools of abstract philosophy when it comes to understanding freedom, Smith proves a helpful interlocutor. His contributions to that extent remain of continued relevance, and deserve consideration above and beyond the act of interpretative recovery that has been the main aim of this chapter.

Conclusion

Smith cared deeply about domination and the imperative to replace this with robust forms of liberty. Yet central to his political thought was the conviction that understanding the modern liberty that Europe had chanced upon required recognising it to be a complex historical phenomenon, dependent upon centuries of political and economic evolution which had unleashed myriad unintended consequences not controlled or directed by specific individuals. This was something no purely philosophical analysis, much less a definition, could hope to capture. Furthermore, modern liberty was—in the properly global perspective of pervasive political domination that Smith urged his

75. Bernard Williams, 'From Freedom to Liberty: The Construction of a Political Value', in *In the Beginning Was the Deed: Realism and Moralism in Political Argument*, ed. G. Hawthorn (Princeton: Princeton University Press, 2005), 75.

76. Matthew Longo and Bernardo Zacka, 'Political Theory in an Ethnographic Key', *American Political Science Review* 113, no. 4 (2019): 1069.

audience to recognise—a major historical achievement, to be celebrated precisely because its benefits extended to unprecedented numbers of ordinary people.

From our current historical vantage point Smith's insistence on the security of property and the importance of regular forms of impartially administered justice can seem unduly insensitive to the fact that under conditions of modern liberty many continue to suffer at the hands of the richer and more powerful, and that independence in the market nonetheless still leaves a great many in positions of real and severe disadvantage.[77] All of this is true. But what Smith's work still correctly urges us to remember is that whilst life under modern liberty is by no means perfect, in politics nothing ever is, and lack of perfection ought not to blind us to what may be real and significant achievements, properly recognised as such only when placed in an appropriately wide frame of historical reference. Furthermore, and as Samuel Fleischacker has demonstrated, Smith was highly alert to the many sources of domination, and which he recognised were liable to arise from more than just public (i.e., state) power, and could pose just as serious a threat.[78] Thus Smith recognised that the Church had historically been a major source of domination, as detailed in Book V of *WN*, whilst there was every reason to believe that private actors of sufficient size and scope would proceed in just as domineering and cruel a manner as any arbitrary political despot, as Book IV's attack on the East India Company illustrated (and will be explored in more detail in chapter 5 below). Indeed, and as Fleischacker also notes, one of the reasons that Smith was hostile to republicanism was precisely that such a form of political organisation struggled to override the partial interests of powerful private citizens, who were (at least in the ancient world) typically slave owners, and whose perceived economic self-interest and 'tyranic' dispositions pointed firmly in the direction of continued institutionalised domination of the worst sort.[79] It is

77. On this see especially Anderson, *Private Government*, chap. 2. Berry also draws our attention to the fact that 'for those whose chief aim is (say) anti-colonialism, freedom may be more important than opulence, while for those who seek ordered economic growth in order to induce opulence, liberty may need to be directed' (Berry, 'Smith on Liberty', 399). It is also worth noting that Smith may have been overly optimistic about the independence ordinary people had in fact acquired under conditions of modern liberty: on this see Ann Hughes, 'Learning from the Levellers?', in Anderson, *Private Government*, 80–85.

78. Fleischacker, *On Adam Smith's* Wealth of Nations, 236–57.

79. Fleischacker, *On Adam Smith's* Wealth of Nations, 246–49. I am grateful to Glory Liu for discussion on these points.

a serious mistake, therefore, to think that Smith's emphasis on the rule of law, the security of property, and the restriction of arbitrary power is focused exclusively on state actors, or that he thinks it is only the state that can be a source of domination and therefore unfreedom. On the contrary, what his perspective urges is that precisely because domination is the default norm in human affairs, we should expect the threat from it to be more or less ubiquitous, and to manifest whenever some have the ability to put others under their power. Controlling that power through the rule of law will thus need to apply widely, and not only to 'the state' as narrowly conceived. This, of course, is not to deny that our world has changed in dramatic ways since Smith's day. It is right that we should now think also about forms of domination that continue to subsist, as well as those that have come into being since he wrote, whilst also recognising how and why others have now been largely eradicated. In these regards we must do our own thinking for ourselves. Nonetheless, Smith remains an exemplary guide regarding the seriousness and difficulty that any such thinking will properly involve.

———

Appendix 1: Liberty and Commercial Society

Readers will likely have noticed that the term 'commercial society' has not appeared in the above chapter. This is entirely deliberate. As laid out in chapter 1, commercial society is for Smith a technical term pertaining to the internal relations of a society as regards how its members secure subsistence, and is highly indeterminate with regards to the form of politics it may be coupled with. Accordingly, any attempt to properly understand Smith on the issue of liberty means prioritising not the underinformative label 'commercial society', but Smith's analysis of specific, historically located forms of government. Nonetheless we can usefully ask: what is the relationship between liberty and commercial society?

On the one hand there will be a strong elective affinity between societies in which individuals live from exchange, and liberty understood as a form of nondomination. In the first instance this is because—as many commentators already note—living from exchange promotes interdependence through a web of market interactions, and this is a vastly superior mode of living vis-à-vis securing nondomination than being directly dependent upon social and economic superiors for subsistence.[80] If one lives from exchange, one is not a retainer—and is thus much less likely to be dominated, and much more likely to be free. Closely connectedly, the *dignity* of individuals who live by exchange is likely also to be enhanced: recall Smith's famous observation in *WN* that 'nobody but a beggar chuses to depend chiefly upon the benevolence of his fellow citizens' (*WN* I.ii.2). A commercial society is likely to foster psychological as well as economic independence, at least for those able to find work, and to that extent reduce domination as experienced by ordinary people. Finally, living from exchange will be most feasible, and collectively successful, in a social setting whereby there is widespread security of property and predictable governance according to the rule of law. A commercial society and modern liberty are thus obvious mutual complements to each other.

They are not, however, identical, and their connection is not a historical necessity. The ancient republics were, on Smith's view, various species of commercial society, although they were ones founded on massive slave populations. In ancient Rome or Athens, for example, it was not *every* man who lived as 'in some measure a merchant', but only those granted the privileges of free citizenship, a condition enabled by supervening on a base of mass social and economic repression. Recall here Smith's technical definition of commercial society:

> When the division of labour has been once thoroughly established, it is but a very small part of a man's wants which the produce of his own labour can supply. He supplies the far greater part of them by exchanging that surplus part of the produce of his own labour, which is over and above his own consumption, for such parts of the produce of other men's labour as he has occasion for. Every man thus lives by exchanging, or becomes in some measure a merchant. (*WN* I.iv.1)

80. Luban, 'Smith on Vanity'; Berry, *Idea of Luxury*, 156–58; Berry, 'Adam Smith', 327–31; Winch, *Smith's Politics*, 78–80; Ryan Patrick Hanley, *Adam Smith and the Character of Virtue* (Cambridge: Cambridge University Press, 2009), 19–22; Schmidtz, 'Smith on Freedom', 210–12. Rasmussen, *Problems and Promise*, 3, puts it well: 'Building on Smith's description . . . we can say that a commercial society is one in which we find an extensive division of labor and hence a high degree of interdependence, the protection of property rights and the rule of law, and a good deal of social, economic, geographic, and occupational mobility'. Rasmussen further explores the connection between economic independence and liberty in *Problems and Promise*, chap. 4.

Strictly speaking, then, the premodern republics were not 'properly' commercial societies vis-à-vis their entire populations, because only some privileged individuals lived from exchange. Yet vis-à-vis the citizen populations specifically, they qualified as such. Something similar might be said of the China of Smith's day: subsistence peasant farmers in remote rural provinces might not live from exchange, but they might nonetheless be part of a wider national grouping wherein a great many do, meaning that on balance and as a whole the state may be considered a commercial society. The point is that the status of commercial society is, in practice, likely to exhibit gradation. Indeed, a 'properly' commercial society wherein literally *every* man lives from exchange is likely best thought of as an ideal type in Smith's overall thought, rather than being intended as a literal description of any actually existing society he knew of.[81] However, what this means in turn is that societies that nonetheless on balance qualify as 'commercial' from Smith's perspective (because there is an advanced division of labour, and many individuals do accordingly live from exchange) need not necessarily be coupled, in actual fact, with high degrees of liberty, let alone 'modern' liberty. The ancient republics are the standout example, and China illustrates the same. This is a function of the point made in the previous chapter: that the designator 'commercial society' is radically underdeterminate as regards the politics and form of government it goes along with, and so it is quite possible—indeed it has often happened in history, Smith thinks—that a commercial society could arise *without* widespread promotion of liberty in wider political affairs, and certainly without freedom 'in our present sense of the word'. However, if one is interested in promoting liberty—and especially modern liberty—then operating a commercial society rooted in market interdependence, where a right to participate in the exchange economy is extended to all members of the community who more fundamentally enjoy guarantees of security in property, is from Smith's perspective bound to be a favourable and mutually complementary state of affairs.

---

81. As the presence of some who cannot work due to incapacity or disability (and children, the indolent rich, the old in receipt of charity, etc.) indicates, Smith cannot have thought that *any* actual existing society was characterised by literally *every* person living from exchange. Hence the designator 'commercial society' is best thought of not as an all-or-nothing evaluation but as a general mode of securing subsistence, with various levels of real-world actualisation.

Appendix 2: The System of Natural Liberty

The elective affinity between liberty as nondomination and commercial society points to another aspect of Smith's thought that has purposefully not been discussed above: 'the system of natural liberty'. Purposefully, because this is distinct from Smith's account of modern liberty and must be handled accordingly, the tendency of scholars to inaccurately equate 'the system of natural liberty', 'commercial society', and 'modern liberty' notwithstanding.[82]

The 'system of natural liberty' in Smith's usage is a precise label used to pick out the regulation of economic affairs as a matter of national policy.[83] Writing in the eighteenth century Smith had no conception of 'the economy' in our modern sense of a discrete (if necessarily abstract) unit of analysis subject to the management of the state.[84] Nonetheless the 'system of natural liberty' can usefully (if anachronistically) be viewed as a recommendation for what we would now call *economic policy*, as indicated by Smith's own presentation of it as *a system*.[85] Specifically, it was offered as a direct counter to the two other 'systems of political economy' (*WN* IV.intro) that Smith identified as existing by the late eighteenth century: the actually existing mercantile system of monopolies, drawbacks, and nefarious merchant manipulation which the majority of Book IV of *WN* was dedicated to condemning, and the theoretical reforming plans of the French Physiocrats with their call for the economies of western Europe to be forcibly reformed via an interventionist programme favouring agriculture over manufacturing. Smith took himself to have demonstrated the folly of both the actually existing mercantile system as well as any attempt to implement the Physiocrats' radical reforms. He thus presented his

---

82. For example, Hill, *Smith's Pragmatic Liberalism*, 130–31; Berry, 'Adam Smith', 337; Charles L. Griswold, *Adam Smith and the Virtues of Enlightenment* (Cambridge: Cambridge University Press, 1999), 301–10.

83. For accurate discussions of Smith's system of natural liberty as precisely a system of political economy, see Winch, *Smith's Politics*, chap. 4; Winch, *Riches and Poverty*, chap. 3; Hont, 'Adam Smith and the Political Economy', 376–88; Keith Tribe, 'The "System of Natural Liberty"': Natural Order in the *Wealth of Nations*', *History of European Ideas* (forthcoming); and especially Vivienne Brown, *Adam Smith's Discourse: Canonicity, Commerce, and Conscience* (London: Routledge, 1994), chap. 7, which identifies it as founded in the sectoral analysis which constitutes the theoretical foundation of the economic argument of *WN*.

84. On the much more recent genesis of the idea of 'the economy', see Timothy Mitchell, 'Fixing the Economy', *Cultural Studies* 12, no. 1 (1998).

85. On this see Tribe, '"System of Natural Liberty"'.

own preferred alternative of 'natural liberty'—wherein 'every man, as long as he does not violate the laws of justice, is left perfectly free to pursue his own interest his own way, and to bring both his industry and capital into competition with those of any other man, or order of men' (*WN* IV.ix.51)—as winning the intellectual case by default, validated by the fact that it avoided the pitfalls that the other two systems fell into.

Yet the idea of a system of *natural* liberty in the realm of political economy was, in Smith's handling, necessarily paradoxical. When Smith wrote of a system of natural liberty in Book IV, he used the term 'natural' as he did in Book III (and as discussed in the previous chapter): to describe an economically logical progression as would be expected to occur absent political interference, that is, disruption caused by (as he put it) 'human institutions' (*WN* III.i.4). The 'obvious and simple' system of natural liberty meant allowing individuals to pursue their own reasonable self-interest in webs of market exchange, with the state understanding its task as the mere facilitator of this 'natural' process, rather than attempting to forcibly channel it towards specific ends, and in the process obstructing rather than advancing collective opulence. Yet the irony— indeed paradox—was that the system of natural liberty did not, and indeed could not, itself come about 'naturally' (i.e., spontaneously and without direction) precisely because political interference and the accumulated sediment of several millennia of distorting 'human institutions' prevented it from doing so. Artifice would thus be required to make way for the natural progress of opulence, in the form of purposeful intervention by the state, but with the ultimately self-denying aim of *reducing* distorting interferences as facilitated by already existing 'human institutions'.[86] Given the point that modern Europeans in particular had reached by the time that Smith wrote—that is, the legacy of an unnatural and retrograde economic order where the towns had developed ahead of the agricultural base due to the legacy of Roman collapse and feudal misrule—the system of natural liberty could only ever be inaugurated via *un*natural means.

Smith famously judged that because so many vested private interests were aligned with keeping the mercantile system in place, whilst the 'love of system' that was apt to take hold of the minds of reformers tended to enchant them with the love of specific schemes and plans directed at imagined ideal outcomes (*TMS* VI.ii.2.10–18), the system of natural liberty was in fact highly

---

86. On this see also Hont, 'Adam Smith and the Political Economy', 380, on 'the apparently paradoxical idea of regulating in order to arrive at a non-regulated system'.

unlikely ever to be brought about in practice: 'To expect, indeed, that the freedom of trade should ever be entirely restored in Great Britain, is as absurd as to expect that an Oceana or Utopia should ever be established in it. Not only the prejudices of the publick, but what is much more unconquerable, the private interests of many individuals, irresistibly oppose it' (*WN* IV.ii.43).[87] The system of natural liberty would certainly not come about 'naturally' (i.e., spontaneously, without political direction), but nor was it likely to come about artificially (i.e., through political direction) either. Some of the implications and consequences of this are discussed in chapter 5. In the meantime, we may note the relationships between Smith's 'system of natural liberty' and other connected, but distinct, aspects of his thought.

In the first place, the system of natural liberty is not identical with 'commercial society'. On Smith's view it is quite possible for individuals to live from exchange under other forms of economic organization. Indeed, this was precisely the case in Smith's own day: the modern European commercial societies with which he was intimately familiar operated the mercantile system, not that of natural liberty. Second, the system of natural liberty is distinct in Smith's handling from the idea of modern liberty. The 'liberty' of the system of natural liberty pertains to individual market transactions free from excessively distorting effects of perverting institutional interference, which are left to the discretion of individual agents so long as they conduct themselves within the bounds of justice (i.e., that individuals may engage in fierce market competition, but they must in the process refrain from violations of the physical integrity of others, whilst likewise respecting the sanctity of property holdings: *WN* IV.ix.51). By contrast the 'liberty' of modern liberty refers to nondomination secured under the rule of law via property security and the separation of powers as achieved in modern western Europe. As with 'commercial society', there is certainly an elective affinity between these two phenomena: modern liberty complements—and would be complemented in turn by—the system of

87. Smith's language of natural liberty as being 'restored', versus a Utopia being 'established', should not be read as his thinking that the *system* of natural liberty ever obtained in human history. Instead, Smith is here invoking the idea of natural liberty as being pre-political, and hence any system that put it in place would restore the 'natural' (i.e., economically logical) condition that would obtain absent the interference of politics, or in his locution, 'human institutions'. Smith may here be drawing on an older natural law discourse whereby correctly administered politics was an attempt to restore the harmony that ought to obtain in nature but which had been distorted by human history—on which see especially Hont, 'Adam Smith and the Political Economy', 387–88.

natural liberty. But the former does not *need* the latter. Indeed, the history of modern Europe demonstrates, Smith thinks, that modern liberty arose *in the absence of* the system of natural liberty. This is because the former is a political value understood in a historical frame, whereas the latter is a mode of economic organisation. Whilst the political value would certainly be augmented by the addition of the economic policy, and the two are thus natural complements, modern liberty had, as a matter of historical fact, emerged in the absence of the system of natural liberty—and Smith saw no reason to expect that situation to change anytime soon. Chapter 5 considers some of the reasons for, and implications of, this important aspect of his thought.

3

Smith and Rousseau, after Hume and Mandeville

IN WRITING the history of political thought there is a danger that one's estimation of a thinker becomes unduly influenced by the subsequent reputation, no matter how well deserved, that the thinker has come to possess.[1] This can lead not only to distorted and anachronistic readings of past texts, but also to mistakes about the significance of those texts to contemporaries, where the subsequent eminence of a thinker may cloud our assessment of how they were received by their immediate readership. The argument of this chapter is that in recent scholarly treatments this is precisely what has happened as regards

---

1. This chapter originally appeared as Paul Sagar, 'Smith and Rousseau, After Hume and Mandeville', *Political Theory* 46, no. 1 (2018), and is republished here with minor amendments. Since its original acceptance and online publication (2016), several other studies have in different but to some degree complementary ways called into question the extent to which Smith was animated by a perceived need to respond to Rousseau, notably Robin Douglass, 'Morality and Sociability in Commercial Society: Smith, Rousseau—and Mandeville', *Review of Politics* 79, no. 4 (2017); Michelle Schwarze and John T. Scott, 'Mutual Sympathy and the Moral Economy: Adam Smith Reviews Rousseau', *Journal of Politics* 81, no. 1 (2019); Claire Pignol and Benoît Walraevens, 'Smith and Rousseau on Envy in Commercial Society', *European Journal of the History of Economic Thought* 24, no. 6 (2017). Nonetheless, I take it that the mainstream view still remains the one that I challenge below. I do not consider here the arguments put forward more recently by Charles Griswold, *Jean-Jacques Rousseau and Adam Smith: A Philosophical Encounter* (London: Routledge, 2018). This is because Griswold conducts a primarily philosophical investigation, one less interested in the extent to which Smith himself actually responded to Rousseau, but seeks rather to put the two thinkers' ideas into dialogue on various questions, regardless of whether they ever actually responded to each other as a matter of historical fact. I agree with Griswold (xx, n. 7) that what I say in this chapter (and the original article it reprints) need not necessarily impugn his philosophical investigation—we are for the most part pursuing different lines of enquiry.

the intellectual encounter between Smith and Jean-Jacques Rousseau.[2] For against the thrust of most of what has recently been written on this matter I believe that Smith did not take Rousseau particularly seriously as an intellectual opponent, and instead took his positions to be neither particularly novel nor uniquely challenging. This is revealed by returning to Smith's intellectual context in the 1750s, during which he both reviewed Rousseau's *Second Discourse* and published *TMS*, but where a proper appreciation of the significance of David Hume and Bernard Mandeville pushes Rousseau firmly into the background.

The argument proceeds in four main sections. The first situates my case by using the publication of István Hont's 2009 Carlyle Lectures as a critical foil for interrogating the Smith-Rousseau interface. The second challenges the view that Smith was impressed by Rousseau due to the latter's conception of pity by suggesting that Smith's much richer British philosophical context meant that the Genevan's intervention would have been received by him as far behind the best available English-language work. The third considers Smith's distinction between praise and praiseworthiness, and argues that although this functions as a reply to Rousseau, its original target was Mandeville. The final section examines the roles of utility, vanity, and economic consumption in the context of Smith's paraphrasing of Rousseau's rhetoric from the *Second Discourse*, but suggests that a careful reading indicates that Hume is the primary interlocutor, with Rousseau featuring as collateral damage. The reorientation effected in this chapter sets up a revisionist interpretation of Smith in the next, regarding the moral status of 'commercial society' and the prospects of the individuals who live within such arrangements.

Smith and Rousseau: The Question of Influence

My argument is indebted to the posthumous publication of Hont's 2009 Carlyle Lectures as *Politics in Commercial Society*. My aim, however, is not to straightforwardly endorse or extend Hont's positions, but to take his central point of departure and argue that if properly worked out it yields a very different picture of the Smith-Rousseau relationship to that which presently prevails. This may seem surprising, or even redundant, insofar as Hont *already*

---

2. It was an intellectual encounter only. As far as we know the two never met in person or corresponded, although Smith certainly knew of Hume's later unhappy interactions with Rousseau.

presents himself as offering a position distinct from that to be found in the existing scholarship. But where that difference lies is a matter that needs careful consideration, and one that we must review before proceeding.

Hont claims that Rousseau is typically taken to be a fierce critic of commercial modernity, whilst Smith is standardly depicted as its defender (or apologist). Hont himself rejects this dichotomy: both Smith and Rousseau ought to be considered theorists of commercial society, who are attempting to explain its foundations, predicaments, and possibilities.[3] Hont does not deny that Smith and Rousseau's political visions are very different, but he does contend that they share the same, or at least very similar, 'theories of moral foundations'.[4] Given this, Hont suggests that the interesting question is why their politics nonetheless diverged, and how each might be evaluated in the light of the other. Yet even if Hont's analysis differs from what he presents as the inadequate traditional dichotomy, he shares with the established literature the view that Rousseau was important to Smith, and exercised meaningful influence on the development of his ideas. Hont does not state this as explicitly as, for example, Pierre Force, for whom Smith was an 'admirer' of Rousseau,[5] or Dennis Rasmussen, who claims that Smith took Rousseau's arguments 'quite seriously, for in his view they pointed to the deepest and seemingly most intractable problems of the emerging commercial societies of his time'.[6] But he does credit Rousseau's concept of pity as leaving a direct mark on Smith's

3. István Hont, *Politics in Commercial Society: Jean-Jacques Rousseau and Adam Smith*, ed. B. Kapossy and M. Sonenscher (Cambridge, MA: Harvard University Press, 2015), 2.

4. Hont, *Politics in Commercial Society*, 22.

5. Pierre Force, *Self-Interest Before Adam Smith: A Genealogy of Economic Science* (Cambridge: Cambridge University Press, 2003), 20–24. Force's reading of Smith is convincingly critiqued in Christopher J. Berry, 'Smith Under Strain', *European Journal of Political Theory* 3, no. 4 (2004).

6. Dennis C. Rasmussen, *The Problems and Promise of Commercial Society: Adam Smith's Response to Rousseau* (University Park: Pennsylvania State University Press, 2008), 70. Similar endorsements of Rousseau's importance to Smith can be found in Charles Griswold, 'Smith and Rousseau in Dialogue: Sympathy, *Pitié*, Spectatorship and Narrative', in *The Adam Smith Review Vol. 5*, ed. V. Brown and S. Fleischacker (London: Routledge, 2010), 59; Michael Ignatieff, 'Smith, Rousseau and the Republic of Needs', in *Scotland and Europe 1200–1850*, ed. T. C. Smouth (Edinburgh: Edinburgh University Press, 1986); E. J. Hundert, *The Enlightenment's Fable: Bernard Mandeville and the Discovery of Society* (Cambridge: Cambridge University Press, 1994), 105–115, 220–21; John Robertson, *The Case for the Enlightenment: Scotland and Naples 1680–1760* (Cambridge: Cambridge University Press, 2005), 392–96; Donald Winch, *Riches and Poverty: An Intellectual History of Political Economy in Britain, 1750–1834* (Cambridge: Cambridge University Press, 1996), chap. 3.

thought, and suggests that crucial aspects of the Scot's political system are specific replies to the Genevan.[7] Overall, Hont agrees with most other commentators that when Smith read Rousseau, he registered him as a major intellectual interlocutor and challenger.

Of course, believing that Rousseau influenced Smith by itself settles nothing of further significance. There is protracted debate about *how* Rousseau did so, to what extent and where Smith responded, and who had the better of things on a variety of intellectual fronts. Yet all of these further questions are affected by whether Smith *did* take Rousseau particularly seriously, and was in various ways preoccupied with responding to his challenge(s). If that turns out not to be so, or at least not in the regards often supposed, then the proffered answers will be in varying ways inadequate because the wrong starting questions will have been asked. To see why the wrong questions may indeed have been asked, we must bring the foundations of Hont's own project more clearly into focus.

The editors of *Politics in Commercial Society* suggest that a key difference between Hont's analysis and the majority of the existing literature is that whereas the latter tends to analyse Smith in ways that make him look more like Rousseau, Hont brings out the ways in which Rousseau resembles Smith.[8] This is fair enough, but it is not the most illuminating way to draw the comparison. A more important difference between Hont and other commentators is that whilst the latter tend to compare Smith and Rousseau primarily as theorists of morality, Hont begins the analysis a step further back, with the question of sociability. A root concept in eighteenth-century debates on morality and politics, sociability (as Hont has shown elsewhere) was the foundational issue that had to be settled before anything else could be determined.[9] Hont maintains that neither Smith nor Rousseau countenanced the idea that man was naturally sociable, and hence explaining the emergence of stable society

---

7. Hont, *Politics in Commercial Society*, 26–27, 51.

8. Béla Kapossy and Michael Sonenscher, 'Editor's Introduction', in *Politics in Commercial Society*, xi.

9. István Hont, 'Introduction', in *Jealousy of Trade: International Competition and the Nation-State in Historical Perspective* (Cambridge, MA: Belknap, 2005), 40–45; Hont, 'The Language of Sociability and Commerce: Samuel Pufendorf and the Theoretical Foundations of the "Four Stages" Theory', in *Jealousy of Trade*; Hont, 'Commercial Society and Political Theory in the Eighteenth Century: The Problem of Authority in David Hume and Adam Smith', in *Main Trends in Cultural History: Ten Essays*, ed. Willem Melching and Wyger Velema (Amsterdam: Rodopi, 1994).

required some appeal to artifice. We can therefore label both thinkers in this regard 'epicureans', albeit without expecting too much theoretical precision from that label.[10] However—and as I argue below—when we more fully develop the claim that both Smith and Rousseau were primarily sociability theorists, pressure is put on the idea that Smith was seriously influenced or impressed by Rousseau. This is because Smith was the inheritor of an advanced British sociability discourse to which Rousseau had no access because he could not read English, and largely constructed his own intervention from a working out of Hobbes's *De Cive* and secondary discussions of Hobbes's positions in French.[11] In other words, when encountering Rousseau in the mid-1750s, the Scott would have registered the Genevan as a highly able, but very behind-the-curve, thinker, any shared 'epicureanism' notwithstanding.

It may nonetheless remain the case that there is much value to be had in comparing Smith and Rousseau's positions regardless of the question of influence. Hont's own wider analysis of political, moral, and economic theory indicates as much, as do (for example) Ryan Patrick Hanley's detailed and illuminating comparative studies of Smith and Rousseau, which typically proceed without putting heavy weight on matters of influence.[12] Nonetheless, our understanding of exactly how Smith and Rousseau should be compared, and what those comparisons ultimately yield, may come to change if we end up believing that one viewed the other's positions as largely obsolete, or without particular force—as indeed I shall argue in chapter 4 below. Furthermore, there are also ramifications for the wider conceptualization of the history of political thought. The efforts of a so-called Cambridge School notwithstanding, there is still typically held to be a canon of great historical political thinkers in the Western tradition. Rousseau is most definitely a member. Smith, despite recent healthy interest in his political thought, is not typically granted

10. Hont, *Politics in Commercial Society*, 14–18, 20–21.

11. That this was Rousseau's relationship to the sociability debate, via his complex engagement with Hobbes and Hobbes's French critics, see Robin Douglass, *Rousseau and Hobbes: Nature, Free Will, and the Passions* (Oxford: Oxford University Press, 2015), introduction (esp. 16–20) and chaps. 1 and 2.

12. Ryan Patrick Hanley, 'Commerce and Corruption: Rousseau's Diagnosis and Adam Smith's Cure', *European Journal of Political Theory* 7, no. 2 (2008); Hanley, 'From Geneva to Glasgow: Rousseau and Adam Smith on the Theatre of Commercial Society', *Studies in Eighteenth Century Culture* 35, no. 1 (2006); Hanley, 'Enlightened Nation Building: The Science of the Legislator in Adam Smith and Rousseau', *American Journal of Political Science* 52, no. 2 (2008).

inclusion. Yet the discovery that Smith was unimpressed by Rousseau is potentially disruptive to established evaluations, especially if we come to believe that Smith was *right* not to be impressed. In either case, there follow implications not just for how we read Rousseau as well as Smith, but regarding what should count for inclusion in a canon, and whether such a thing should be thought to exist at all. Those are some of the wider matters raised. In the rest of this chapter, however, I limit myself to making the case regarding Rousseau's lack of serious influence upon, or importance to, Smith, before turning in the next chapter to cash out some of the implications of my reading.

The Amiable Principle of Pity

In 1756, Smith famously offered Scottish readers an extended consideration of Rousseau's *Second Discourse* through a 'Letter' to the short-lived *Edinburgh Review*. Demonstrating Smith's direct engagement with Rousseau's ideas, the 'Letter' has unsurprisingly served as a principal source of evidence for the influence on, or importance of, Rousseau to Smith in recent discussions.[13] After calling for Scottish readers to extend their gaze both to English and French achievements in natural and moral philosophy, whilst indicating that the most exciting future advances were likely to come from the continent, Smith certainly dedicates the bulk of his 'letter' to summarizing (as he sees it) the key features of Rousseau's *Discourse*, listing its main claims and providing translations of three long passages from Part 2 of the work. But it is by no means obvious that in doing so Smith was signalling the particular importance, novelty, or urgency of Rousseau's intervention. In fact, he may be read as indicating precisely the opposite, once we unpack the content of his remarks in the context of 1750s British intellectual advances.

Of especial importance is Smith's declaration that 'whoever reads this last work with attention, will observe, that the second volume of the Fable of the

---

13. For discussions of Smith's review, see Griswold, *Rousseau and Smith*, 94–102; Nicholas Phillipson, *Adam Smith: An Enlightened Life* (London: Allen Lane, 2010), 144–48; Rasmussen, *Problems and Promise*, 59–71; Eric Schliesser, 'Adam Smith's Benevolent and Self-Interested Conception of Philosophy', in *New Voices on Adam Smith*, ed. Leonidas Montes and Eric Schliesser (London: Routledge, 2006), 329–57; Shannon C. Stimson, 'The General Will after Rousseau: Smith and Rousseau on Sociability and Inequality', in *The General Will: The Evolution of a Concept*, ed. J. Farr and D. Lay Williams (Cambridge: Cambridge University Press, 2015), 253–58; Winch, *Riches and Poverty*, 66–76; Hont, *Politics in Commercial Society*, 18–21, 26; Douglass, 'Morality and Sociability', 600–606.

Bees has given occasion to the system of Mr. Rousseau'. Yet despite drawing attention to this alleged connection, Smith also claimed that there was an important difference. Rousseau's account differed from Mandeville's insofar as it was 'softened, improved, and embellished, and stript of all that tendency to corruption and licentiousness which has disgraced them in their original author'. The reason for this was that Rousseau maintained that the 'amiable principle' of pity was capable of producing all the virtues the reality of which Mandeville denied (*EPS* 250–51).

Hont takes Smith's zeroing in upon pity as evidence that he was a fellow traveller in making the capacity for shared affective sentiment foundational for any satisfactory 'epicurean' account of sociability. Hont must be correct that by 1755 Smith would have had the argument of *TMS* largely in place, hence his own system cannot have had its genesis in reading Rousseau. Instead, Hont suggests, when Smith read the *Discourse* this must have helped him 'more easily decide that the way ahead was through the generalization of the pity model'.[14] The problem with this latter claim is that although it is true, when we restore the intellectual context—which Hont hints at, but does not explore—it turns out to be trivial. Yet that triviality in turn gives reason to suspect that when Smith encountered Rousseau's ideas he cannot have registered them as especially important.

In Britain, debate over the capacity to feel on behalf of others had been raging for decades by the time Smith read Rousseau. The principal point of antagonism was originally Thomas Hobbes's infamous supposition that human beings were entirely selfish and incapable of genuine feeling on behalf of others. As he put it in *Leviathan*,

> *Griefe*, for the Calamity of another is PITTY; and ariseth from the imagination that the like calamity may befall himselfe; and therefore is called also COMPASSION, and in the phrase of this present time a FELLOW FEELING: And therefore for Calamity arriving from great wickedness, the best men have the least Pitty; and for the same Calamity, those have least Pitty, that think themselves least obnoxious to the same.[15]

14. Hont, *Politics in Commercial Society*, 34.

15. Thomas Hobbes, *The Clarendon Edition of the Works of Thomas Hobbes, Leviathan*, 3 vols., ed. N. Malcolm (Oxford: Oxford University Press, 2012), II, 90; cf. Thomas Hobbes, *The Elements of Law, Natural and Politic*, ed. F. Tönnies and M. M. Goldsmith (London: Frank Cass, 1969), 44.

This position was part and parcel of Hobbes's denial of natural sociability. Once one dismissed Aristotelian notions of a *zoon politikon*, and also denied that human beings were capable of non-selfish affective sentiments directed towards others, then, as Hobbes put it in *De Cive*, human beings could form 'large and lasting' society only from the materials of 'honour' and 'advantage', that is, from attempts to further utility, or out of the desire to secure recognition in the eyes of peers.[16] Yet for Hobbes the interplay of honour and advantage was inherently unstable.[17] The desire for unequal recognition (in Hobbes's language, pride) overwhelmed efforts to live peaceably in order to secure utility and the mutual satisfaction of the need to be liked. As a result, large and lasting society could not be stabilized from the materials of honour and advantage. The only solution was 'fear', that is, the imposition of an over-aweing power to terrorize potential defectors into obedience, thus making large-scale society possible.[18]

This vision was resisted by many of Hobbes's British successors.[19] Particularly important to Smith's intellectual context were Bishop Butler and Francis Hutcheson, who both drew upon the Earl of Shaftesbury's anti-Hobbesian 'An Inquiry Concerning Virtue and Merit' to further attack the Hobbesian edifice. Butler's 1726 *Fifteen Sermon's Preached at the Rolls Chapel* argued directly against Hobbes's claim that human beings were incapable of genuine fellow feeling, offering a refutation of the supposition of necessary motivational egoism.[20] Butler similarly appealed to capacities for fellow feeling as providing the 'cement' to society, which he believed disproved the Hobbesian supposition of natural unsociability.[21] Influenced by Butler, Hutcheson in his 1728 *Essay on the Nature and Conduct of the Passions* invoked the idea of a 'public

---

16. Thomas Hobbes, *On the Citizen*, ed. R. Tuck and M. Silverthorne (Cambridge: Cambridge University Press, 1998), 21–22.

17. Hont, *Politics in Commercial Society*, 10–12.

18. Hobbes, *On the Citizen*, 24; for detailed discussion, see Sagar, *The Opinion of Mankind: Sociability and the Theory of the State from Hobbes to Smith* (Princeton: Princeton University Press, 2018), 27–39.

19. For an overview of some relevant theories of pity, see Christian Maurer, 'Facing the Misery of Others: Pity, Pleasure and Tragedy in Scottish Enlightenment Moral Philosophy', in *The Poetic Enlightenment: Poetry and Human Science 1650–1820*, ed. T. Jones and R. Boyson (London: Pickering & Chatto, 2013).

20. Joseph Butler, *Butler's Fifteen Sermons*, ed. T. A. Roberts (London: SPCK, 1970), 49–63.

21. Butler, *Butler's Fifteen Sermons*, 23.

sense', which operated alongside his earlier idea of an innate 'moral sense' that disinterestedly detected virtue in others.[22] This 'public sense' accounted for men's capacity for fellow feeling, 'our Determination to be pleased with the *Happiness* of others, and to be uneasy at their *Misery*', which Hutcheson presented as giving the lie to Hobbesian and Mandevillean suppositions of irreducible selfishness.[23] Regarding sociability, Hutcheson's 1730 inaugural lecture as Professor of Moral Philosophy at the University of Glasgow—where he would of course teach Smith in the late 1730s—invoked the idea of 'sympathy' (or in the original Latin *contagio*) to offer a theory of natural sociability that was targeted at Hobbes, Mandeville, and Pufendorf.[24] After these more major theorists, the now little-known Scottish philosopher Archibald Campbell offered a sophisticated reworking of Hobbes's concept of pity, which he labelled 'sympathy', in the 1733 reissue of his *An Enquiry into the Original of Moral Virtue*.[25]

Most important of all, however, was David Hume. In his *Treatise of Human Nature*, published in 1739 and 1740, Hume supplied a complex theory of sociability rooted in the most advanced theory of fellow feeling yet deployed. Hume's 'sympathy' posited that human beings literally shared each other's sentiments, in his parlance transforming the 'idea' of an other's affective state into an 'impression'. As he memorably put it in a metaphor later picked up and developed by Smith, 'the minds of men are mirrors to one another', reflecting passions back and forth.[26] Sympathy allowed Hume to block the Hobbesian supposition that pride destabilized the capacity to form society. On the contrary '*vanity* is rather to be esteem'd a social passion, and a bond of union among men'.[27] Due to the capacity to sympathize with others, man was 'the creature of the universe, who has the most ardent desire of society, and is fitted

22. On the moral sense, see Francis Hutcheson, *An Inquiry into the Original of Our Ideas of Beauty and Virtue*, ed. W. Leidhold (Indianapolis: Liberty Fund, 2004), 85–182.

23. Francis Hutcheson, *An Essay on the Nature and Conduct of the Passions and Affections, with Illustrations on the Moral Sense*, ed. A. Garrett (Indianapolis: Liberty Fund, 2002), 17.

24. Francis Hutcheson, 'Inaugural Oration', in *Logic, Metaphysics, and the Natural Sociability of Mankind*, ed. J. Moore and M. Silverthorne (Indianapolis: Liberty Fund, 2006).

25. Archibald Campbell, *An Enquiry into the Original of Moral Virtue* (Edinburgh, 1733), 30–48, 215–55.

26. David Hume, *A Treatise of Human Nature*, ed. D. F. Norton and M. J. Norton (Oxford: Oxford University Press, 2007), T.2.2.5.21; SBN 365; cf. *TMS* III.I.3.

27. Hume, *Treatise*, T.3.2.2.12; SBN 491.

for it by the most advantages'.[28] But Hume did not maintain that man was therefore straightforwardly naturally sociable. The trouble came not from 'honour', as Hobbes had supposed, but from 'advantage'. The pursuit of material interests led men into conflict, threatening to destabilize social arrangements because of the coordination problems generated by the instability of possessions combined with the limited generosity of men in conditions of moderate scarcity. Artifice was ultimately required in order for humans to achieve large and lasting society, but it was not that of overawing sovereign power, as Hobbes had supposed, or the invention of systems of morality and honour by legislator figures, as Mandeville claimed. Rather, it was the convention (and subsequently, virtue) of justice: a spontaneously developed, but artificial, response to the need to coordinate utility seeking across groups of self-interested, but nonetheless sympathetically capable, individuals. Hume's theory of justice was an 'epicurean' account of sociability, but one that hoped to avoid the licentious and scandalous implications associated with Hobbes and Mandeville.[29]

There is no doubt that Smith knew Hume's position intimately. Not only had he read the *Treatise* whilst an unhappy visiting undergraduate at the University of Oxford,[30] but in *TMS* he supplied a compact summary of Hume's view,[31] and endorsed his central conclusion (albeit with technical modifications) that the organization of utility seeking was the central sociability question, hence why justice was to be considered the 'main pillar' that upheld society, benevolence its mere 'ornament' (*TMS* II.ii.3.4).[32] The point of this for present purposes, however, is that compared to Hume's complex position, Rousseau's

---

28. Hume, *Treatise*, T.2.2.5.15; SBN 363.

29. On Hume as an epicurean theorist, see especially James Moore, 'Hume and Hutcheson', in *Hume and Hume's Connexions*, ed. M. A. Stewart and J. P. Wright (Edinburgh: Edinburgh University Press, 1994), and Robertson, *Case for the Enlightenment*, chap. 6.

30. Phillipson, *Adam Smith*, 64–66.

31. *TMS* II.ii.3.6, the entirety of which is an explication of Hume's utility-centred theory of justice, predicated upon first granting that man has a 'natural love for society' as manifested in the primitive family, but requiring utility-regarding artifice to attain large and lasting associations, i.e., the real sociability problem. For detailed discussion of *TMS* as a response to Hume's earlier sentimentalist ethical theory, see Paul Sagar, 'Beyond Sympathy: Smith's Rejection of Hume's Moral Theory', *British Journal for the History of Philosophy* 25, no. 4 (2017).

32. Sagar, *Opinion of Mankind*, 168–73.

account of pity in the *Discourse* would have struck Smith as extremely basic, far behind the best English work available.[33]

Rousseau's claim was that (as Smith put it in his review) pity was 'in itself no virtue' (*EPS* 251) but was more like an instinct, possessed by many animals as well as savage man in his primitive condition: 'a natural sentiment which, by moderating in every individual the activity of self-love, contributes to the mutual preservation of the entire species.'[34] The central function of pity in Rousseau's sociability story was to discredit Hobbes's claim that in the state of nature man was naturally aggressive and violently competitive for status: 'in the state of Nature', pity 'takes the place of Laws, morals, and virtue, with the advantage that no one is tempted to disobey its gentle voice; pity that will keep any sturdy Savage from robbing a weak child or an infirm old man of his hard-won subsistence if he can hope to find his own elsewhere.'[35] Hobbes's vision was a back projection of civilized man into his primordial state.[36] The proof that it was a back projection, and a false one at that, was that it would have been impossible for men to ever group together long enough to escape their situation of primitive indolence if they were naturally aggressive in the way Hobbes supposed. Instead, Rousseau deduced, man had originally been solitary (Hobbes was right that there was no principle of natural sociability), yet nonetheless nonaggressive due to the possession of pity. He had ultimately entered society not by being overawed by superior power, but—as Smith summarized—because of some 'unfortunate accidents having given birth to the unnatural passions of ambition and the vain desire of superiority' (*EPS* 250). Crucial to Rousseau's story, however, was that natural pity was extensively suppressed after his *amour propre*—that is, the desire for recognition—became pathologically inflamed due to contact with economic inequality and the rise of luxury.[37] According to Rousseau, in modern conditions when pity

33. For detailed discussion of the early modern British sociability debate, see Sagar, *Opinion of Mankind*, chaps. 1–2.

34. Jean-Jacques Rousseau, 'Second Discourse', in *The Discourses and Other Early Political Writings*, ed. V. Gourevitch (Cambridge: Cambridge University Press, 1997), 154.

35. Rousseau, 'Second Discourse', 154; Douglass, *Rousseau and Hobbes*, 68–69, 90–93.

36. Rousseau, 'Second Discourse', 132, 138–40.

37. Rousseau, 'Second Discourse', esp. 171–72, on how 'Nascent Society gave way to the most horrible state of war' after the 'unbridled passions of all' lead to the 'stifling of natural pity and the still weak voice of justice' at the point when the state was invented by the rich as a way of enforcing property rights, whilst tricking the poor into their own subjection. Rousseau does say that the force of natural pity sometimes resists even 'the most depraved morals', as evidenced

was suppressed and *amour propre* was inflamed, yet *amour de soi*-même—that is, the material needs of the body—remained still active, the only materials human beings had to form society were, as Hobbes claimed, honour and advantage. Hobbes's mistake was thinking that human beings had always been like this. What he was not wrong about was how they were now.

Yet from Smith's perspective in 1756 this story would have appeared far behind the advances achieved in Britain, by Hume in particular. Compared to the sophistication of Hume's sympathy matrix, Rousseau's pity was a primitive notion. Furthermore, in order to explain the emergence and stability of large-scale societies, whereas Hume had his complex theory of justice, on top of which he grafted an account of allegiance rooted in affective sentiment, which Smith himself directly picked up and extended, Rousseau posited the systematic deception of the poor by the rich after the point at which runaway inequality and inflamed *amour propre* meant that the state of nature was left behind forever (something we shall return to below). And it is important to emphasize that in Rousseau's story pity becomes fatally suppressed when humanity enters advanced large-scale society. For although Rousseau dismissed Mandeville for failing to see that pity could be the source of natural virtue, that is, criticizing the Dutchman for supposing that no natural virtue was possible at all, this was a very specific point. What Rousseau did not deny was that now, in conditions of modernity, with *amour propre* pathologically inflamed and when pity *was* extensively suppressed, most individuals did not act virtuously but only out of selfish regard to their own desire for recognition.[38] Rousseau's corrective of Mandeville was a technical point about the capacity for virtue amidst uncorrupted human beings, not a claim that pity enabled the widespread practice of virtue in the here and now. Yet when compared to Hume's complex and detailed ethical theory—which took sympathy as its starting point, and which his 1751 *Enquiry Concerning the Principles of Morals* made clear told decisively against theorists like Mandeville who denied the reality of moral distinctions due to suppositions of irreducible selfishness—Rousseau's

---

by people being moved to weeping in theatres (Rousseau, 'Second Discourse', 152), but the overall point is that inflamed *amour propre* had effectively negated pity as a source of virtue for almost all who live in advanced society.

38. This is spelled out explicitly at the close of the *Discourse*, with Rousseau summarizing that 'everything being reduced to appearances, everything becomes facetious and play-acting . . . we have nothing more than a deceiving and frivolous exterior, honour without virtue, reason without wisdom, and pleasure without happiness' ('Second Discourse', 187).

intervention cannot have struck Smith, despite its rhetorical power, as anything other than a variation on a theme that had already been surpassed.[39]

All of which throws into doubt Hont's contention that there is a 'direct imprint' of Rousseau's influence on the very first page of Smith's *TMS*.[40] Smith certainly declares that 'however selfish soever man may be supposed, there are evidently principles in his nature which interest him in the fortune of others' and gives "pity . . . the emotion which we feel for the misery of others", as a prime example' (*TMS* I.i.1.1). Yet rather than Smith here offering an endorsement, or continuation, of Rousseau's basic insight, it is something like the opposite. Not only could Smith have taken the claim that we are capable of pity from a long line of previous British thinkers, he should anyway be read as saying that theorists like Rousseau are simply wrong. No matter how selfish we may be supposed, the principle of pity can 'evidently' be discerned in us, and not as a rarely encountered residue from an uncorrupted age, but as a quotidian fact of present existence. Furthermore, immediately after making this declaration in the first paragraph, Smith moves into a discussion of full-blown sympathy, expanding greatly beyond the rudimentary capacity of pity with which he opens. Explicitly taking over Hume's term, and developing the older philosopher's framework, Smith's opening chapter laid the foundations of an account of sympathy which constituted a bold new intervention in the ongoing British debate. Ultimately, from Smith's vantage point in Glasgow during the mid-1750s, Rousseau's softened and embellished Mandevilleanism would have had nothing new or important to add to what had already been achieved in Britain.

39. David Hume, *An Enquiry Concerning the Principles of Morals*, ed. T. L. Beauchamp (Oxford: Oxford University Press, 1998), esp. appendix 2. Indeed, it is not even clear that Rousseau was as far away from Mandeville as he presented himself, or as Smith credited him with being. Mandeville after all does discuss pity, but rather than seeing it as a building block of sociability and morality, simply dismisses it as a self-regarding and thereby ipso facto vicious motivation: Bernard Mandeville, *The Fable of the Bees Volume 1*, ed. F. B. Kaye (Indianapolis: Liberty Fund, 1988), 56. Nonetheless, it is striking that in remark 'P' of the *Fable of the Bees Volume 1*, Mandeville explicitly talks of the 'strong remains of Primitive Pity and Innocence, which all the arbitrary Power of Custom, and the violence of Luxury, have not yet been able to conquer' (174). Mandeville does not develop this claim any further—indeed it looks like he ought not to make it at all given his other theoretical commitments—but this may put him even closer to Rousseau than I have suggested in my main line of argument. I am grateful to an anonymous reader at *Political Theory* for pointing this out: as they suggest, this may mean that Smith is *even less* interested in Rousseau—as opposed to Mandeville—than I have indicated above.

40. Hont, *Politics in Commercial Society*, 26–27.

This raises the question of why Smith chose to review the *Discourse* at all. It is doubtful that we will ever have an entirely satisfactory answer. One suggestion, made in light of the above, might be that rather than seeing Smith's 'Letter' as straightforward evidence of his interest in Rousseau, we might instead read it as something like an advertisement for his own forthcoming intervention. Smith may have been priming his readers, telling them that the interesting part of Rousseau's thesis—the only thing that separates him from Mandeville—is the attempt to build a theory of morality on the capacity for fellow feeling. Rousseau hadn't gotten it right, but Smith would soon offer his own, much more sophisticated, explication of how to do it properly. Admittedly, this explanation is limited: an advertisement appearing three years before the advertised product has obvious drawbacks. But be that as it may, we are not entitled to assume that the mere fact of the review is by itself evidence for Rousseau's influence upon, or importance to, Smith. To assume that it must be is to back project contemporary estimations of these thinkers' respective importance, and invest the 'Letter' with a meaning to Smith that we cannot know that it had. After all, motivations for reviewing the works of others are many and various: of those of us writing book reviews today, who would wish such things to be taken as a clear and unambiguous evidence of influence, or one's estimations of importance, in two hundred fifty years' time? The fact is that we simply do not know why Smith reviewed Rousseau for his Scottish audience, and in light of that ignorance we ought not to assume that the review clearly signals anything one way or the other. To arrive at a more reliable judgement on the matter, we must instead consider the wider evidence from Smith's own published positions.

Praise and Praiseworthiness

Ryan Patrick Hanley has argued that Smith's central distinction between the love of mere praise, and the love of being genuinely praiseworthy, functions as a response to Rousseau's claim that 'commercial society is fundamentally driven by a vanity that threatens to corrupt its participants.'[41] According to Rousseau, 'commercial society stimulates in men a desire for esteem and consideration such that they can only live in the eyes and opinions of others. Such individuals, plagued by solicitude for recognition, can no longer achieve the

41. Hanley, 'Commerce and Corruption', 138.

simple goodness natural to them in their uncorrupted, self-sufficient state'.[42] Living always in the eyes of others, men developed the distinction between being and appearing to be—between *être* and *paraître*—and in the process lost the capacity for virtue, possessing only its simulacrum in the gratification of *amour propre*. Smith recognised this danger, but believed that it could be resisted. 'To avoid such slavishness, nature invested man with a second side . . . in which the praises of others are mitigated by a natural regard for what is praiseworthy'.[43] Man desired not simply to appear virtuous, but to *be* virtuous. Indeed, Smith went so far as to claim that 'so far is the love of praiseworthiness from being derived altogether from that of praise; that the love of praise seems, at least in a great measure, to be derived from that of praiseworthiness' (*TMS* III.2.4). As Hanley concludes, 'Through the love of praiseworthiness, nature has supplied not simply a cure for an existing malady but an inoculation against an illness to come, for in a renewed appeal to our natural love of praiseworthiness lies what Smith takes to be the key to recovering virtue in civil society, and thereby returning civilized man from a concern with *paraître* to the love of *être*'.[44]

Putting aside for now Hanley's problematic use of the term 'commercial society' (on which see chapter 1 above) I agree that Smith's distinction between praise and praiseworthiness operates as a reply to Rousseau. But a philosophical argument may function effectively against a particular position without that position being the original intended target. Hanley takes it that Rousseau was indeed Smith's original target. I believe the evidence points in another direction.

Matters are complicated here by the fact that Smith's most comprehensive discussion of the praise/praiseworthiness distinction was added at the very end of his life, to the sixth and final 1790 edition of *TMS* in the heavily revised and extended chapter 2 of Part III. At first glance it would appear that this is an area of Smith's thought that cannot be posited as having been significantly formed prior to contact with Rousseau. Indeed, some commentators see the final edition as bearing indelible marks of the long-lasting influence of the Genevan. John Robertson, for example, has claimed that perhaps Smith's most famous final addition to *TMS*—his claim that 'the disposition to admire, and almost to worship, the rich and the powerful' is 'the great and most universal

---

42. Hanley, 'Commerce and Corruption', 139.
43. Hanley, 'Commerce and Corruption', 143.
44. Hanley, 'Commerce and Corruption', 143.

cause of the corruption of our moral sentiments' (*TMS* I.iii.3.1)—evidences Smith's 'wrestling over his answer' to Rousseau, 'finally conceding the point' that modern European commercial society corrupts the individuals who must live within it.[45] But we must be cautious here. With regards to the claim that excessive regard for the rich and the powerful corrupts our moral sentiments, Smith immediately states that this has been 'the complaint of moralists in all ages' (*TMS* I.iii.3.2). If Rousseau is indeed the primary interlocutor, Smith is expressly denying his originality. And in what follows, Smith actually paints a very different picture to that found in Rousseau's thought. For whereas the Genevan depicts advanced society as a state in which pretty much all individuals are corrupted by the love of fame and fortune, and thus lose their natural capacity for virtue, Smith denies this. In the 'middling and inferior stations of life' the 'road to virtue and that to fortune' usually coincide (*TMS* I.iii.3.5). The real problem is a specifically and narrowly political one: that those in positions of power can be consistently materially rewarded for unethical behaviour, and are surrounded by flatterers who exacerbate the problem (two factors which do not hold in ordinary life). In other words, Rousseau's general worry (if indeed he is even the target) about the ethical corruption of all individuals in advanced societies is misplaced, and he misses the real issue: how political leaders can be corrupted by their position, and what needs to be done, institutionally, to stymie and control that. This is not to suggest that Smith was therefore blasé about the potential for ethical corruption unleashed by inequality, a desire for material possessions, and the servility towards the rich and the great that the human predilection for sympathy with superiors generated—and we shall explore precisely what he had to say about these matters in the next chapter. Nonetheless, the present point is a specific one: that Smith held these concerns independent of his engagement with Rousseau, and the Genevan's polemic cannot satisfactorily be viewed as a, let alone the, decisive spur to Smith's concerns about moral corruption in conditions of advanced European modernity.

With regards to praise and praiseworthiness, although it is true that Smith's most thorough articulation of this distinction appeared only in 1790, it can nonetheless be identified in the earliest version of *TMS*, to which the late addition refers when answering 'some splenetic philosophers' who have 'imputed to the love of praise, or to what they call vanity, every action which ought to be ascribed to that of praise-worthiness' (*TMS* III.2.27). This

---

45. Robertson, *Case for the Enlightenment*, 394.

discussion is located in Part VII, and is trained explicitly upon the sceptical theory of Mandeville.

Part VII is the written-up version Smith's student lectures on moral philosophy and the history of ethics, dating in part from his 1748–50 stint at Edinburgh, and thereafter from his appointment at Glasgow, first as Professor of Logic in 1751, then as Professor of Moral Philosophy from 1752.[46] Part VII is thus likely to be one of the oldest sections of *TMS*, and what we find there is even more likely to predate Smith's encounter with Rousseau than other sections of the book. And one thing we find is the distinction between praise and praiseworthiness being used to refute Mandeville's 'licentious' system. As Smith puts it, 'Dr. Mandeville considers whatever is done from a sense of propriety, from a regard to what is commendable and praise-worthy, as being done from a love of praise and commendation, or as he calls it from vanity' (*TMS* VII.ii.4.7). Against this Smith maintains that 'the love of virtue' is 'the noblest and best passion in human nature', and that even 'the love of true glory' whilst inferior to the love of true virtue, 'in dignity appears to come immediately after it' (*TMS* VII.ii.4.8). Men of real magnanimity will still desire to be praised for their virtues, but they are conscious that this is because their virtues are deserving of real glory and this holds even if they don't actually receive the praise they are owed. By contrast, 'none but the weakest and most worthless of mankind are delighted with false glory'. Although Smith had not yet worked out the most powerful statement of his view as it would appear in the final additions to Part III, it is nonetheless clear in his 1759 rejoinder to Mandeville that a man of true virtue, who is unfortunate enough to be thought vicious by his peers 'though he despises the opinions which are actually entertained of him, he has the highest value for those which ought to be entertained of him'. Although Smith admitted that only a very few robust individuals could live from praiseworthiness alone—most people needed frequent doses of psychologically stabilizing praise to keep them going—he nonetheless took the possibility of living for praiseworthiness alone, and the admission of the legitimate enjoyment of praise for behaviour that was indeed praiseworthy, as refuting Mandeville's claim that we only ever acted to selfishly secure our 'vanity' (*TMS* VII.ii.4.10).

Yet recognising that Smith employs the praise/praiseworthiness distinction in the first edition of *TMS* implies a particular significance regarding his claim that Rousseau was a softened and embellished Mandeville. Recall that,

46. See the editor's introduction, *TMS*, 1–5.

according to Smith, Rousseau presented the same essential system as Mandeville but without the *apparent* scandal and licentiousness of the earlier version, because Rousseau claimed that natural pity meant that we were not always incapable of virtue, as Mandeville provocatively claimed. Yet by the mid-1750s Smith already knew what he thought was wrong with the kind of debunking theory which posited that because we act out of a desire for recognition in order to satisfy *amour propre*—or as Mandeville termed it in *The Fable of the Bees Volume 2*, 'self-liking'[47]—so all putative ethical behaviour is necessarily fraudulent or normatively compromised. This kind of argument could be defeated via the distinction between praise and praiseworthiness—and was originally worked out as a refutation of Mandeville. Certainly, it operated *pari passu* against Rousseau. But that was because the Genevan was restating the same ideas as the Dutchman, albeit in a manner that deceptively made them appear to have all the 'purity and sublimity' of the 'morals of Plato' (*EPS* 251).

Why, then, did Smith in 1790 offer an expanded and more thorough articulation of the praise/praiseworthiness distinction? We need not posit the special or lasting influence of Rousseau. Rather, the answer lies in the underlying structure of Smith's own ethical theory. As Hont encourages us to see, Smith's theory of morals may be understood as an extension of the insight Hume had applied to justice, but to all of the virtues: their origin in repeat experience of social interaction.[48] Hume divided the virtues into 'natural' and 'artificial', where the existence of the former was evidenced by immediate sympathetic responses to the imputed motivations of other agents, whilst the latter required some external convention to be in place before they could be made intelligible.[49] Smith, by contrast, backed up the story to ask how it was possible that there could be any virtues at all, even the putatively natural ones. This was a facet of the question of sociability: before one could examine the content of morality, one had to know where it came from—and that meant exploring the origins of society. This Smith did in Part III of *TMS*, where he offered a conjectural history of human ethical capacities as rooted in repeat iterations of judging and being judged over long periods of time. Morality for Smith was ultimately socially composed, an outcome of having to live in the gaze of others (*TMS* III.I.1–7).

47. Bernard Mandeville, *The Fable of the Bees Volume 2*, ed. F. B. Kaye (Indianapolis: Liberty Fund, 1988), 128–36.

48. Hont, *Politics in Commercial Society*, 35.

49. Hume, *Treatise*, T.3.2.1–2; SBN 477–84, T.3.3.1–2; SBN 574–91.

By doing this, however, Smith sailed much closer to Mandevillean shores than Hume. For the older Scott, precisely because there were 'natural' virtues antecedent to reflection, Mandeville's claim that all moral virtue was fraudulent—in his notorious phrase merely 'the Political Offspring which Flattery begot upon Pride'—could be straightforwardly dismissed.[50] And Mandeville was also wildly off target with regards to the artificial virtues: the manipulation of sociable behaviour by self-interested legislator figures mistook a secondary reinforcement effect for a primary cause of sociability, which Hume instead located in the artifice of justice.[51] Smith had to take Mandeville much more seriously because he essentially agreed with the Dutchman that the origins of all morality lie in repeat experiences of social interaction with judging peers. As Hanley writes, 'Insofar as sympathy is natural', nonetheless 'Smith seems to argue that it is natural for our natures to be shaped by convention. But at the same time, Smith foresaw the possible consequence of such an ethics if pursued to its conclusion—namely that an individual shaped by the morality of sympathy would be preeminently a slave to the strong need that men have for the approbation of their fellows'.[52] This explains why Smith could write that 'how destructive soever' Mandeville's system might appear, 'it could never have imposed upon so great a number of persons, nor have occasioned so general an alarm among those who are the friends of better principles, had it not in some respects bordered upon the truth' (*TMS* VII.ii.4.13).[53] This was an assessment Hume would never have countenanced, but which Smith did because his own account of the foundations, if not the normative validity, of morals travelled along much more similar lines to Mandeville's than Hume's had done.

The praise/praiseworthiness distinction was required to secure the possibility of genuine virtue in a world where ethical practices and values were ultimately a function of deep-rooted conventions of social interaction—of judging others and being judged in turn—whilst equipped with the capacity to share each other's sentiments. Smith needed such a distinction to prevent his own theory from collapsing into the sceptical debunking genealogy of

50. Mandeville, *Fable of the Bees Volume 1*, 51.

51. Hume, *Treatise*, T.3.2.6.11; SBN 533–34, T.3.3.1.11; SBN 578–79. On this see especially Hundert, *Enlightenment's Fable*, 62–86.

52. Hanley, 'Commerce and Corruption', 143.

53. For differing assessments of Smith's response to Mandeville, compare Hundert, *Enlightenment's Fable*, chap. 5, with Force, *Self-Interest*, chap. 1.

Mandeville's 'licentious' system. By 1790 he judged that his earlier attempts had not adequately or most powerfully explicated what separated him from Mandeville. Yet Smith's felt need to make good on his arguments was a product of the demands incumbent upon his own system, given his unwavering commitment not to cede the field to Mandeville, instead consistently denying that a socially composed origins theory of the foundations of morals must therefore be a sceptical or debunking one. As a result, Rousseau featured not as a source of any great influence or intellectual threat, but as merely repeating a challenge that Smith had already long registered, and knew that his own position needed to address.

Utility and Deception

What of Part IV of *TMS*, where Smith directly paraphrases Rousseau's arguments from the *Discourse*? Surely here we can discern the latter's profound influence upon the former? I suggest not. The reasons are revealed by paying close attention to Smith's wider purposes and strategy of argument.

Part IV is primarily a response to Hume's claim, stated in the *Treatise* and repeated even more forthrightly in the second *Enquiry*, that a regard for utility is the dominant factor in explaining value judgements. According to Hume, Smith reminded his readers, the 'utility of any object . . . pleases the master by perpetually suggesting to him the pleasure or conveniency which it is fitted to promote', with spectators able to share in this pleasure via sympathy (*TMS* IV.I.2). Despite the initial plausibility of this account, Smith insisted that it was subtly and importantly mistaken. In fact, human psychology exhibited a pervasive and wide-ranging quirk, such that the 'fitness, this happy contrivance of any production of art, should often be more valued, than the very end for which it was intended'. Bizarrely—at least to a sober philosophical eye—'the exact adjustment of the means for attaining any conveniency or pleasure, should frequently be more regarded, than that very conveniency or pleasure, in the attainment of which their whole merit would seem to consist' (*TMS* IV.I.3). Smith took himself to be the first to have noticed this, yet pointed to a multitude of everyday examples to prove its truth: the man who expends much effort arranging the chairs in a room to achieve an order which costs him more in convenience than is gained by having the floor clear; the person who is excessively curious about watches and rejects one model on the grounds that it loses two minutes in a day, replacing it with a much more expensive one that only loses a minute in a fortnight, despite both being perfectly adequate for the basic function of telling the time; he who adores 'trinkets of frivolous utility' and walks about 'loaded with a multitude of baubles' which cost him more inconveniency to constantly carry about than can ever be gained from having them to hand (*TMS* IV.I.4–6).

Taken alone these examples would constitute little more than a simple refinement of Hume's account. But Smith's next case—that of 'the poor man's son, whom heaven in its anger has visited with ambition'—opened up the deeper implications (*TMS* IV.I.8). It is vital to recognise that the poor son in Smith's example is *not* primarily motivated by *amour propre*. One might expect Smith to suggest that a desire for esteem and status underlies such 'ambition', especially in the context of his having read both Mandeville and Rousseau, and what he himself appears to say in *TMS* Part I. Indeed, this is how he is usually interpreted. Hanley writes that 'Smith in his own name advances the claim originally made in his translations of the *Discourse*: that markets are driven by solicitude for praise and recognition, and that such dependence on the esteem of others is also the source of the corruption of all our moral sentiments'.[54] Jerry Z. Muller similarly states that for Smith 'the dominant motive for engaging in economic activity—beyond providing for one's bodily needs—is the non-material desire for social status'.[55] Hont likewise claims that Smith 'rehearsed' Hume's point that continuous consumption of material goods beyond the point of needs satiation was not simply about utility but about the 'beauty of their design that pleased their owners', but he nonetheless concludes that 'Smith conceded Rousseau's case, also describing the hectic culture of status seeking as a giant deception'.[56] These readings, however, subtly misconstrue Smith's argument.[57]

For it is categorically *not* status recognition that does the central work in Smith's account, at least in Part IV. The 'love of distinction so natural to man', he tells us, is at best only a secondary consideration in explaining the human tendency towards luxury consumption. The primary factor is the quirk of

---

54. Hanley, 'Commerce and Corruption', 141.

55. Jerry Z. Muller, *Adam Smith in His Time and Ours: Designing the Decent Society* (New York: Free Press, 1993), 133.

56. Hont, *Politics in Commercial Society*, 92. Hont is wrong to say that Smith 'rehearses' Hume's points; Smith is correcting what he takes to be Hume's mistakes.

57. For a reading of Smith on the role of utility in the psychology of consumption that is closer to mine, although still different in important technical respects, see Daniel Diatkine, 'Vanity and the Love of System in *Theory of Moral Sentiments*', *European Journal of the History of Economic Thought* 17, no. 3 (2010).

human rationality that Smith takes himself to be the first to have identified. The poor man's son feels his daily inconveniences and compares those to what he imagines are the pleasure of the rich, afforded to them by their many devices for promoting utility. Whereas he must walk, they ride in carriages; whereas he must labour for all his wants, they have a retinue of servants. The poor son sees these conveniences and imagines that because they are fitted to promote pleasure they therefore make the rich happy—and that if he had them, then he too would be happy. Accordingly, the poor son becomes 'enchanted with the distant idea of felicity', and devotes himself to the endless 'pursuit of wealth and greatness'. But the outcome is a paradox: the poor son spends his life toiling to achieve wealth as a means of securing instruments of pleasure, and in the process expends far more effort, and incurs far more inconvenience, than could ever be compensated for by the riches he manages to amass. 'Through the whole of his life he pursues the idea of a certain artificial and elegant repose which he may never arrive at, for which he sacrifices a real tranquility that is at all times in his power'. The situation ends in irony: because the poor son is enchanted with the idea of utility promotion rather than utility itself, he will never achieve the levels of wealth that he thinks will make him happy. For such levels are constantly receding from him, due to the very quirk of human psychology that makes him pursue the imagined means of pleasure rather than solidly attainable pleasures themselves. In old age such a man may finally come to see, with regret and bitterness, the error of his ways: that 'wealth and greatness are mere trinkets of frivolous utility, no more adapted for procuring ease of body or tranquility of mind than the tweezer-cases of the lover of toys'. But by then it will largely be too late, and he will realise that he has wasted most of his life in chimerical pursuits (*TMS* IV.I.8).[58]

I will return to this crucial passage in much more detail in the next chapter, but for now it is important to recognise that Smith's poor man's son is intended as an *extreme* example. He is not supposed to represent how all people typically think and behave, but merely illustrates, in acute and dramatic form, those tendencies that are less pronounced in ordinary, well-adjusted people. Smith did not deny that the condition of the rich and the great received widespread admiration, and that this forwarded the desire of ordinary people to themselves become rich and great. However,

---

58. I discuss the poor man's son in detail in chapter 4 below, showing that it has been widely misread by commentators as a parable about vanity, which it is not.

if we examine . . . why the spectator distinguishes with such admiration the condition of the rich and the great, we shall find that it is not so much upon account of the superior ease or pleasure which they are supposed to enjoy as of the numberless artificial and elegant contrivances for promoting this ease or pleasure. He does not even imagine that they are really happier than other people: *but he imagines that they possess more means of happiness*. And it is the ingenious and artful adjustment of those means to the end for which they were intended, *that is the principal source of his admiration*. (*TMS* IV.I.8, emphasis added)

Yet matters are complicated by the fact that Smith appears to take a much more Rousseau-like position in *TMS* Part I. He there writes that 'to be observed, to be attended to, to be taken notice of with sympathy, complacency, and approbation, are all the advantages which we can propose to derive' from 'that great purpose of human life which we call bettering our condition'. Indeed, Smith even seems to contradict what he later says in Part IV, declaring that 'it is the vanity, not the ease, or the pleasure, which interests us' (*TMS* I.iii.2.1). This passage is what commentators seem to have in mind when they claim that Smith concedes Rousseau's claim about *amour propre* as the underlying driver of material consumption beyond bare necessity. But we must read carefully here. The context of these passages is Smith's claim that 'mankind are disposed to sympathize more entirely with our joy than our sorrow', where he follows Hume's view that we tend to love and esteem, rather than hate and envy, the rich and powerful.[59] Yet Smith's 'vanity' is not Rousseau's *amour propre*. The notes of the *Discourse* specified *amour propre* to be 'a relative sentiment . . . which inclines every individual to set greater store by himself than by anyone else, inspires men with all the evils they do one another'.[60] In contrast to this, what Smith claims in *TMS* Part I is that individuals pursue riches because observers sympathize with the pleasure that the rich ought to receive from their wealth, and this in turn augments the pleasures the rich themselves expect from their material affluence.[61] 'The rich man glories in his riches, because he feels that they naturally draw upon him the attention of the world, and that mankind are disposed to go along with him in all those agreeable

59. Hume, *Treatise*, T.2.1.10–11; SBN 309–24.

60. Rousseau, 'Second Discourse', 218.

61. The contempt the poor receive, through lack of spectator sympathy with their poverty, operates in exactly the reverse manner.

emotions with which the advantages of his situation so readily inspire him'
(*TMS* I.iii.2.1). According to Rousseau we primarily desire riches to rub other
people's noses in our superiority: 'the ardent desire to raise one's relative fortune less out of genuine need than in order to place oneself above others, in-
stills in all men a black inclination to harm one another . . . and always the
hidden desire to profit at another's expense'.[62] For Smith, by contrast, we
pursue riches to augment the pleasures that wealth brings by the added pleasure that arises from having others themselves take pleasure, via sympathy, in
our prosperous condition. Hence 'that emulation which runs through all the
different ranks of men' is not a zero-sum game of brute status competition, but
a complex product of the capacity to share each other's sentiments, made in
the context of Smith's central claim that having other people agree with our
sentiments via sympathy is inherently pleasurable.[63]

The difference between Smith and Rousseau is therefore ultimately pronounced. The *Discourse* postulated that a figure like the 'poor man's son' was
motivated primarily by competitive *amour propre*, in a zero-sum competition
for status (and inevitably so since pity had been fatally suppressed, meaning
that men could only compete with each other and not share each other's sentiments). Furthermore, following the introduction of private property and the
advent of inequality, the poor man's son was not the extreme, but the arche-
type, of how corrupted human beings behaved in contemporary conditions.
Smith rejected both these claims. The desire for riches and greatness and the
admiration of the rich and the great were primarily motivated not by the competitive seeking of recognition in the eyes of peers, but by two other features
of human psychology. First, the quirk of rationality which encouraged men to
value the means of utility-promotion more than utility itself. Second, the propensity, via sympathy, to take pleasure not in the actual pleasures of the rich,
but in the pleasure one imagined that they *ought* to take (even if they in fact
didn't) from their possessions (their means of promoting utility), and in turn
the pleasure, via sympathy, that the rich themselves took from knowing that
others took pleasure in observing their condition. Yet this view was one that
Smith arrived at through a correction of Hume's ideas, both with regards to

---

62. Rousseau, 'Second Discourse', 171, also 184 on how the rich 'value the things they enjoy
only to the extent that the others are deprived of them'.

63. See *TMS* I.i.2, 'Of the Pleasure of Mutual Sympathy', which also lays out Smith's core
claim about how 'mutual' sympathy brings pleasure and hence is the foundation of normative
approbation and disapprobation.

the quirk of rationality regarding utility as explicated in Part IV, but also with the claim that individuals pursue luxuries to augment their pleasures as a function of Smith's central contention that 'mutual sympathy pleases'—the very aspect of Smith's system that Hume labelled its 'hinge', but believed to be a mistake.[64] Insofar as Rousseau was also answered, that was a secondary effect, and one that in any case essentially addressed a vision of the motivations behind luxury consumption that had already (and notoriously) been stated in Mandeville's *Fable of the Bees Volume 1* as long before as 1714.

This brings us to the question of the role of deception in human psychology, where Smith is often read as (in Hont's phrase) 'conceding Rousseau's case'. But this is not an accurate construal. First of all, we need to be aware and keep in mind that there are two metrics of deception in play when we compare Smith and Rousseau. The first relates to the matter we have just been discussing: the psychological processes underpinning market activity and the pursuit of material, and especially luxury, goods. What should already have been established is that Smith did not 'concede' Rousseau's case in this regard. Whereas the Genevan posited that market activity was driven by an irreducibly competitive desire for superior status—luxury was both the focus of *amour propre*, and pathologically inflamed it in turn—Smith claimed that the majority of material appropriation beyond the satisfaction of bare necessity was the result of a product of the quirk of our rationality when it came to estimating pleasures, their means of attainment, and the corresponding connection to happiness. Smith certainly described this as a deception—but it was not the one that Rousseau supposed.

The second metric along which the notion of deception may be considered relates to how economic inequality, arising from market interactions and the rise of luxury, interacted with the basis of political power in large-scale advanced societies. Rousseau's claim in the *Discourse* was that the rich originally tricked the poor into accepting the property rights that formalized and entrenched material inequality, fooling them into believing that this would be to their own advantage. 'All ran toward their chains in the belief that they were securing their freedom; for while they had enough reason to sense the advantages of a political establishment, they had not enough experience to foresee its dangers.'[65] The 'deception' therefore amounted to a form of false

64. David Hume, 'Letter to Adam Smith, July 1759', in *Hume's Letters: Volume 1, 1727–65*, ed. J. Y. T. Greig (Oxford: Oxford University Press, 1932), 313.

65. Rousseau, 'Second Discourse', 173.

consciousness.[66] Smith entertained no such thing, by contrast, and opted to follow Hume's alternative in locating the stability of large-scale political societies in a theory of natural authority. Although its full sophistication and power has long lain obscured from modern readers, Book 3 of Hume's *Treatise* contained a detailed theory of allegiance rooted in what his later essays called the 'opinion of mankind'.[67] Thanks in part to sympathy's ensuring that ordinary people tended to admire and esteem the rich and powerful, men typically deferred to the authority of their rulers, initially out of utilitarian self-interest, but eventually—and as was typically the case in stable and advanced societies—out of a belief in the rightfulness of the political authority they found themselves living under. Certainly, significant abuses of power led to the forfeiture of the basis of allegiance with regards to (in Smith's later phrase) 'utility' and 'authority' (*LJ(B)* 12–15). But in ordinary circumstances human beings did not need to be deceived in order to live under conditions of material and political inequality, instead spontaneously submitting to established modes of authority.[68]

Smith certainly knew Hume's account of natural authority—indeed, he spent much of his working life attempting to extend and improve it. *TMS* offered a compact endorsement of the thesis as the basis of political rule when explaining 'the distinction of ranks, and the order of society' (*TMS* I.iii.2.3), whilst Book V of *WN* would offer a more developed analysis of the psychological foundations of natural authority than Hume ever supplied (*WN* V.ii.1–25), and *LJ* featured a sustained attempt to supply a historically grounded political theory organised around natural authority and the opinion of mankind.[69] The

66. Michael Rosen, *On Voluntary Servitude: False Consciousness and the Theory of Ideology* (Cambridge: Polity, 1996), 80–95. Rosen also compares Smith's theory of natural authority with Rousseau's account and notes the considerable further complexity and sophistication of the former, 95–100, 117–29.

67. David Hume, 'Of the First Principles of Government', in *Essays Moral, Political, and Literary*, ed. E. F. Miller (Indianapolis: Liberty Fund, 1985), 32–33. For a full explication of Hume's theory of natural authority, see Paul Sagar, 'The State without Sovereignty: Authority and Obligation in Hume's Political Philosophy', *History of Political Thought* 37 (2016), reprinted in *Opinion of Mankind*, chap. 3.

68. Hume, *Treatise*, T.3.2.8–10; SBN 539–67; cf. 'Of Passive Obedience' and 'Of the Original Contract', in *Essays Moral, Political, and Literary*.

69. On this see especially István Hont, 'Adam Smith's History of Law and Government as Political Theory', in *Political Judgement: Essays for John Dunn*, ed. R. Bourke and R. Geuss (Cambridge: Cambridge University Press, 2009) and Sagar, *Opinion of Mankind*, chap. 5. Smith's intellectual biographer suggests that the lectures were first delivered by Smith in Edinburgh in the

point of this for present purposes is that with Hume's theory already in hand, Rousseau's false consciousness explanation of the basis of advanced political society would have struck Smith as crude, and anyway redundant. Indeed, it would have looked rather like Mandeville's claim that society was founded in the systematic manipulation of the weak and stupid by the powerful and cunning. Which is exactly what Smith stated in his 1756 review, where he wrote that both Rousseau and Mandeville held that the 'laws of justice, which maintain the present inequality amongst mankind, were originally inventions of the cunning and the powerful, in order to maintain or to acquire an unnatural and unjust superiority over the rest of their fellow-creatures' (EPS 251).

With these wider matters in focus we can now appreciate the proper context and import of Smith's paraphrasing of Rousseau in TMS Part IV. As is well known Smith claimed that with regards to the 'deception' underlying the pursuit of material goods 'it is well that nature imposes upon us in this manner. It is this deception which rouses and keeps in continual motion the industry of mankind' (TMS IV.i.10). Echoing Rousseau's rhetoric from one of the passages of the Discourse that he had translated for readers of the Edinburgh Review, he continued,

> It is this which first prompted them to cultivate the ground, to build houses, to found cities and commonwealths, and to invent and improve all sciences and arts, which ennoble and embellish human life; which have entirely changed the whole face of the globe, have turned the rude forests of nature into agreeable and fertile plains, and made the trackless and barren ocean a new fund of subsistence, and the great high road of communication to the different nations of the earth. (TMS IV.i.10)[70]

Although it was the designs of the rich for their own pleasure that originally stimulated much economic activity, the paradoxical outcome was to improve the lot of all, as market consumption stimulated demand and the rising tide of economic productivity lifted all boats.[71] As Hont notes, by making this move

---

late 1740s, meaning Smith's attempts to develop his own theory of natural authority significantly predate his encounter with Rousseau: Phillipson, Adam Smith, 90–92.

70. See also Ignatieff, 'Smith, Rousseau and the Republic of Needs', 191.

71. TMS IV.I.10. This fundamental point is reiterated, although applied in a different direction, in WN, with Smith's famous declaration that 'it is not from the benevolence of the butcher, the brewer, or the baker, that we expect our dinner, but from their regard to their own interest' (WN I.ii.2).

Smith firmly aligned himself with Locke and Mandeville, and against Rousseau, in the tradition of thought that held that the division of the world into unequal propertied holdings was justified insofar as the result of the economic activity such inequality stimulated made the worst off vastly better off than they could have been if the earth remained communally owned and yet uncultivated.[72]

But let us now put all of the pieces together. Smith is typically read as first conceding Rousseau's fundamental case about the way markets are driven by competitive *amour propre* and in turn tend to corrupt participants through processes of deception, but then offering, as a consolation, and via what Hont terms a 'rudimentary theodicy', the beneficial effects this deception had in terms of the overall gains to mankind.[73] But this is not right. Smith's deployment of Rousseau's rhetoric takes place in a discussion whose primary target is Hume's theory of utility, and where Smith did *not* endorse the 'deception' that Rousseau posited, either with regards to the personal pursuit of luxury, or the basis of political societies exhibiting high levels of material inequality. In Part IV Smith located the primary 'deception' that gave rise to property, productivity, market exchanges, and eventually large-scale inequality, not in the desire for recognition—and not even in his own, sympathetically modified, account from Part I—but in the quirk of human rationality regarding utility seeking he took himself to be the first to have noticed. In other words, both the premises *and* the conclusions of Rousseau's case were mistaken. The more general point for present purposes is that in seeing this we can also appreciate that rather than Rousseau being Smith's primary target in Part IV, he featured as something more like collateral damage. Once Hume's account of utility was properly corrected to make the central 'deception' in human psychology the quirk of rationality with regards to the means rather than the ends of pleasure, Smith could in passing also explain what was wrong with the recent polemic from the continent, recycling the key passages he'd translated in his earlier review to this effect. In this case, one prominent thinker's paraphrasing of another corresponds to their marginal, rather than central, importance.

The extent to which Smith's own view of the 'deception' that lies behind economic consumption is darkly pessimistic, or ultimately more sanguine than might be supposed, is a matter requiring further interpretation, and which I consider in the next chapter. But whatever the outcome of that question, we

---

72. Hont, *Politics in Commercial Society*, 80.

73. Hont, *Politics in Commercial Society*, 92.

should recognise Smith's intervention for what it was: a new innovation, self-consciously moving beyond Hume's earlier framework of combining the capacity for sympathy with regard for the effects of utility, that was neither a concession to, nor an adoption of, Rousseau's Mandevillean emphasis on bare competitive *amour propre* as the primary motor of economic activity.

Conclusion

Despite what might reasonably be supposed, and indeed as is assumed in much of the existing literature, when Smith read Rousseau's *Discourse* he did not register it as the work of a particularly important or challenging interlocutor. As a result, the influence of Rousseau upon Smith is at best minimal and secondary. One reason for this, I have tried to suggest, is that it is a mistake (even if an understandable one) to assume that because the *Discourse* was published in 1755 and *TMS* in 1759, and because both survey much of the same or similar terrain, they must therefore share the same intellectual context.[74] As Robin Douglass has shown, Rousseau's sources were relatively limited when he was developing his ideas. When it came to the debate over sociability he effectively worked out of the French translation of *De Cive*, and contemporary French criticisms of Hobbes and Pufendorf of extremely varying reliability (as well, presumably, as the French translation of Mandeville's *Fable of the Bees* available after 1740).[75] That Rousseau could write the *Discourse* from such materials makes his achievement, if anything, that much more impressive. But Smith was a more fortunate genius. Not only did he have greater access to published works than Rousseau, first as a student and then as a teacher in a university setting, he was also the inheritor of long-standing British debates that Rousseau did not know. In particular, Smith was able to read and absorb

74. Smith apparently recognized the intellectual power of Rousseau's later *Social Contract*, which he is supposed to have claimed 'will one day avenge all of the persecutions he experienced': Barthélémy Faujas de Saint-Fond, *Travels in England, Scotland and the Hebrides, Undertaken for the Purpose of Examining the State of the Arts, the Sciences, Natural History and Manners, in Great Britain* (London: James Ridgway, 1799), II, 242. Yet Smith clearly constructed a very different kind of politics to Rousseau—for a start, one was a republican who drew directly on the Mediterranean ancients, and the other rejected this form of politics as in the long run incompatible with European modernity. Appreciation of ability is distinct from either influence or agreement.

75. Douglass, *Rousseau and Hobbes*, 'Introduction', 16–20 especially, and chap. 1 on the French reception of Hobbes.

Hume's revolutionary contributions, in the light of which Rousseau's *Discourse* must have paled by comparison, as I have tried to indicate above. This matters, however, because if we approach Smith's texts not as a response to Rousseau, but as part of a sustained programme of enquiry rooted firmly in the British intellectual context from which he emerged, then our assessment of the precise nature of the claims that Smith makes about the status of 'commercial society' under conditions of European modernity must shift. The next chapter shows in detail some of the ways that this is so.

4

Whose Corruption, Which Polity?

Fixing the Targets

The previous chapter sought to establish that Smith viewed Rousseau's *Discourse on Inequality* as neither particularly novel, nor especially challenging. If this is correct then we are invited to reassess Smith's own contributions, but now without the assumption that he was either responding to Rousseau or animated by the same basic concerns or beliefs as the Genevan. More specifically, we are invited to consider whether recent treatments of Smith's moral and political thought have erred precisely by imposing Rousseau's (or at least Rousseauvian) concerns onto Smith's works. Such is the contention of this chapter: that whether realising it or not, commentators have distorted Smith's thought by reading it through a Rousseauvian lens. Take that lens away and a different picture emerges.

One way to remove the Rousseauvian lens is by focusing on the issue of *corruption*. It has become something of a commonplace in the recent literature to say that Smith was preoccupied, to varying degrees and for varying reasons, about the capacity for 'commercial society' to be 'corrupting'.[1] Yet the language

---

1. Ryan Patrick Hanley, *Adam Smith and the Character of Virtue* (Cambridge: Cambridge University Press, 2009), chap. 1; Hanley, *Love's Enlightenment: Rethinking Charity in Modernity* (Cambridge: Cambridge University Press, 2017), 120–29; Hanley, 'Commerce and Corruption: Rousseau's Diagnosis and Adam Smith's Cure', *European Journal of Political Theory* 7, no. 2 (2008); Hanley, 'Adam Smith on Living a Life', in *Adam Smith: His Life, Thought, and Legacy*, ed. R. P. Hanley (Princeton: Princeton University Press, 2016); Dennis C. Rasmussen, *The Problems and Promise of Commercial Society: Adam Smith's Response to Rousseau* (University Park: Pennsylvania State University Press, 2008), chaps. 2–3; Rasmussen, 'Adam Smith on What Is Wrong with Economic Inequality', *American Political Science Review* 110, no. 2 (2016); Charles L. Griswold, *Adam Smith and the Virtues of Enlightenment* (Cambridge: Cambridge

of corruption is rarely used with theoretical precision, often being applied more or less indiscriminately across a range of distinct issues and across different aspects of Smith's texts, that are frequently run together but which we do better to handle discretely. The following aims to put this right by showing precisely where, how, and why Smith did—and crucially, did not—think corruption was of pertinent concern. Furthermore, it is anyway getting off on firmly the wrong foot to talk—as so many commentators are presently happy to do—about 'commercial society' as being somehow a privileged locus for discussions of corruption in Smith's thought. This is because, as established in chapter 1, 'commercial society' is simply too imprecise a designator. We need to ask *what kind* of commercial society we are discussing in relation to Smith's views of corruption, as well as whether Smith is even talking about corruption with relation to specific kinds of society, or in more general terms, at all. Having said that, it is plain that what commentators typically have in mind when discussing Smith and corruption vis-à-vis 'commercial society' is not Smith's minimal technical definition of living from exchange—which as we saw in chapter 1 properly includes polities like ancient Athens and Rome, as well as contemporary China—but rather *modern Europe*, that is, the large eighteenth-century trading states of Smith's own day that were characterised by high

University Press, 1999), chap. 7; Samuel Fleischacker, *On Adam Smith's* Wealth of Nations: A *Philosophical Companion* (Princeton: Princeton University Press, 2005), chap. 6; Lisa Hill, 'Adam Smith on the Theme of Corruption', *Review of Politics* 68, no. 4 (2006); Hill, '"The Poor Man's Son" and the Corruption of Our Moral Sentiments: Commerce, Virtue and Happiness in Adam Smith', *Journal of Scottish Philosophy* 15, no. 1 (2017); Hill, *Adam Smith's Pragmatic Liberalism: The Science of Welfare* (Cham: Palgrave Macmillan, 2019), chap. 5; John Robertson, *The Case for the Enlightenment: Scotland and Naples 1680–1760* (Cambridge: Cambridge University Press, 2005), 392–96; Michelle A. Schwarze and John T. Scott, 'Mutual Sympathy and the Moral Economy: Adam Smith Reviews Rousseau', *Journal of Politics* 81, no. 1 (2018); Christopher J. Berry, 'Commerce, Liberty and Modernity', in *Essays on Hume, Smith and the Scottish Enlightenment* (Edinburgh: Edinburgh University Press, 2018); Spiros Tegos, 'Adam Smith: Theorist of Corruption', in *The Oxford Handbook of Adam Smith*, ed. C. J. Berry, M. P. Paganelli, and C. Smith (Oxford: Oxford University Press, 2013); David Schmidtz, 'Adam Smith on Freedom', in Hanley, *Adam Smith*, 212–20. See also Claire Pignol and Benoît Walraevens, 'Smith and Rousseau on Envy in Commercial Society', *European Journal of the History of Economic Thought* 24, no. 6 (2017), which although it does not discuss 'corruption' explicitly is in large measure a response to the anxieties raised in the above literature. Similarly, Pierre Force's *Self-Interest Before Adam Smith: A Genealogy of Economic Science* (Cambridge: Cambridge University Press, 2003), 42–47, draws parallels between Smith and Rousseau on themes picked up by later commentators, although he does not tend towards explicit use of the language of corruption.

degrees of material opulence as generated by an extensive internal division of labour (and which many commentators now treat as straightforwardly synonymous with our own socioeconomic situation).[2] Yet lack of theoretical precision over the meaning both of 'corruption' and of 'commercial society' in Smith's thought prevents proper understanding of his precise claims and arguments. To properly understand Smith, we must put this right.

We can begin by fixing at the outset more precisely the idea of corruption.[3] Here it is helpful to draw upon the distinction made by John Joseph Wallis between 'venal' and 'systemic' corruption:

> **Systemic corruption**: a concrete form of political behavior and an idea. In polities plagued with systematic corruption, a group of politicians deliberately create rents by limiting entry into valuable economic activities, through grants of monopoly, restrictive corporate charters, tariffs, quotas, regulations, and the like. These rents bind the interests of the recipients to the politicians who create them. The purpose is to build a coalition that can dominate the government. Manipulating the economy for political ends is systematic corruption. Systematic corruption occurs when politics corrupts economics.

2. For example, Samuel Fleischacker discusses 'the reasons for Smith's moral approval of the economic system we call "capitalism" (what he called "commercial society")' (*On Adam Smith's Wealth of Nations*, 55), whilst Rasmussen, *Problems and Promise*, 'Conclusion', connects Smith's analysis to a consideration of 'commercial society's record over the past two centuries and more since he lived and wrote, in relation not only to precommercial societies but also to the alternatives to commercial society that were advocated and implemented in the twentieth century' (161–62), implicitly equating 'commercial society' with 'capitalism'. On similar lines, Griswold, *Adam Smith and the Virtues of Enlightenment*, 17, states, 'As the continuing litany of complaints today about the moral decadence of materialistic Western culture demonstrates, this problem is still with us'. This equation of commercial society with what we call capitalism, and the further conflation of capitalism with *consumerism*, is now standard amongst commentators, even if not all of them state the matter as explicitly as Fleischacker. In the conclusion of this book I offer considerations for why such an equation—or rather, conflation—must necessarily be a mistake.

3. For an alternative reading of how to think about corruption and with regards to Smith specifically, see Hill, 'Adam Smith on the Theme of Corruption', 636–48. Although I disagree with Hill on important points of interpretation, her essay is valuable insofar as it considers Smith in his own terms, and not as shaped by the Rousseauvian concerns that have since come to dominate—and I suggest, distort—more recent readings of Smith on these matters. Hill has also more recently offered a helpful overview of Smith's attitude to political corruption—which shows Smith as operating within the emergent eighteenth-century discourse of what Wallis (below) labels systemic corruption: Hill, *Smith's Pragmatic Liberalism*, chap. 5.

Venal corruption: the pursuit of private economic interests through the political process. Venal corruption occurs when economics corrupts politics.[4]

To this however we must add a third category, which I here tailor specifically to fit Smith's style of ethical outlook and analysis:

Moral corruption: a condition whereby the moral sentiments of an agent have been distorted in such a way as to no longer function most optimally, and in a manner which they might otherwise be expected to do.

The focus of this chapter is primarily on phenomena that fall under the headings of moral corruption. In the next chapter I examine Smith with regards to systemic corruption, giving particular focus to his account of the nefarious activities of the merchant and manufacturing classes. Venal corruption tends not to attract much of Smith's direct attention; when it does feature it is as a subset of what he has to say about moral corruption. Of course, Smith did not employ these terms or distinctions himself. Nonetheless, they help to elucidate his thought, and in a way that serves to clarify his ideas, rather than simply adding a new distorting lens in the place of a removed Rousseauvian one (as I hope to show below).

This, however, brings us to a further important conceptual point: that proposing a relatively firm distinction between categories of systematic, venal, and moral corruption presupposes underlying political-theoretic commitments which would not have been granted at all points in human history by all interested observers. Most obviously and pertinently to the present study, the republican (or civic humanist) tradition that predated Smith's interventions was in part premised on *denying* any effective distinction between moral, venal, and systemic corruption of the sort that Wallis draws, and that I extend. On the classical republican outlook, the moral virtue of the citizenry was directly linked to the political health of the republic, these being two sides of a single coin: citizens who were primarily preoccupied with their own personal gain and aggrandisement would lack the civic virtue—itself a simultaneously moral *and* political disposition to sacrifice personal interest for the good of the community either through domestic service and/or military participation—required to uphold

---

4. John Joseph Wallis, 'The Concept of Systemic Corruption in American History', in *Corruption and Reform: Lessons from America's Economic History*, ed. E. L. Glaiser and C. Goldin (Chicago: University of Chicago Press, 2006), 25.

the free institutions of an independent, self-governing, *res publica*. Aside from the very ideas of 'the economy' and 'economics' in our contemporary senses not being available to earlier republican thinkers, the notion that the corruption of individuals could even in principle be separated out from the health of the body politic is a fundamental and straightforward error according to the base logic of classical republican thought. Hence, in turn, its long-standing and deep hostility to luxury as a threat not just to the private virtue and martial capacity of the citizenry, but to the stability and longevity of the entire political community.[5] This already tells us something important about Smith (or indeed any other thinker): that insofar as his thought can be mapped effectively in terms of a distinction between concerns about 'venal', 'systemic', and 'moral', corruption—as I suggest that it can—this indicates its fundamentally non-republican nature.[6] Indeed, one thing that is noteworthy about Smith's discussions of individual corruption in *TMS* is the extent to which he does *not* draw further conclusions regarding the purported health or longevity of the body politic. And although some commentators argue that Smith implicitly draws upon an earlier civic humanist discourse in his famous discussion of standing armies in *WN*, even if this is true as a matter of intellectual genealogy (itself a controversial claim), the overall *effect* of any such appropriation (if so it be) is to move Smith's ideas firmly outside of earlier republican preoccupations.[7]

5. On this, see István Hont, 'The Early Enlightenment Debate on Commerce and Luxury', in *The Cambridge History of Eighteenth Century Political Thought*, ed. M. Golide and R. Wokler (Cambridge: Cambridge University Press, 2005), 380–83; Christopher J. Berry, *The Idea of Luxury: A Conceptual and Historical Investigation* (Cambridge: Cambridge University Press, 1994), chaps. 2–4.

6. Accordingly, I do not share Lisa Hill's view that Smith employed an 'eccentric', 'hybrid' conception of corruption blending classical republican notions with more modern ideas about systemic inequality ('Adam Smith on the Theme of Corruption', 646), but present him instead as aligned firmly with the moderns. The reasons for this will become clear below. Similarly, Hanley (*Adam Smith and the Character of Virtue*, 24–36) claims that Smith was not much concerned with 'political' corruption whilst being centrally preoccupied with 'moral' corruption, whereas I take essentially the reverse view here, which Hill appears to share in her more recent writings (e.g., *Smith's Pragmatic Liberalism*, chap. 5).

7. For a civic humanist reading of Smith, see Leonidas Montes, *Adam Smith in Context: A Critical Reassessment of Some Central Components of His Thought* (London: Palgrave Macmillan, 2004), chap. 3, but in reply Samuel Fleischacker's review in *Journal of the History of Economic Thought* 28, no. 1 (2006): 128–29. Montes is drawing upon J. G. A. Pocock's suggestion that Smith (like Hume) is a 'commercial humanist' (*Virtue, Commerce, and History: Essays on Political Thought, Chiefly in the Eighteenth Century* [Cambridge: Cambridge University Press, 1985], 50,

That this is so becomes especially clear when we recall that 'corruption' properly designates a form of decay, a deterioration from good health to poor. When used accurately it is not a synonym for something's being merely bad or undesirable, but denotes a degradation from a superior prior state. This was at the heart of earlier republican usages of the idea of corruption, and indeed is central to why earlier republican political theorists were consistently preoccupied with corruption as simultaneously a supreme moral *and* political threat. From Aristotle through Polybius and later Machiavelli, a central presumption of republican political thought is that the *polis* or *res publica* inevitably passes through cycles of health, decline, corruption, and possibly then renewal, and that whilst the process can be mitigated and slowed at the political level by militating against the civic decay of the citizenry, it cannot ultimately be stopped.[8] Building on the work of J. G. A. Pocock, István Hont has shown however that this understanding of time—and hence of politics—as being necessarily cyclical underwent a major transformation in the eighteenth century, with Smith being a foremost innovator in a new conceptual framework which operated without being premised on the assumption that corruption and decline is the inevitable fate of all political communities.[9] Indeed, this reconfiguration of the understanding of time—and the emergence in turn of the belief that a state could at least in principle last forever—constitutes one of the intellectual preconditions for the emergence of liberal political thought, the intellectual strata of the tradition that has come to dominate Western politics in both theory and practice, and which Smith's own work points firmly in the direction of. Although Smith does make use of the language of corruption, he is doing so outside of the earlier republican tradition—and this again puts important distance between him and Rousseau, insofar as the Genevan

---

194). For a clear overview of the essentially non-republican nature of Smith's thought, and with which I broadly concur, see Christopher J. Berry, 'Commerce, Liberty and Modernity' and 'Adam Smith and the Virtues of the Modern Economy', in *Essays on Hume*, and Hill, *Smith's Pragmatic Liberalism*, 123–25.

8. For details, see Wallis, 'Concept of Systemic Corruption', 27–30; Hill, 'Adam Smith on the Theme of Corruption', 636–42.

9. István Hont, 'The "Rich Country–Poor Country" Debate in the Scottish Enlightenment', in *Jealousy of Trade: International Competition and the Nation-State in Historical Perspective* (Cambridge, MA: Belknap, 2005); J. G. A. Pocock, *The Machiavellian Moment: Florentine Political Thought and the Atlantic Republican Tradition* (Princeton: Princeton University Press, 1975).

continued to operate firmly within republican parameters, albeit via a series of original innovations.[10]

Focusing in this chapter on phenomena captured under the headings of 'venal' and especially 'moral' corruption, and having identified Smith as breaking with earlier republican ideas on these matters, we must carefully consider two specific areas of his thought. For whilst often run together in recent scholarly treatments, and whilst they do exhibit a degree of dynamic interplay, these two areas are best handled separately if we wish to get clear on exactly what Smith believed to be the relationship between moral corruption and modern European states—that particular form of commercial society that commentators typically have in mind when they discuss Smith in this regard. To that end the following are considered in turn:

10. We should certainly not take the mere fact that Smith uses the word 'corruption' in his corpus as by itself indicating that he is taking over in any substantive or interesting sense specifically republican concerns. The case is analogous to the language of 'class' today. In the twenty-first century one may straightforwardly talk and write about 'the working class' without being in any way committed to (say) a Marxist analysis of politics and society. Indeed, we today now freely talk about corruption without ordinary users of the word being committed to republican political ideas, let alone undergirding structural beliefs about the nature of time. Individual words and concepts can continue to function in general usage long after having become detached from earlier theoretical baggage. In this regard Smith is closer to us than to prior republican thinkers: he (mostly) uses the word 'corruption' accurately to describe a degradation from a healthier prior state, but in and of itself the word for him does not signal more substantive, let alone specifically republican, political commitments, any more than it does for us. Something similar can be said of Montes, *Adam Smith in Context*, chap. 3, which argues that Smith's language regarding the standing army debate (more on which below) is firmly, consciously, and significantly civic humanist in origin. I find this unconvincing: Smith may use words like 'martial virtues' and discuss the importance of courage, but this is hardly surprising given the subject matter, and more needs to be shown than that he might plausibly have derived these from specifically republican sources if this claim is to be enlightening. In particular, it needs to be shown that Smith meant to do so, and did so with a specifically civic humanist purpose in mind. More fundamentally, Montes's case rests on the idea that Smith is a synthesiser of two predecessor discourses: civic humanism on the one hand, and natural jurisprudence on the other. It is more plausible, however, to read him as a major innovator, following Hume, who broke free of both these earlier traditions and helped forge a new political idiom founded in the centrality of opinion and explicated via Hume's new 'science of man', as I argue at length in *The Opinion of Mankind: Sociability and the Theory of the State from Hobbes to Smith* (Princeton: Princeton University Press, 2018).

1. The extent to which Smith thought that *individual agents* suffer from a threat of being morally corrupted in modern European commercial societies.

2. The extent to which modern European commercial societies *are themselves* to be considered as morally corrupt, or at least compromised, to some degree.

I argue that in both cases it is inaccurate to read Smith as thinking that there is any special, or especially worrying, sense in which modern European states are peculiarly vulnerable to threats of moral corruption. Indeed, if anything such states are in some crucial regards likely to be *better off* than alternative forms of society have proven themselves to be. In order to see this, however, we must return in detail to some of the passages examined in the previous chapter, but this time reading them primarily in their own light, rather than beginning by juxtaposing them with Rousseau.

Commerce and the Corruption of Our Moral Sentiments?

In surveying the recent literature on Smith's moral thought it is easy to come away with the impression that a—if not indeed *the*—primary aim of *TMS* is to 'defend' economically advanced societies from the charge that such arrangements are morally corrupting of the individuals who live in them, as well as being themselves normatively suspect for essentially the same reasons. Insofar as this impression obtains, however, it is a mistake.

TMS is, first and foremost, a work of moral philosophy whose primary aim is to explain the functioning of the ethical sentiments, and hence account for various moral phenomena and practices. It grows directly and primarily out of Smith's immediate intellectual context and personal philosophical formation, most especially an engagement with David Hume's moral philosophy (as found in *The Treatise of Human Nature*, as well as the later *Enquiry Concerning the Principles of Morals*), but also major works by the previous generation of British moral philosophers, notably Smith's teacher Francis Hutcheson, as well as the work of Bishop Butler, and to some extent Lord Kames.[11] Standing

---

11. On Smith as primarily taking over, but also repurposing and fundamentally altering, key aspects of Hume's sentimentalist ethical theory, see Paul Sagar, 'Beyond Sympathy: Smith's

behind those authors were of course the infamous contributions of Bernard Mandeville, and behind him in turn Hobbes and Locke, as well as the Earl of Shaftesbury. More generally, Smith was well versed in the thought of Plato, Aristotle, and the ancient Stoics and Epicureans, as demonstrated by Part VII of *TMS*, which draws extensively on the material he had for several years used in his moral philosophy lectures at the University of Glasgow.[12] The overwhelming majority of *TMS*, in other words, has *nothing* to say about the effects upon the moral sentiments of commerce, luxury, inequality, or any of the other issues typically associated with the conditions of advanced modern European societies operating extensive market economies. Such discussions that do take place are the exceptions, not the rule, in what is first and foremost a work of moral philosophy in a traditional sense.[13] Indeed, if we straightforwardly enumerate the space given over to issues pertaining to commercial relations in *TMS*, they are but a small fraction of the whole.[14] Smith's primary aim in writing the book was to offer, precisely, a theory of moral sentiments, not to 'defend' something called 'commercial society' (a term Smith never even uses

---

Rejection of Hume's Moral Theory', *British Journal for the History of Philosophy* 25, no. 4 (2017). For further discussion of sympathy in Smith in the light of Hume's earlier claims, see John McHugh, 'Ways of Desiring Mutual Sympathy in Adam Smith's Moral Philosophy', *British Journal for the History of Philosophy* 24, no. 4 (2016); McHugh, 'Working Out the Details of Hume and Smith on Sympathy', *Journal of the History of Philosophy* 56, no. 4 (2018); McHugh, 'Hume's General Point of View, Smith's Impartial Spectator, and the Moral Value of Interacting with Outsiders', *Journal of Scottish Philosophy* 19, no. 1 (2021).

12. For detailed discussion, see Gloria Vivenza, *Adam Smith and the Classics: The Classical Heritage in Adam Smith's Thought* (Oxford: Oxford University Press, 2001), chap. 2.

13. Indeed, I would go so far as to say that there is unambiguously only *one* such discussion, in Part IV, for reasons that are established below.

14. To wit: using the Glasgow Edition of *TMS*, we might include (somewhat generously, given reasons adduced below) the following as relating to anything that might be classed as pertinent to considerations about 'commercial society'. Rounding up in all cases: I.iii.2.1–11 (on vanity and ranks): 10 pages; I.iii.3.1–8 (on the 'corruption of our moral sentiments): 5 pages; IV.1.1–11 (on utility, deception, the invisible hand, etc.): 9 pages; VII.ii.4.1–14 (generously including the entirety of the discussion of 'Licentious Systems'): 9 pages; III.3.4. (a passing remark about European commerce): 1 page; VI.ii.2.3 (the discussion of national antagonism, which extends to considering commerce as a reason of state): 2 pages. Generous total: 36 pages. The Glasgow Edition runs to 342 pages. So, at a generous estimate, considerations pertinent to 'commercial society' feature in around 10.5 percent of the book. Whilst of course page numbers do not correlate neatly to conceptual importance, if *TMS* really is primarily structured by concerns about 'commercial society', it ought to be somewhat puzzling that most of the book is given over to discussing other things entirely.

in *TMS*). Insofar as he did or did not undertake that latter task, it was at most a subsidiary, and never a primary, aim.

This point matters because if commentators set out by working (errone-ously, I suggest) from the assumption that Smith aimed to write *TMS* as a 'defence' of something called 'commercial society', they are encouraged to feel permitted to cherry-pick from various distinct and separate discussions in the text, taking what Smith says in disparate parts of the book and reading them back into part of an allegedly more fundamental and unified project of 'defend-ing commercial society'. The effect is to surreptitiously inflate the degree to which Smith is talking about the ill effects of commerce on our moral senti-ments, by reading what are separate and unrelated discussions as responses to the alleged all-pervasive ill effects of 'commerce'. (In this way, a second error compounds the first, yet both appear to legitimate each other in turn.) At its most advanced, this approach generates a reading of the entirety of *TMS* as fundamentally an attempt to philosophically cure the ills that 'commercial society' allegedly generates.[15] The reasons for this flawed pattern of interpre-tation are not bad or dishonest scholarly practice, but precisely the effects of the error I have argued above should be resisted: reading Smith as primarily *responding to Rousseau*. After all, if the framework one is working with is that Rousseau attacked 'commercial society', and Smith set out to 'defend' it from that attack, the result is to reorientate one's entire reading of *TMS* to fit this framework, permitting one to integrate discussions about distinct moral phe-nomena (such as vanity, prudence, the love of praiseworthiness, and so forth), into a unified agenda whose primary aim is taken to be the 'defence' of 'com-mercial society' from one of its most ferocious critics. Hence, what I take to be cherry picking just looks, in this framework, like good textual interpreta-tion. But if I am correct, and Smith did *not* find Rousseau's thought particularly

---

15. Hanley, *Adam Smith and the Character of Virtue*, is a singular example in this regard: see especially chap. 1, at 15–17, 24–25, 31–34, 36–38, 52; see also his 'Commerce and Corruption', 144. Much the same pattern can be found in, e.g., Griswold, *Adam Smith and the Virtues of Enlighten-ment*; Rasmussen, *Problems and Promise*; Fleischacker, *On Adam Smith's* Wealth of Nations, though somewhat less forcefully stated. István Hont has gone further and suggested that *WN* was fundamentally motivated by a perceived need to refute Rousseau's claims in the *Discourse*: 'Introduction', in *Jealousy of Trade*, 91–99; see also (with Michael Ignatieff) 'Needs and Justice in the *Wealth of Nations*', in *Jealousy of Trade*, 397–403. I find this implausible: it attributes far too much importance to the alleged influence of Rousseau on Smith, and drastically underval-ues the intended scope of *WN*, as well as the wide range of questions Smith was responding to therein, and his varying motivations for responding to them.

novel or troubling, and was not in significant measure attempting to respond to him, then what I read as cherry picking is precisely that, and serves to compound distortions of Smith's thought rather than clarifying it.

I propose instead that we focus exclusively on those passages of *TMS* where Smith is explicitly talking about the effects of commercial relationships upon the moral sentiments (although even here questions will immediately need to be raised as to whether this is even so), and ask if there is evidence that Smith thought economically advanced European states were particularly prone to exposing their populations to corruption. Ryan Patrick Hanley, for example, has claimed that for Smith 'the desire for esteem and recognition is at once the animating passion of commerce as well as the origin of commercial corruption'.[16] This is presented as a major problem, because 'if commerce corrupts "moral sentiments", then the effects of corruption extend to the whole range of subjects to be treated in a theory of moral sentiments'.[17] The implication in turn is that there is something *special* about advanced modern European states in his regard. By contrast, I argue that this is not so.

Vanity

A key locus for recent discussions of Smith and corruption is *TMS* I.iii.2, titled 'Of the Origin of Ambition, and the Distinction of Ranks', and which contains Smith's account of vanity. According to Hanley, 'Smith was particularly sympathetic to Rousseau's insistence that commercial society is fundamentally driven by a vanity that threatens to corrupt its participants', something with which many commentators agree.[18] But what does Smith actually say about vanity in *TMS* I.iii.2.2, and to what extent does it support a reading of him as viewing the citizens of modern European states as especially prone to corruption due to a conjunction of commerce and vanity, and hence agreeing with Rousseau? It is helpful here to analyse this specific portion of the text in isolation, and only later consider how it relates to other parts of the book (namely

16. Hanley, *Adam Smith and the Character of Virtue*, 36.

17. Hanley, *Adam Smith and the Character of Virtue*, 34.

18. Hanley, 'Commerce and Corruption', 138. See below for discussion of whether (as commentators widely maintain) it is *true* that Smith thinks large-scale commercial economies are primarily driven by vanity. I suggest it is not. For an accurate summary overview of the moves Smith makes in his discussion, one tied closely to the text, see Craig Smith, *Adam Smith* (Cambridge: Polity, 2020), 78–82.

IV.I.1–11 on 'Why Utility Pleases'). For the precise relationship between Smith's specific arguments needs more careful and discrete handling than it typically receives, and we do well here to go slowly.

The very first paragraph of I.iii.2 contains Smith's discussion of vanity as regarding the effects of wealth and poverty, and what he argues is as follows. First, 'It is because mankind are disposed to sympathize more entirely with our joy than our sorrow, that we make parade of our riches and conceal our poverty'. Crucially, he goes on, 'it is chiefly from this regard to the sentiments of mankind, that we pursue riches and avoid poverty. For to what purpose is all the toil and bustle of the world? what is the end of avarice and ambition, of the pursuit of wealth, of power, and preheminence? Is it to supply the necessities of nature? The wages of the meanest labourer can supply them'. Smith makes this point at length: riches are not pursued as instruments to securing the necessities of life, and indeed everybody already admits this when we get clear on the issue, so riches must be desired for some other reason. 'From whence, then, arises that emulation which runs through all the different ranks of men, and what are the advantages which we propose by that great purpose of human life which we call bettering our condition?' The answer: 'To be observed, to be attended to, to be taken notice of with sympathy, complacency, and approbation, are all the advantages which we can propose to derive from it. It is the vanity, not the ease, or the pleasure, which interests us. But vanity is always founded upon the belief of our being the object of attention and approbation' (*TMS* I.iii.2.1).

Smith is thus unambiguous: people pursue riches primarily because of the approbation that they believe others will grant them if they secure those riches, and which pleases via sympathy. The wealthy bask in the approving attention that they believe others pay to them for their riches, whilst the poor are hurt by the disapproval that they sympathetically feel relayed by those who look down upon them. In turn, *observers* also take pleasure in looking at 'those of rank', as they share by sympathy with the pleasure they imagine the rich feel from being rich and appearing in the gaze of others: 'Every body is eager to look at him, and to conceive, at least by sympathy, that joy and exultation with which his circumstances naturally inspire him' (*TMS* I.iii.2.1). By the reverse process observers feel pained looking at the poor, and so shun them. This complex process of mutually sympathising with other people's imputed initial estimations *and* their imputed return sympathizing—a multilevelled dynamic process—leads to the reason why 'greatness' is respected despite the evident and serious costs that the great themselves must incur to achieve it:

In a great assembly he is the person upon whom all direct their eyes; it is upon him that their passions seem all to wait with expectation, in order to receive that movement and direction which he shall impress upon them; and if his behaviour is not altogether absurd, he has, every moment, an opportunity of interesting mankind, and of rendering himself the object of the observation and fellow-feeling of every body about him. It is this, which, notwithstanding the restraint it imposes, notwithstanding the loss of liberty with which it is attended, renders greatness the object of envy, and compensates, in the opinion of mankind, all that toil, all that anxiety, all those mortifications which must be undergone in the pursuit of it; and what is of yet more consequence, all that leisure, all that ease, all that care-less security, which are forfeited for ever by the acquisition. (*TMS* I.iii.2.1)

Let us here take stock, noting two things. First, that the aim of this long opening paragraph is twofold, and indicated by the chapter title. On the one hand, to explain the origin of ambition (which Smith has just done, locating it in the processes of mutual sympathy and the pleasure derived from approbation). On the other, to set up what comes next, the discussion of the nature and origins of ranks, and hence of political subordination. Notice that *nowhere* in this paragraph does Smith mention either commerce (which is *not* the same thing as attempting to acquire riches so as to acquire approbation: one can trade for many other reasons, and one can attain riches in many ways besides commerce), nor indicate that he is speaking here specifically of a phenomenon unique to, nor especially prevalent in, modern European societies, nor indeed in any other form of 'commercial society'. On the contrary, Smith is describing a *universal* tendency to seek riches and avoid poverty, based on underlying psychological processes present in all humans, because generated by the baseline fact (as Smith sees it) that mutual sympathy pleases. There is therefore nothing in this paragraph, at least taken alone, to suggest that Smith thinks there is anything distinctive or unusual about advanced civilizations running, for example, luxury-based economies featuring high levels of commerce, at least when it comes to the desire to be looked at and taken notice of. Indeed, the point should rather be taken the other way around: that insofar as such societies have emerged, what gave rise to them was the underlying human psychology rooted in sympathy and the desire for approbation which interacts with the desire for riches as a desire to be thought well of. Now it *may* be that modern European states running large luxury-fuelled economies featuring high levels of commerce have a special effect upon the underlying processes of human psychology that first gave rise to them. Rousseau in the *Discourse* certainly suggests that something like this is the case. But Smith has said nothing, in this specific passage, to indicate that he believes it to be so. Thus, we must be very wary of reading this one-paragraph discussion of vanity as evidence for a view that Smith thought modern Europe corrupted its citizens because of a desire for riches, and hence the fuelling of ambition amongst at least some of its members, and thus as in agreement with Rousseau. As things stand, Smith has said nothing of the sort, and given no indication of believing that modern Europeans are any different to any other people, at any other point in history. In fact, given what he says about shepherd and feudal warlord politics in the *LJ* and *WN*—whose entire raison d'être is the acquisition of wealth and power for those who sit atop the political hierarchy—we can go further: Smith *cannot possibly* have thought that the desire for riches and the thirst of ambition were somehow unique to, or especially prevalent in, 'commercial societies' (whether ancient, modern, or any other form they might take) vis-à-vis other forms of social organisation, given that the main historical alternatives were shepherding and quasi-shepherding systems of domination and extraction that were centrally organised around precisely the getting of wealth and power as concentrated in the hands of political elites.

Having noted this, we may also observe that Smith does not say anything, in the subsequent ten subsections that make up I.iii.2, about commerce specifically, nor about the condition of modern Europeans generally. On the contrary, the remaining discussion is given over, first, to how ranks are established and why human beings tend to defer to the authority of others based on external signals of wealth and power, before assessing the pitfalls of ambition and the ways in which seeking to satisfy a lust for riches and power is often self-defeating for the individual, despite the social usefulness of politics being founded in what Hume had called opinion, that is, the psychological dispositions of the ruled to indeed be ruled (*TMS* I.iii.2.2–11).[19] In this subsequent discussion Smith explains that it is the tendency to sympathise more strongly with the rich and powerful than the poor and miserable (something Hume had already called attention to in the *Treatise*)[20] that underpins the

---

19. David Hume, 'On the First Principles of Government', in *Essays Moral, Political, and Literary*, ed. E. F. Miller (Indianapolis: Liberty Fund, 1985), 32–33. For detailed discussion on this regarding both Hume and Smith, see Sagar, *Opinion of Mankind*, chaps. 3 and 5.

20. David Hume, *A Treatise of Human Nature*, ed. D. F. Norton and M. J. Norton (Oxford: Oxford University Press, 2007), T.2.1.10–11; SBN 309–24.

establishment of ranks, hierarchy, and hence political authority. But again, there is nothing *special* here about modern European societies: the same process underlies *every* form of human social organisation in which ranks are established and political authority emerges. Indeed, Smith illustrates the pain of falling from a comparative position of status to one of lowliness with an example drawn from ancient Rome, not modern Europe (I.iii.2.6, on being paraded as a slave in the capital city of one's conquerors). In this chapter, Smith is describing what he takes to be universal phenomena, grounded in a universal human psychology of the pleasures and pains associated with mutual sympathy, which is itself the core explanatory tool of Part I of *TMS*. There is simply nothing special here to be noted about modern European, or indeed any other kind of, 'commercial society'.

On the evidence adduced thus far, therefore, there is nothing to suggest that Smith thought modern European commercial societies were especially prone to corrupting their citizens. Indeed, regarding the portion of the text so far considered, Smith does not even use the language of either commerce or corruption *at all*.[21] These passages simply do not provide evidence that Smith thought 'commerce' was 'corrupting', still less that he agreed with Rousseau. What they say is that we sympathise more readily with the pleasures and pains of the rich and the great than we do with those of the poor and the lowly, and that this explains the origin of ranks and political authority. And this was an insight Smith was developing primarily through engagement not with Rousseau but with Hume, and it is in turn presented as a universal claim about all human beings, not a specific claim about the effects of commerce upon some humans in economically advanced societies. If Smith thinks that 'commerce' tends to 'corrupt' our moral sentiments, the evidence must come from elsewhere.

'The Universal Cause of the Corruption of Our Moral Sentiments'

Of course, Smith does introduce talk of corruption in the immediately succeeding section of *TMS*, namely I.iii.3, 'Of the corruption of our moral sentiments, which is occasioned by this disposition to admire the rich and the

---

21. Indeed Smith uses the term 'commerce' in the entirety of Part I of *TMS* only twice, in a single sentence, and which is dedicated to the exchange not of goods via markets but of sentiments amidst personal relationships: *TMS* I.ii.4.1.

great, and to despise or neglect persons of poor and mean condition'. Famously added to the sixth and final edition in 1790, this chapter is sometimes cited as direct evidence that Smith was preoccupied, right up until his death, with answering—and perhaps even finally conceding—Rousseau's challenge in the *Discourse*.[22] But this is incorrect. To see why, we can begin by considering Smith's opening declaration in full:

> This disposition to admire, and almost to worship, the rich and the power-ful, and to despise, or, at least, to neglect persons of poor and mean condi-tion, though necessary both to establish and to maintain the distinction of ranks and the order of society, is, at the same time, the great *and most uni-versal cause* of the corruption of our moral sentiments. That wealth and greatness are often regarded with the respect and admiration which are due only to wisdom and virtue; and that the contempt, of which vice and folly are the only proper objects, is often most unjustly bestowed upon poverty and weakness, *has been the complaint of moralists in all ages.* (*TMS* I.iii.3.1, emphasis added)

Several things should be noted here. First, Smith again gives no indication of singling out European modernity, or indeed even commerce or its effects, for special treatment (riches and poverty are hardly the preserve of commercial relationships, as amply demonstrated by the violently acquisitive practices of a Mongol khan or a feudal baron). Second, in any case excessive admiration for the rich, whilst necessary for political authority to function, is not only the greatest, but the *most universal,* cause of the corruption of our moral senti-ments. In other words, it happens always and everywhere. Second, that this is so has been the complaint of moralists *in all ages;* that is, it is a long noticed and widely condemned phenomenon, reflecting its universal prevalence. Again, there is no indication that Smith thinks modern Europe, or indeed any form of 'commercial society', is especially bad in this regard. Finally, it is not even clear to what extent Smith is himself endorsing the claim about corrup-tion, because it is not clear to what extent he considers himself a 'moralist', as opposed to (say) a dispassionate philosopher attempting to understand the functioning of the moral sentiments.[23]

---

22. Robertson, *Case for the Enlightenment*, 394.

23. These essential points have previously been made by Rasmussen, *Problems and Promise*, 77–78, although as explained momentarily, I do not believe he puts them to use in quite the correct way. See also Hill, 'Adam Smith on the Theme of Corruption', 650–51.

The chapter continues with Smith observing that 'two different roads are presented to us, equally leading to the attainment of this so much desired object [the approval and approbation of others]; the one, by the study of wisdom and the practice of virtue; the other, by the acquisition of wealth and greatness'. Given that the rich and great tend to have their vices diminished and their virtues exaggerated in the estimations of those who sympathize more easily with riches than poverty, however, this exacerbates a situation whereby the 'wise and virtuous' turn out to be but a 'small party' amongst all humanity, whereas 'the great mob of mankind are the admirers and worshippers, and, what may seem more extraordinary, most frequently the disinterested admirers and worshippers, of wealth and greatness' (*TMS* I.iii.3.2). Note again however that Smith is here talking of mankind as such, and says nothing about modern Europe, nor any other commercial society, in particular, nor indeed anything about commerce generally. And he then goes on to claim that things are anyway not so bad as they initially seem. This is because (as noted in the previous chapter) Smith thinks that it ordinarily *doesn't matter* that excess admiration for the rich and powerful tends to corrupt the moral sentiments, because most people are sufficiently sheltered from contact with the rich and powerful such that they are not unduly affected in this regard. 'In the middling and inferior stations of life, the road to virtue and that to fortune, to such fortune, at least, as men in such stations can reasonably expect to acquire, are, happily in most cases, very nearly the same' (*TMS* I.iii.3.5). The constraints of the law, the correlation between right conduct and ordinary success in most walks of life, the judgements of one's immediate peers—all ensure that the bulk of mankind, even if they are prone (as all humans are) to excessively admiring the rich and powerful, do not themselves end up corrupted in their day-to-day lives.[24] The real problem, Smith insists, applies only to that small

---

24. Rasmussen, *Problems and Promise*, 77–78, suggests a distinction here between one's *sentiments* being corrupted and yet one's *actions* being kept in check by wider social forces. However it is unclear that the text of *TMS* supports reading Smith as making this precise distinction or claim. Indeed, such a reading may well be conceding too much to the causes of corruption: Smith may instead be read as saying that the other facts of life in the 'middling and inferior' stations are jointly capable of keeping the moral sentiments in a healthy state, our disposition to over-admire the rich and powerful notwithstanding. Rasmussen's distinction implies that wider social forces act as a sort of social control mechanism, keeping secretly corrupt moral sentiments amongst ordinary people in check by preventing their expression in action—an altogether Mandevillean (and hence Rousseauvian) interpretation that we should be cautious about reading into the text without good warrant.

portion of people in 'the superior stations of life', where 'the case is unhappily not always the same' (*TMS* I.iii.3.6). In the courts of princes and the drawing rooms of the great, flattery, dissimulation, falsehood, and other forms of vicious behaviour are frequently more expedient for self-advancement than virtue and wisdom—and so it is amongst *this* class of people that one should expect individual corruption to flourish (and expect it on both 'venal' and 'moral' metrics). But again, this is a worry not about commerce and the effects of luxury and market transactions in a modern European society, but about the conduct of individuals who seek political power and influence. Yet such conduct is universal to any human society in which politics takes place, and hence where some seek to gain influence and favour from those who rule—which, once again, is hardly the preserve of any form of 'commercial society'.

Some of these points have previously been made by Dennis Rasmussen, although he uses them to present Smith as defending 'commercial society' from precisely the critique mounted by Rousseau in the *Discourse*, which for the reasons suggested above is a subtle but important misinterpretation of the passages themselves (which are not about commerce, but about riches and sympathy, two different and distinct phenomena), and is also a misreading of Smith's overarching project (he wasn't trying, at least in the passages surveyed so far, to 'defend' something called 'commercial society').[25] However in more recent work Rasmussen has suggested a reason for thinking that in these passages Smith might, after all, have thought that 'commercial society' or, more accurately speaking, advanced European modern societies with large luxury-driven economies based on extensive commerce *are* especially problematic as regards the corruption of our moral sentiments. This is because, as Rasmussen's analysis shows, what Smith really seems to think is dangerous in terms of the corruption of the moral sentiments is not riches and power per se, but the *inequality* that they give rise to. As Rasmussen shows, Smith holds that insofar as there is found extreme inequality in wealth and power, the effects of this are debilitating upon our moral sentiments, and that *this* is the prime source of individual moral corruption: 'Smith suggest that extreme economic inequality tends to corrupt the morals of the very wealthy, who are freed from having to behave morally in order to earn the sympathy and approval of others, as well as the morals of the many others

---

25. Rasmussen, *Problems and Promise*, 126–30.

who admire these unadmirable individuals and/or strive to join their ranks, often through unscrupulous means'.[26]

Rasmussen's analysis is convincing on the point that it is inequality, and not mere riches and poverty, that makes the real difference for Smith. Yet we must resist falling into a Rousseauvian trap in explicating what, if anything, this means for Smith's wider analysis. This comes in the form of taking a further step, and assuming that modern European societies are especially marked out by the fact that they are somehow *more unequal* than other forms of society—and must therefore be more corrupting of the moral sentiments of their inhabitants.[27] If we do indeed assume this, then it would follow that modern European commercial societies are indeed more problematic than other forms of society regarding the issue of individual-level sentimental corruption. And perhaps this is true. Yet *Smith* did not seem to think that modern European societies were more especially marked by inequality than other forms of politics. Here it is again crucial to avoid mistakenly importing Rousseau's arguments or assumptions into Smith's texts. For whilst Rousseau in the *Discourse* postulates humanity as falling away from a prepolitical, materially egalitarian, and psychologically balanced halcyon idyll—a state of nature prior to the invention of metallurgy and agriculture, that is, of economic exchange powered by the division of labour, which birthed property, material inequality, and eventually the state—Smith has no time for philosophical conjectures about an economically egalitarian, psychologically harmonious paradise lost.[28] On the contrary, Smith is adamant that material inequality was a major feature of shepherdic politics in particular, hence for example he states in *WN* that 'the second period of society, that of shepherds, admits of very great inequalities of fortune, and there is no period in which the superiority of fortune gives so great authority to those who possess it. There is no period accordingly in

26. Rasmussen, 'Smith on What Is Wrong with Economic Inequality', 349; see also Daniel Luban, 'Adam Smith on Vanity, Domination, and History', *Modern Intellectual History* 9, no. 2 (2012): 288–92.

27. See for example the claim by Pignol and Walraevens ('Smith and Rousseau', 1231) that 'Smith and Rousseau both state that inequality tends to increase with the progress of wealth in commercial societies and that it may give birth to envy'.

28. Jean-Jacques Rousseau, *The Discourses and Other Early Political Writings*, ed. V. Gourevitch (Cambridge: Cambridge University Press, 1997), 164–74. For my detailed reading of what Rousseau did and did not achieve, see *Opinion of Mankind*, chap. 4. Note that for Smith whilst primitive 'hunter' societies may have been relatively egalitarian, this came at the cost of extensive material destitution, and hence was in no way a desirable condition to be in.

which authority and subordination are more perfectly established' (*WN* V.i.b.7).[29] One way to read this passage is that if authority and subordination are most perfectly established under shepherd warlordism, that is because economic inequality in such arrangements is at its most pronounced. Furthermore, such inequality concerns Smith because it tends to translate into very direct inequalities of power, and in turn to the domination of the powerless by the powerful. Likewise, and extrapolating from the above (i.e., what Smith says in *TMS* I.iii.3.5), we can suggest in turn that from Smith's perspective modern European citizens would if anything be relatively sheltered from the effects of inequality as a mechanism of sentimental corruption, as well as a vehicle for abuse of power, compared to, for example, those living in close proximity to the court of a feudal baron, or having to beg for crooked justice in the tent of a Mongol khan. In these kinds of sociopolitical arrangements, smaller scale associations and direct economic dependence upon political superiors would typically put ordinary people into far more direct contact with those possessed of vastly greater inequality in material holdings than would be experienced by the average individual in a large, diffuse, economically interdependent, modern European society like the Britain of Smith's day. Hence against the implication that Smith must have been troubled by 'commercial society' because this tends to create extreme levels of inequality, this may simply not be the case as regards Smith's own position. If anything, from Smith's perspective modern European states may have had the great advantage of exhibiting *less* inequality than the shepherdic forms of domination that he believed to be the historical norm.

29. See also the claim at *LJ*(A) iv.8 that 'in this period of society the inequality of fortune makes a greater odds in the power and influence of the rich over the poor than in any other'. Although it is ambiguous here as to whether Smith is saying that the *inequality itself* is greater in shepherd conditions than under modern politics, what is not ambiguous is Smith's insistence that the *effects* of such inequality are there more pronounced. Note also Smith's remark at *LJ*(A) iv.116 that following the fall of Rome, 'These allodial lords, possessing great territories and having great wealth in rents of the produce itself, came to have a great number of dependents as they possessed the whole or the greatest part of the lands of the kingdom. This inequality of property would, in a country where agriculture and division of land was introduced but arts were not practisd, introduce still greater dependance than amongst shepherds, tho there too it is very great'—clearly indicting that Smith took significant inequality to be a core feature of the allodial rule that preceded feudalism, and hence modern European economic development, meaning the latter is unlikely to be a privileged locus of economic inequality in his view.

To be clear, the above has not sought to deny that Smith thinks that our moral sentiments are vulnerable to being corrupted, nor that he rejects the claim (which he evidently advances to some degree in his own voice) that a leading source of such corruption is excessive admiration for wealth and power, which leads people to overvalue the virtues (and downplay the vices) of the rich. What it *has* sought to deny is that regarding two of the most oft-cited sections of *TMS* in discussions of Smith and corruption there is any evidence for thinking that in Smith's view 'commerce' generally, and European modernity in particular, is a privileged site for, or prone to exacerbating threats of, individual-level corruption. Smith's analysis in these passages is not about 'commerce', still less 'commercial society' (either in its narrow technical Smithian sense, or as commentator-imposed synonym for the phenomenon of consumer capitalism). His object of analysis is more fundamentally the human condition, some of the things that constitute it, and that can serve in different ways to make it go well or badly, with particular regards to some aspects of our moral sentiments, and hence of wider ethical phenomena and practices. Which is entirely appropriate, for that is what *TMS* as a whole is principally attempting to do, and hence its constituting components contribute to this overarching aim. What Smith is not trying to do in these passages is 'defend' something called 'commercial society'.

The Working Poor, Faction, and Religious Fanaticism

Does not Smith, however, famously claim that commercial relationships are damaging to the well-being of the working poor in modern economic arrangements, going so far as to state that 'some attention of government is necessary in order to prevent the almost entire corruption and degeneracy of the great body of the people' (*WN* V.i.f.49)?[30] The answer is a qualified yes. But we must again proceed carefully, for Smith's discussion of the ill effects of the division of labour must be carefully distinguished from any claims that he saw 'commerce' as 'corrupting' of the moral sentiments, and hence that modern European commercial societies are particularly open to criticism on this score.

Strictly speaking, Smith is erring in using the language of 'corruption' in *WN* to describe the debilitating effects of the division of labour. This is

---

30. For more detailed discussions of Smith on the debilitating effects of the division of labour, see Griswold, *Adam Smith and the Virtues of Enlightenment*, 292–301; Hill, 'Adam Smith on the Theme of Corruption', 256–58; Rasmussen, *Problems and Promise*, 73–76.

because, as noted above, corruption technically refers to the degradation of a healthy state into an unhealthy one, whereas what Smith actually describes in these passages is a stunting of the capacities of human beings, that is, the prevention of their achieving a healthier state of flourishing that their natures would otherwise be capable of. Nonetheless, and without getting unduly hung up on a linguistic technicality, let us consider what Smith says in *WN* about such individual corruption.

Smith sees the negative effects of the labouring classes being forced to specialize in a small number of tedious and endlessly repetitive tasks as multifold. In the first instance the lowly labourer has no opportunity to regularly exercise his understanding, and he 'naturally loses, therefore, the habit of such exertion, and generally becomes as stupid and ignorant as it is possible for a human creature to become'. The effect of this is felt on a number of metrics: the mentally stunted worker becomes incapable of engaging in or relishing 'rational conversation'; he cannot conceive 'of any generous, noble, or tender sentiment, and consequently of forming any just judgement concerning many even of the ordinary duties of private life'; he is ignorant about, and anyway incapable of properly judging, matters of wider political importance; and he fails to cultivate any sort of martial capacity 'for defending his country in war' because 'the uniformity of his stationary life naturally corrupts the courage of his mind, and makes him regard with abhorrence the irregular, uncertain, and adventurous life of a soldier', whilst even his physical capacities are stunted and decayed beyond those strictly required for his labouring. The effects of the division of labour are therefore severe in terms of ordinary workers' 'intellectual, social, and martial virtues' (*WN* V.i.f.50).

These are serious ills on Smith's assessment. However, Smith is identifying these ills not with 'commerce', but specifically with *the division of labour*.[31] Such effects would still obtain, we can say, even if the products of the division of labour were not traded in subsequent commercial relationships but (for example) piled up in a giant warehouse and never brought into the light of day. Of course, there is therefore indeed a sense in which 'commercial

---

31. It is true that in *LJ* Smith is recorded as saying 'another bad effect of commerce is that it sinks the courage of mankind, and tends to extinguish martial spirit' (*LJ(B)* 331). Yet we should remember here that the hand that wrote these words is not Smith's, and even if Smith did put it this way in the early version of his ideas as presented in his student lectures, he does not make the claim this way in the final version put forward in *WN*, where he focuses specifically on the division of labour.

societies'—wherein every man lives from exchange precisely because 'the division of labour has been once thoroughly established' (*WN* I.iv.1)—are liable to 'corrupt' the moral sentiments of ordinary workers. But this is not because of the commercial transaction themselves, has nothing to do with vanity or the effects of our disproportionately admiring the rich and powerful, does not affect everybody (only the labouring poor, who are forced into menial repetitive work), and furthermore cannot primarily be a result of the pursuit of, for example, luxury status goods, because by definition the poor have at best very limited access to and means of acquiring those. In other words, whilst Smith certainly thinks that the moral sentiments of ordinary people can become corrupted in advanced economic conditions, the reasons for this stem from an entirely different source than those posited by a thinker like Rousseau, for whom such corruption was a function of enflamed *amour propre* and the need to constantly appear in the gaze of others.

Second, Smith in his analysis does not claim that these stunting effects of the division of labour are unique to modern European commercial societies. On the contrary, they are common to 'every improved and civilized society this is the state into which the labouring poor, that is, the great body of the people, must necessarily fall, unless government takes some pains to prevent it' (*WN* V.i.f.50). A pin factory is certainly a modern European invention, elevating the division of labour to an historically unprecedented degree. But the same basic principle underpinned the economic prosperity of the ancient Romans and Greeks, and so their labouring poor were likewise subjected to the same risk of mental degradation as the moderns, even if it is true that the moderns are further along in terms of the level of degradation experienced.[32] Indeed, Smith goes on to illustrate his point by explaining that the advanced civilizations—the commercial societies—of the Greek city-states and early Rome staved off the stultifying effects of the division of labour through the extensive encouragement of military exercises as part of a state militia, which helped offset otherwise degrading effects upon the social, intellectual, and martial capacities of the male labouring classes. Interestingly, Smith claims that these regimes did not however set out with this goal principally in mind. The ancient republican commercial societies were different from modern European commercial societies in that they relied entirely on militias for their

---

32. Though we should also note that Smith was writing prior to the industrial revolution, and so we must not project back onto his thought what we now know about the effects of the division of labour upon the industrial working poor of the following century.

security and defence, and so had a permanent and independent incentive to provide public 'education' in the form of military training. The unintended—but welcome—consequence of this was to offset the debilitating effects of the division of labour on the minds and sentiments of ordinary workers. By contrast, the modern European states of Smith's day no longer relied on citizen militias for their defence, having turned instead to the more effective (itself an instantiation of the division of labour) innovation of standing armies, and so they also neglected the cultivation of the martial virtues, hence failing to provide a publicly organized remedy for the negative effects of the division of labour. For this reason, Smith suggests that regardless of whether or not a militia can make any difference to the military capacity of modern European states (something he is highly dubious about), a government's providing something like militia-style training for ordinary working people would nonetheless still be valuable. 'Even though the martial spirit of the people were of no use towards the defence of the society, yet to prevent that sort of mental mutilation, deformity and wretchedness, which cowardice necessarily involves in it, from spreading themselves through the great body of the people, would still deserve the most serious attention of government' (WN V.i.f.60). The wider point for present purposes is that there is nothing *unique* to modern European commercial societies regarding the effects of the division of labour, although it is true that generating the solutions to its negative effects will need to be done differently now to how it was in the ancient world.[33] Similarly,

---

33. One difference relates to the fact that insofar as commercial societies tend to become opulent, in turn exchanging military prowess for pacific commercial activities amongst the general male population, such societies risk becoming greater targets for—and also less capable of defending themselves from—shepherd assault. Indeed, whereas the ancient commercial societies were ultimately brought down by their inability to defend themselves from the barbarian threat, modern commercial societies are much better placed in terms of crucial technological advances that have reversed the balance of power between civilized and barbarian powers, in particular the invention of firearms (WN V.i.a.44). Furthermore, modern commercial societies have established the use of standing armies, and these are, Smith insists, far more effective in resisting barbarian threats than militias, of the sort which had of course conspicuously failed in the ancient world. On this see especially Ryan Patrick Hanley, 'The "Wisdom of the State": Adam Smith on China and Tartary', *American Political Science Review* 108, no. 2 (2014): 378–81. However, whereas Hanley presents Smith as offering a solution to the problem of 'commercial corruption', and which he reads Smith as situating vis-à-vis an ongoing barbarian threat to even contemporary European states, I suggest that Smith thinks that the innovations of gunpowder and standing armies have permanently neutralised the barbarian threat—and hence the only metric upon which the 'corruption' of ordinary individuals is of concern to Smith is not the loss

given that the division of labour is more advanced under the conditions of modern Europe than in the past, it is reasonable to suppose that its negative effects will be more pronounced than in earlier forms of commercial society. But this is a difference of degree, not kind.

Smith, then, does not deny that the sentiments of ordinary individuals are vulnerable to being 'corrupted' (by which he really means stunted, prevented from flourishing as they otherwise might) in modern European societies. But this is an effect not of 'commerce' generally, nor of the pursuit of status goods, luxury purchases, or our market exchange relationships more specifically, and nor is it unique to European modernity. It is, instead, an effect of how goods and services are produced *before* they can be exchanged in advanced economic conditions, namely the extensive division of labour. Commercial society—in Smith's narrow technical understanding—does give rise to a threat of corruption of the moral sentiments, precisely because when the division of labour has become sufficiently wide and extensive, every man lives from exchange, and the working poor in particular (the great body of the people) live by exchanging their dull, repetitive, 'mentally mutilating' labour for the means of survival (and if they are lucky, something more than merely that). This, we might note, is not an argument advanced by Rousseau, and indeed is very far away from the arguments about the ill effects of commerce, inequality, status competition, and enflamed *amour propre* that Rousseau does put forward. Hence, again, why it is a severe mistake to read Rousseau's concerns into Smith's works, because in doing so we are liable to miss what Smith is actually saying, and to fail to notice when he is operating at a different level of analysis, with different aims and results.

Smith was also very much alert to other sources of corruption which might threaten the moral sentiments, besides our disproportionate admiration for the rich and powerful and the mentally mutilating effects of the extensive division of labour. Most especially, the prevalence of political factionalism, and the power of religious fanaticism to capture people's minds, both of which have the potential to severely distort the moral sentiments.[34] The first thing

---

of military virtue vis-à-vis the capacity for defence, but the attendant loss of an unintended but highly effective means of preventing the mental degradation of ordinary workers brought on by the extensive division of labour.

34. Smith's discussion of these phenomena has been helpfully analysed in Griswold, *Adam Smith and the Virtues of Enlightenment*, 266–92, and Hill, 'Adam Smith on the Theme of Corruption', 658–61; Eric Schliesser, *Adam Smith: Systematic Philosopher and Public Thinker* (Oxford:

to note, however, is that political factionalism and religious fanaticism are again hardly unique to modern Europe, nor indeed to any kind of commercial society. Insofar as these things corrupt moral sentiments, they are liable to do so everywhere, and at all times. Having said that, Smith does suspect that the threat of religious fanaticism and/or political factionalism may be especially acute in advanced economic conditions. This is once again precisely because of the stultifying effects of the division of labour: those rendered ignorant and stupid by the monotony of the pin factory are, Smith thinks, more easily deceived, and hence more easily led astray by political and religious pied pipers. There is thus, beyond the intrinsic good it would do to the happiness and flourishing of the labouring poor themselves, a compelling instrumental reason for modern governments to actively attempt to counter the negative effects of the division of labour:

> Though the state was to derive no advantage from the instruction of the inferior ranks of people, it would still deserve its attention that they should not be altogether uninstructed. The state, however, derives no inconsiderable advantage from their instruction. The more they are instructed, the less liable they are to the delusions of enthusiasm and superstition, which, among ignorant nations, frequently occasion the most dreadful disorders. An instructed and intelligent people besides are always more decent and orderly than an ignorant and stupid one. They feel themselves, each individually, more respectable, and more likely to obtain the respect of their lawful superiors, and they are therefore more disposed to respect those superiors. They are more disposed to examine, and more capable of seeing through, the interested complaints of faction and sedition, and they are, upon that account, less apt to be misled into any wanton or unnecessary

Oxford University Press, 2017), 158–59; Sandra J. Peart and David M. Levy, 'Adam Smith and the Place of Faction', in *The Elgar Companion to Adam Smith*, ed. J. Young (Cheltenham: Edward Elgar, 2009). Interestingly, Smith writes in *TMS* Part III that 'of all the corruptors of moral sentiments, therefore, faction and fanaticism have always been by far the greatest' (III.3.43)—and given that he did not remove this sentence in the sixth and final edition, despite adding the observation to Part I that 'moralists in all ages' have held admiration for the rich and powerful to be the leading cause of our sentimental corruption, this provides further evidence that Smith should perhaps not be taken as straightforwardly talking *in propria persona* with regards to the negative effects of admiration for the rich and powerful in Part I. On this see also Lisa Hill, '"The Poor Man's Son" and the Corruption of Our Moral Sentiments: Commerce, Virtue and Happiness in Adam Smith', *Journal of Scottish Philosophy* 15, no. 1 (2017): 18.

opposition to the measures of government. In free countries, where the
safety of government depends very much upon the favourable judgment
which the people may form of its conduct, it must surely be of the highest
importance that they should not be disposed to judge rashly or capriciously
concerning it. (*WN* V.f.i.61)

Again, the point to be noted is that insofar as political factionalism and religious fanaticism are found to be more of a problem in modern European societies than elsewhere (if indeed they really are), this is a result not of commerce
or market relations, but more fundamentally of the effects of the division of
labour on the psychological functioning of the poor. Smith therefore does not
deny that individual corruption is a real possibility, nor that it is a bad thing,
but his account of why this is so is not an anxiety about market relationships
specifically, or commerce generally, but more fundamentally about what
makes extensive market relationships and commerce possible. This however
means that there is no special or privileged connection between advanced
European modernity and problems of corruption, because such problems will
afflict (to varying degrees) *all* commercial societies, of which modern European states are only one particular subspecies.

What, however, of the normative status of market relationships, and thus
of a society that relies extensively on them, and that permits their effects to
obtain? Does Smith not here agree with Rousseau that there is something
deeply morally suspect about commercial transactions as experienced, in particular, by modern Europeans? The answer, as the next sections seeks to show,
is again no.

The Motor of Prosperity

It may be objected against the reading offered thus far that my analysis of
Smith is crucially incomplete because I have failed to connect his discussion
of vanity and admiration for the rich and powerful in Part I of *TMS* to his account of economic consumption in Part IV. Even if I am right that Part I does
not discuss commerce (it might be claimed), Part IV does, and yet Part I underpins Part IV, and this licenses us to read Smith's earlier discussion of vanity
back and forth with his later discussion of economic activity. Indeed, this is
now an entirely standard approach in the scholarly literature. It is however a
mistake, one resting on a widespread misreading of Part IV. This section explains how and why this is so, and why it matters.

With regards to Smith's estimation of the nature of, and potential justifications for, large-scale market societies of the sort found in the modern Europe of his day, the following framework is broadly accepted by most commentators as being Smith's position (differences of specific technical interpretation notwithstanding):

1. Markets are (a) driven by *vanity*, which (b) consists in a form of *deception* over the minds of ordinary people.[35]
2. Markets in turn create *inequality*.
3. But markets simultaneously result in massive *absolute poverty reduction*.[36]
4. Modern European society has replaced economic dependence on political superiors with economic interdependence in the market, as well as establishing the liberty of subjects more generally through the destruction of feudal power. Markets thus generate *political freedom*.[37]

35. See especially Fleischacker, *On Adam Smith's* Wealth of Nations, chap. 6, which is a reply to Griswold, *Adam Smith and the Virtues of Enlightenment*, 217–27, 292–301, both of which were replied to by Rasmussen, *Problems and Promise*, chap. 3. I do not discuss the details of this dispute insofar as I take all three to be misguided from the outset in that they all start from the incorrect premise that Smith thinks markets are primarily driven by vanity, and all in turn erroneously jump back and forth between Parts I and IV, compounding misreadings in turn. This will become clearer below. See likewise Hanley, 'Commerce and Corruption', 138–39, 141–42; Hanley, *Adam Smith and the Character of Virtue*, 18, 36–38, 52, 101–3; Hill, 'Poor Man's Son', 11; Rasmussen, 'Smith on What Is Wrong with Economic Inequality', 349–51; Schwarze and Scott, 'Mutual Sympathy', 75–78; Force, *Self-Interest*, 42–47, 161; Schmidtz, 'Smith on Freedom', 216; Luban, 'Smith on Vanity', 284; István Hont, *Politics in Commercial Society: Jean-Jacques Rousseau and Adam Smith*, ed. B. Kapossy and M. Sonenscher (Cambridge, MA: Harvard University Press, 2015), 91–102; Jerry Z. Muller, *Adam Smith in His Time and Ours: Designing the Decent Society* (New York: Free Press, 1993), 133; Vivienne Brown, *Adam Smith's Discourse: Canonicity, Commerce, and Conscience* (London: Routledge, 1994), 188–89. Craig Smith (in *Adam Smith*, 82–83) avoids the mistake of reading the poor man's son passage (more on which below) as primarily about vanity, although he unfortunately leaves out the crucial matter of the quirk of rationality, and later (84) identifies the generation of wealth as rooted in vanity, thus ultimately aligning himself with mainstream interpretation.

36. See especially Fleischacker, *On Adam Smith's* Wealth of Nations, chaps. 9–10, but also Griswold, *Adam Smith and the Virtues of Enlightenment*, chap. 6; Hont and Ignatieff, 'Needs and Justice'; Rasmussen, *Problems and Promise*, 103; Smith, *Adam Smith*, 82–87; Schliesser, *Adam Smith*, chap. 8.

37. Rasmussen, *Problems and Promise*, chap. 4, is an exemplar here, and provides a helpfully clear overview.

In this framework, (1) and (2) are held to be the *negative downsides* of 'commercial society' (by which commentators usually mean modern Europe), but (3) and (4) are its *positive upshots*. On balance, we are standardly told, Smith thinks (3) and (4) outweigh (1) and (2). Hence, 'commercial society' is in the end justified, even if Smith thinks (= concedes to Rousseau) that it comes at a real normative cost, namely that it is based on vanity, deception, and the unbridling of inequality that is instrumentally, if not intrinsically, justified due to its correlating to increased prosperity for ordinary people,[38] as well helping to inaugurate modern liberty.[39] On the recently prevalent view of Smith, therefore, the fact that markets are powered primarily by vanity (a vice) is a concession to a Rousseauvian outlook whereby the fundamental normative status of markets is impugned, as by implication is any kind of society—no matter how free and prosperous, and thus to the widespread benefit of ordinary people—that relies on the existence of markets. Hence, we are told, Smith thinks that 'commercial society' can on balance be justified, because the good outweighs the bad, so long as we take things in the round. (Indeed, this is precisely what makes him a 'defender' of 'commercial society', one opposing the critique that was levelled by Rousseau.)

I have no quarrel with (3) and (4) in the above framework, at least when taken in isolation. However, as indicated above, (2) is liable to be overstated if commentators forget that from Smith's perspective advanced European societies are not particularly unusual or notable in featuring high levels of inequality: shepherdic forms of politics are for Smith characterised by extensive inequality, and indeed may have been far more unequal than modern European societies, and with more pernicious results. My substantive objection, however, is to (1). For against the majority of recent scholarship on this topic I maintain that it is (a) *false* to claim that Smith thinks most market activity is undertaken from motives of vanity, and (b) that the 'deception' that Smith discusses in Part IV has its origin in an entirely different location. This matters, because if I am correct then Smith is 'conceding' a great deal less to the

---

38. In Smith's words, that 'the accommodation of an European prince does not always so much exceed that of an industrious and frugal peasant, as the accommodation of the latter exceeds that of many an African king, the absolute master of the lives and liberties of ten thousand naked savages' (*WN* I.i.11).

39. We can thus agree with Hont, 'Introduction', 96–97, that Smith is here siding with Locke, against a thinker like Rousseau, in judging that economic inequality is on balance justified if the result is an absolute and massive improvement in the condition of the poor.

Rousseauvian outlook than commentators standardly read him as doing, and in turn he is not best read as mounting a 'defence' in reply to the attack launched by the Genevan. Furthermore, Smith *does not* accept the view that markets—or, more precisely, economic consumption—and the prosperous advanced civilizations that they give rise to are at base normatively problematic, but then nonetheless on balance deciding that they are anyway justified because of their various supervening and/or instrumental benefits. Rather, economic consumption in his estimation is a good deal more normatively neutral than commentators standardly suppose him to believe—and hence he is, again, further away from Rousseau than commentary has tended to suggest. Contrary to Hanley's claim that 'Smith in his own name advances the claim originally made in his translations of the *Second Discourse*: that markets are driven by solicitude of praise and recognition', Smith believed markets were primarily driven by another source entirely: the quirk of human rationality noted in the previous chapter, whereby individuals become preoccupied with the means of promoting utility rather than the utility itself. And *this* is the source of the deception that primarily powers markets, to the aggregate good of the species as a whole. As a result, Smith thinks economic consumption is much less presumptively normatively problematic than Rousseau does, and so the now-standard interpretive frames noted above are wrong, and must be jettisoned.

To see all of this it helps to go slowly and meticulously through the text. Whereas commentators typically jump back and forth indiscriminately between Smith's paragraph about vanity and riches in Part I and the discussion of economic consumption in Part IV, we should immediately pause and note that the title of Part IV is 'Of Utility'. Vanity, however, is properly to do with the regard that others hold us in, and hence is properly contained (as Smith indeed contains it) under a discussion of *propriety*—the subject of Part I. We should thus be very careful before reading claims about vanity (an aspect of propriety) into what is, at least officially, a chapter on the different subject of utility.

Turning now to the relevant substance of that chapter, we can note that Smith begins his discussion by rejecting Hume's claim that utility is the foundation of the majority of our moral judgements. Seeking to replace this account, Smith makes the following point:

But that this fitness, this happy contrivance of any production of art, *should often be more valued, than the very end for which it was intended;* and that the exact adjustment of the means for attaining any convenieney or pleasure, should frequently be more regarded, than that very convenieney or pleasure, in the attainment of which their whole merit would seem to consist, *has not, so far as I know, been yet taken notice of by any body.* That this however is very frequently the case, may be observed in a thousand instances, both in the most frivolous and in the most important concerns of human life. (*TMS* IV.1.3, emphasis added)

It is striking, and a little ironic, that given Smith's own signalling that he has discovered something entirely original, the precise nature, let along significance, of what he is claiming has (as far as I know) gone almost entirely unremarked by any commentator besides myself.[40] What Smith is pointing to here is the phenomenon which I denoted in the previous chapter as the 'quirk of rationality', whereby we become more preoccupied with the means of promoting utility than with the utility itself. Smith, recall, gives us a raft of examples to illustrate the point: the man who neatly arranges the chairs in an empty room though nobody should actually benefit from it; the person who must buy the more accurate watch even though the one he already owns is perfectly adequate to the task of telling the time; those who 'ruin themselves by laying out money on trinkets of frivolous utility'; the 'lovers of toys' who love 'not so much the utility, as the aptness of the machines which are fitted to promote it' (*TMS* IV.1.6). And lest the reader should think that the phenomenon he is identifying is trivial or unimportant, Smith explicitly states otherwise: 'Nor is it only in regard to such frivolous objects that our conduct is influenced by this principle; it is often the secret motive of the most serious and important pursuits of both private and public life' (*TMS* IV.1.7).

Notice that not once has Smith mentioned either vanity or the approbation derived from the gaze of others in anything said so far in building his own account. He is instead focused firmly on the quirk of rationality whereby people fixate on the means of utility production rather than the actual utility that is generated. And it is in this context that he introduces the famous passage about the 'poor man's son, whom heaven in its anger has visited with ambition' (*TMS* IV.1.8), to which commentators have paid a great deal of attention, but as far as I can tell, have systematically misread as being a parable about

---

40. Luban, 'Smith on Vanity', 281–82, touches briefly upon it, but reads Smith here as focusing on a desire for 'aesthetic' pleasure, which is a connected but separate issue.

vanity—which it is not.[41] For what, precisely, does Smith say about this unfortunate person (whom we do well to remember is an extreme case used to illustrate a point, but whom we all sometimes at least to some extent run the risk of resembling)? Certainly, the poor son 'admires the condition of the rich.' But why? Let us break down this crucial paragraph in full, quoting Smith in his entirety to ensure that we have an accurate understanding of the argument being made.

First, note that Smith initially says *nothing at all* about vanity, or the approving or disapproving gaze of others. The primary motivations attributed to the poor son are entirely those based on the getting of utility and his unfortunate fixation on the means of utility rather than the utility those means actually procure for him:

> The poor man's son, whom heaven in its anger has visited with ambition, when he begins to look around him, admires the condition of the rich. He finds the cottage of his father too small for his accommodation, and fancies he should be lodged more at his ease in a palace. He is displeased with being obliged to walk a-foot, or to endure the fatigue of riding on horseback. He sees his superiors carried about in machines, and imagines that in one of these he could travel with less inconveniency. He feels himself naturally indolent, and willing to serve himself with his own hands as little as possible; and judges, that a numerous retinue of servants would save him from a great deal of trouble. *He thinks if he had attained all these, he would sit still contentedly, and be quiet, enjoying himself in the thought of the happiness and tranquillity of his situation. He is enchanted with the distant idea of this felicity.* It appears in his fancy like the life of some superior rank of beings, and, *in order to arrive at it, he devotes himself for ever to the pursuit of wealth and greatness.* To obtain the conveniencies which these afford, he submits in the first

---

41. For example, Hanley, *Adam Smith and the Character of Virtue*, 106, claims that 'the poor man's son is Smith's quintessential expression of "vanity" that drives the pursuit of "wealth and greatness" in order to "gratify that love of distinction so natural to man"'—which I maintain is entirely wrong. For other mistaken readings of the poor man's son as a parable about vanity, see Hill, 'Poor Man's Son', which whilst offering a dispute with Hanley agrees with him in reading the poor man's son as about vanity corrupting the moral sentiments; Lisa Herzog, 'The Normative Stakes of Economic Growth; Or Why Adam Smith Does Not Rely on "Trickle Down"', *Journal of Politics* 78, no. 1 (2015): 59; Fleischacker, *On Adam Smith's* Wealth of Nations, chap. 6; Griswold, *Adam Smith and the Virtues of Enlightenment*, 217–27, 292–301; Rasmussen, *Problems and Promise*, chap. 3.

year, nay in the first month of his application, *to more fatigue of body and more uneasiness of mind than he could have suffered through the whole of his life from the want of them.* He studies to distinguish himself in some laborious profession. With the most unrelenting industry he labours night and day to acquire talents superior to all his competitors. He endeavours next to bring those talents into public view, and with equal assiduity solicits every opportunity of employment. *For this purpose* he makes his court to all mankind; he serves those whom he hates, and is obsequious to those whom he despises. *Through the whole of his life he pursues the idea of a certain artificial and elegant repose which he may never arrive at, for which he sacrifices a real tranquillity that is at all times in his power,* and which, if in the extremity of old age he should at last attain to it, he will find to be in no respect preferable to that humble security and contentment which he had abandoned for it. (*TMS* IV.1.8, emphasis added)

It is at this point that Smith first introduces the idea that the poor son labours under a deception. But the deception has nothing to do with vanity or the approbation of others, and is instead rooted entirely in confusing the means of utility with the ends which they are supposed to promote. The poor son is constantly striving for material goods and social positions in the belief that they will make him satisfied, even though they manifestly cost him far more effort than can ever be compensated for by the utility that they actually give rise to:

It is then, in the last dregs of life, his body wasted with toil and diseases, his mind galled and ruffled by the memory of a thousand injuries and disappointments which he imagines he has met with from the injustice of his enemies, or from the perfidy and ingratitude of his friends, that he begins at last to find that *wealth and greatness are mere trinkets of frivolous utility*, no more adapted for procuring ease of body or tranquillity of mind *than the tweezer-cases of the lover of toys; and like them too, more troublesome to the person who carries them about with him than all the advantages they can afford him are commodious.* There is no other real difference between them, except that the conveniencies of the one are somewhat more observable than those of the other. (*TMS* IV.1.8, emphasis added)

As regards the promotion of genuine utility (which Smith is here equating with contentment and happiness) wealth and greatness are in and of themselves about as useless—Smith is telling us—as a box of trinkets that one purchases when besotted with the idea that the trinkets will make one's life more convenient, and thus happier, but which inevitably turns out not to be the case. Or to take a more modern example, the same phenomenon explains why the present author finds himself with an iPad, an iPhone, an iMac, *and* a MacBook, despite at most needing (and even that is a stretch) perhaps one of these ludicrously expensive Apple products. The others were all bought whilst labouring under the deception that having more means of utility would make him happier. Unsurprisingly, they didn't. As soon as they were purchased, the craving for the next purchase—the next means of utility—set in.[42] If this sounds familiar, it is because Smith is *correct* in these remarkably underappreciated passages, where he is offering, to my mind at least, the most accurate depiction of the bulk consumer psychology in the pursuit of non-necessary purchase goods ever put into print. But let us return to the text and continue to follow the argument.

Vanity does eventually make an appearance in the poor man's son paragraph. But Smith brings it in as a *subsidiary point* to his wider exposition of the quirk of rationality:

> The palaces, the gardens, the equipage, the retinue of the great, are objects of which the obvious conveniency strikes every body. They do not require that their masters should point out to us wherein consists their utility. Of our own accord we readily enter into it, and by sympathy enjoy and thereby applaud the satisfaction which they are fitted to afford him. *But the curiosity of a tooth-pick, of an ear-picker, of a machine for cutting the nails, or of any other trinket of the same kind, is not so obvious. Their conveniency may perhaps be equally great, but it is not so striking, and we do not so readily enter into the satisfaction of the man who possesses them.* They are therefore *less reasonable subjects of vanity* than the magnificence of wealth and greatness; and in this consists the sole advantage of these last. (*TMS* IV.1.8)

42. Whilst revising this chapter in lockdown during the global COVID-19 pandemic of spring 2020, the author became borderline addicted to online shopping for goods of frivolous utility. Insofar as there was literally nobody else who could see these purchases other than the author and his partner (who was decidedly unimpressed), I offer this as compelling evidence that Smith is right about what motivates a great deal of consumption, and indeed helps us to understand the phenomena of shopping addiction and of compulsive purchasing, either online or through things like television shopping channels. The anticipation of perceived future utility—and the augmenting factor of having to wait for the utility good to arrive in the mail, thus heightening the delight via prolonged anticipation—are not trivial pleasures and can be highly motivating to action (most especially during the boredom of a quarantine).

In other words, it makes sense to take pleasure in genuine objects of wealth and greatness via the pleasure one derives in the gaze of others that such acquisitions do indeed bring (vanity is a real thing, and it does bring pleasure; Smith is not denying that). But most consumer activity in the market *cannot* be explained by vanity, because most consumer activity is directed at in-and-of-themselves ridiculous or idiosyncratic purchases that relevant observers *do not* look upon with approbation, because they do not share the individual acquiring agent's excited sentiments at the prospect of the anticipated purchase. Hence, a desire for approbation *cannot* be what is primarily motivating that kind of consumption. What Smith is saying, in other words, is that vanity *is not* the main motor of most economic consumption—the quirk of rationality is.

But what is the 'sole advantage' associated with the vanity that more properly attaches to 'the magnificence of wealth and greatness'? Smith goes on:

> They more effectually gratify that love of distinction so natural to man. To one who was to live alone in a desolate island it might be a matter of doubt, perhaps, whether a palace, or a collection of such small conveniencies as are commonly contained in a tweezer-case, would contribute most to his happiness and enjoyment. If he is to live in society, indeed, there can be no comparison, because in this, as in all other cases, we constantly pay more regard to the sentiments of the spectator, than to those of the person principally concerned, and consider rather how his situation will appear to other people, than how it will appear to himself. (*TMS* IV.1.8)

Given that we live in societies and are by nature determined to care about each other's sentiments and take pleasure in their approbation, it is not surprising that wealth and greatness attract approval in the eyes of onlookers (and we in turn enjoy this if we are wealthy and powerful), whereas frivolous trinkets for the promotion of utility do not. But then, what is really generating the approbation in the eyes of the onlookers, upon which the vanity of the wealth and great is founded?

> If we examine, however, why the spectator distinguishes with such admiration the condition of the rich and the great, we shall find that *it is not so much upon account of the superior ease or pleasure which they are supposed to enjoy, as of the numberless artificial and elegant contrivances for promoting this ease or pleasure.* He *does not even imagine that they are really happier than other people:* but *he imagines that they possess more means of happiness.* And it is the ingenious and artful adjustment of those means to the end for

which they were intended, that is the principal source of his admiration. (*TMS* IV.1.8, emphasis added)

It turns out that the true source of the approbation upon which vanity is founded is *the quirk of human rationality that over-values the means of utility rather than the utility itself.* The rich and great may well take pleasure, via sympathy, in being admired by others. But they could not get that admiration if it weren't for the utility that their wealth and greatness is presumed by onlookers to secure for them. It is utility—or more accurately, the quirk of rationality with regards to the means of utility—that is most fundamental in Smith's analysis, not vanity. The quirk of rationality not only drives frivolous market consumption, but is itself the root cause of why vanity can operate in this area at all, insofar as vanity rests on the imputed sentiments of onlookers, which are calibrated to observing wealth and greatness not for their own sake, but as the means to utility, the thought of which gives pleasure in the imagination, and which is sympathetically reflected back to the rich in turn. Hence it is categorically wrong to say that Smith thinks that economic consumption, and hence markets, are primarily founded on vanity. According to Smith, markets and economic activity beyond the act of getting bare necessities—that is, the vast majority of consumption in any developed economy—are founded principally and most importantly on the quirk of rationality whereby we become fixated on the means of utility rather than utility itself.

In turn, the 'deception' that Smith invokes in Part IV chapter 1 relates likewise not to vanity, but to the quirk of rationality, that is, the mistake of becoming besotted with means and not ends:

But in the languor of disease and the weariness of old age, the pleasures of the vain and empty distinctions of greatness disappear. To one, in this situation, they are no longer capable of recommending those toilsome pursuits in which they had formerly engaged him. In his heart he curses ambition, and vainly *regrets the ease and the indolence of youth, pleasures which are fled for ever, and which he has foolishly sacrificed for what, when he has got it, can afford him no real satisfaction.* In this miserable aspect does greatness appear to every man when reduced either by spleen or disease to observe with attention his own situation, and to consider what it is that is really wanting to his happiness. *Power and riches appear then to be, what they are, enormous and operose machines contrived to produce a few trifling conveniencies to the body,* consisting of springs the most nice and delicate, which must be kept in order with the most anxious attention, and which in spite of all our care are ready every moment to burst into pieces, and to crush in their ruins their unfortunate possessor. They are immense fabrics, which it requires the labour of a life to raise, which threaten every moment to overwhelm the person that dwells in them, and which while they stand, *though they may save him from some smaller inconveniencies, can protect him from none of the severer inclemencies of the season.* They keep off the summer shower, not the winter storm, but leave him always as much, and sometimes more exposed than before, to anxiety, to fear, and to sorrow; to diseases, to danger, and to death. (*TMS* IV.1.8, emphasis added)

The quirk of rationality certainly imposes on us a deception: we are liable to think that by acquiring more means of utility, we will eventually become satisfied. Yet the treadmill never stops, and we risk sacrificing far more utility trying to secure the means of it than those means themselves ever really deliver (in its most extreme manifestation, this is the fate of the poor man's son). We would do better, Smith insists, to try to get off the treadmill at regular intervals rather than attempting to forever pound away, foolishly thinking that one day we will reach the end goal of satiated contentment, as achieved via more and more consumer goods (although as he later explains, we can never entirely stop ourselves from hopping back on at least some of the time). But again, this has nothing to do with *vanity*, which as regards consumption is parasitic upon the more fundamental phenomenon that Smith is here analysing: the quirk of rationality.

I have quoted the poor man's son paragraph in full and examined it in detail because to my knowledge it is universally misread in the commentary, presented as evidence that Smith thought markets were powered by vanity (with commentators here usually moving back and forth between Parts I and IV to establish the textual warrant for such a reading, but which is a distortion rather than an illumination of Smith's argument). Yet once we see that Part IV chapter 1 is in fact about the quirk of rationality when it comes to the pursuit of utility, Smith's subsequent argument emerges in a different light.

Smith goes in IV.1.9 to remark that although the truth of the deception in times of 'sickness or low spirits is familiar to every man, thus entirely depreciates those great objects of human desire, when in better health and in better humour, we never fail to regard them under a more agreeable aspect'. In an 'abstract and philosophical light' the endless pursuit of consumer goods as a means of securing utility is doomed to fail, and indeed is revealed as frankly absurd. However, 'we rarely view it in this abstract and philosophical light. We naturally confound it in our imagination with the order, the regular and harmonious movement of the system, the machine or œconomy by means of which it is produced. The pleasures of wealth and greatness, when considered in this complex view, strike the imagination as something grand and beautiful and noble, of which the attainment is well worth all the toil and anxiety which we are so apt to bestow upon it' (*TMS* IV.1.9). This in turn sets up Smith's invocation of the 'invisible hand' in *TMS*, and the claim that it is *good* that we are—in general and for the most part—deceived in the above manner. For 'it is this deception which rouses and keeps in continual motion the industry of mankind': whilst the 'proud and unfeeling landlord' is entirely selfish in his pursuit of the means of utility, the economic stimulus that this generates prompts further wealth to be generated in turn, whilst the landlord's eyes are bigger than his belly, and he ends up sharing the surplus with others for profit, but which he would never otherwise have given them from 'his humanity or his justice'. Here commentators are certainly right that Smith thinks markets are beneficial insofar as the rising tide lifts all boats: the landlords are 'led by an invisible hand, to make nearly the same distribution of the necessaries of life, which would have been made, had the earth been divided into equal portions among all its inhabitants, and thus without intending it, without knowing it, advance the interest of the society, and afford means to the multiplication of the species'. This is why 'Providence' neither 'forgot nor abandoned' the poor when it divided the earth between a small number of masters, for they 'too enjoy their share of all that it produces'. Smith does not deny that markets generate inequality, and on balance he affirms that this is normatively tolerable insofar as markets also lead to massive absolute gains in material well-being for those towards the bottom of the pile. Crucially, however, because the rich and ambitious are the ones who most extensively labour under the deception that securing the means of utility will make them happy, it is in many ways those *without* riches and power who have the last laugh: 'In what constitutes the real happiness of human life, they are in no respect inferior to those who would seem so much above them. In ease of body and peace of mind, all the different ranks of life are nearly upon a level, and the beggar, who suns himself by the side of the highway, possesses that security which kings are fighting for' (*TMS* IV.1.10).

When correctly interpreted, we can now see that Part IV chapter 1 of *TMS* is anything but a concession to Rousseau's claim that markets are principally powered by vanity. On the contrary, Smith's position is that Rousseau's claim is *false*: markets are primarily powered by the quirk of human rationality. In turn, several things ought to change in our assessment of Smith's overall position. First, markets are on this view *not presumptively normatively problematic*, as they are powered not by the vice of vanity (and especially not in Rousseau's sense of an enflamed *amour propre*), but by a curious, often self-defeating, but not in itself morally vicious, quotidian quirk of human psychology.

Second, although human beings do labour under a deception—and it is true that this deception is liable to be bad for individuals like the poor man's son who are excessively captured by it—nonetheless most of us, at least most of the time, can keep the deception in check, and not let it get out of control in a way that will damage our lives (this is part of the point being made at IV.1.9). As a result, markets are not normatively problematic in anything like as serious a way as if they were systematically predicated on people being widely deceived about promoting their own selfish vanity to an endless and innately pathological degree (as Rousseau suggests).

Third, Smith has said nothing in IV.1 to indicate that he thinks the psychological phenomena which generate economic consumption are unique to modern Europe (or indeed any other form of 'commercial society'), nor that they are especially problematic or made worse under conditions of either modern Europe, or 'commercial society' generally. Instead, Smith is here explaining that *all* human prosperity is driven by these underlying psychological processes. The outgrowth of the unintended consequences of this state of affairs (the effects of the 'invisible hand') eventually culminate—at least in fortuitous circumstances, and at some points in history—in the emergence of commercial societies, that is, that condition wherein everyone is in some measure a merchant and lives from exchange. This first happened in Europe in the ancient Attican republics, and has again come to pass with the collapse of feudalism in modern Europe. The analysis offered in IV.1 is therefore about *what fundamentally and eventually makes commercial societies possible*, and is not narrowly focused on 'commercial society' alone, or modern European states in particular. After all, the process Smith describes in IV.1.10 is presented as the motor of *all* significant human economic prosperity, throughout all of human history, and hence it must both predate and underpin the emergence of complex commercial relations at more advanced points, such as in modern Europe. There is therefore simply no textual warrant for the claim made by Hanley that on Smith's view 'individuals in commercial societies are uniquely sensitive to the opinions of others and are hence potentially vulnerable to corruption'.[43] That may be Rousseau's view, but it is not Smith's.

Fourth, rather than viewing Smith as totting up an 'economic and moral balance sheet'[44] of 'positives' and 'negatives' associated with modern European conditions (or as commentators usually say, 'commercial society'), and cautiously coming out on the side of the 'defence', we do better to see that he rejects entirely the supposition that markets are normatively problematic because they allegedly rest primarily on motives of vanity, that is, craving unwarranted approval in the gaze of others, thus incentivizing people to pursue a vice that corrupts the moral sentiments. Not only is it false to claim that Smith thinks that something called 'commercial society' tends especially to corrupt the individuals who live within it, it is also false to hold that he thinks that societies characterized by high degrees of economic consumption are themselves morally compromised due to a foundation in the pursuit of vanity. Smith does not endorse *either* claim.

Finally, we should note that Part IV of *TMS* is principally concerned with *refuting Hume*, and that Smith's 'quirk of rationality' thesis has its origin in rejecting Hume's claim that utility is the foundation of most of our moral approbations, which Smith then goes on in the rest of Part IV to systematically critique.[45] This reinforces the point made in the previous chapter: insofar as Smith engages Rousseau in Part IV of *TMS*, he does so more or less incidentally, with Rousseau featuring as a passing casualty in the more fundamental task of correcting and replacing Hume's sentimentalist theory, that is, the leading and most sophisticated philosophical competitor theory to that which Smith is putting forward.[46] Rather than writing *TMS* to 'defend' 'commercial society' from an attack by Rousseau, Smith wrote *TMS* to advance a sentimentalist theory of morality rooted in sympathy that aimed to be an improvement

43. Hanley, 'Commerce and Corruption', 142.

44. Rasmussen, *Problems and Promise*, 13.

45. Again see Sagar, 'Beyond Sympathy'.

46. In this regard see also Robin Douglass, 'Morality and Sociability in Commercial Society: Smith, Rousseau—and Mandeville', *Review of Politics* 79, no. 4 (2017), which identifies Smith as primarily responding to Mandeville rather than to Rousseau (a point with which I agree, though I suggest that both are still a good less important to Smith's project than Hume). Smith must have Rousseau at least partially in mind as he paraphrases from the *Discourse* drawing on the passages he had translated in his *Edinburgh Review* piece—but this by itself is not evidence for more than Smith neatly showing, in passing, how he can refute the recent noisy polemic from Europe, as argued in chapter 3 above.

on Hume's earlier account. In the process he happened to reject a recent polemic from the continent, one which he had already openly declared in his
own earlier review to be made up primarily of 'rhetoric' and 'philosophical
chemistry', and hence by implication to be lacking in sound analysis (*EPS* 251).
Part IV of *TMS* makes good on Smith's early review of Rousseau by showing
why, despite his impressive style and his eye-catching repackaging of Mandeville's earlier ideas, Rousseau is seriously off-base. This is not so much a 'defence'
in reply to a 'critique', as explaining that the alleged critique is so fundamentally mistaken that no defence is required. What *is* required is a more accurate
analysis of the factors in play—which is precisely what Smith takes himself to
have offered.

Before concluding this section, an objection might however be made to my
case. This is that on my reading Smith appears to have landed himself in a
contradiction, and yet given his sophistication as an author, and the meticu-
lousness with which he revised *TMS* for over thirty years, this is at least prima
facie a reason to doubt my interpretation. For as noted earlier, in his discussion
of vanity in Part I, Smith explicitly states that 'it is chiefly from this regard to
the sentiments of mankind, that we pursue riches and avoid poverty', before
going on to ask, 'From whence, then, arises that emulation which runs through
all the different ranks of men, and what are the advantages which we propose
by that great purpose of human life which we call bettering our condition. To
be observed, to be attended to, to be taken notice of with sympathy, complacency, and approbation, are all the advantages which we can propose to derive
from it' (*TMS* I.iii.2.1). Here, then, Smith seems to indicate that 'bettering our
condition' is pursued *only* because of the 'sympathy, complacency, and approbation' it yields. But as we have seen above, Smith argues in Part IV that the
quirk of rationality, not the approving gaze of others, is the motor of most
economic activity. Has he contradicted himself?

There is no need to think so. In the paragraph just quoted, Smith is using
the phrase 'bettering our condition' to refer specifically to the topic under
discussion: seeking riches and avoiding poverty in the pursuit of the sympathetic approbation of others, that is, attempting to attain social status via
wealth. This is not meant as a universal claim about how we might better our
condition in all and every regard, but is being used specifically to refer to what
we are up to when pursuing riches as a means to the attainment of rank.[47]

47. Smith uses the same expression in the same way in a famous passage in *WN* in his discussion of the motivations for spending versus saving: 'With regard to profusion, the principle,

This, however, is entirely consistent with supposing that *general consumer market activity* is primarily powered not by the pursuit of status goods that signal the possession of wealth, but by the purchasing of the purported means of utility whereby the agent aims at their own individual pleasure (however self-deflatingly, as in the case of the poor man's son). There are thus two distinct phenomena in play here, but they are also quite compatible. Furthermore, one is to do with propriety, the other with utility, and that helps explain why Smith treats of them separately, in Parts I and IV, respectively.

We should also note that it makes perfect sense for Smith to think that there are indeed two separate motivations in play (the desire for riches as a proxy desire for rank and approbation, and the separate desire for acquiring objects as well as positions in society as a purported means of securing utility). This is for two reasons. First, the great process of multiplying wealth and spreading it beyond the clutches of the proud and selfish landlords that is described in IV.1.10 is likely to have been much more effective if *everybody* is engaged in consumption of utility goods, rather than economic activity above subsistence level being confined solely in the effort to acquire status goods by those who can afford to do so. Smith's case is just more plausible if we read things this way around, and that is at least one reason to favour such a reading.

Second, the two motivations will in practice anyway dovetail: having riches and power not only draws the approval of onlookers, it also makes it easier to acquire the means of utility to indulge the quirk of human rationality. The pursuit of wealth and status and the pursuit of the means of utility will

---

which prompts to expence, is the passion for present enjoyment; which, though sometimes violent and very difficult to be restrained, is in general only momentary and occasional. But the principle which prompts to save, is the desire of bettering our condition, a desire which, though generally calm and dispassionate, comes with us from the womb, and never leaves us till we go into the grave' (*WN* II.iii.28). Smith's usage here is continuous with *TMS*: riches are primarily valued not for their own sake or for the attainment of bare necessities, but for securing the approbation of others and thus the pleasure of mutual sympathy, and that is why we save rather than immediately spending all our disposable income on consumer goods. However, he also uses the same expression in a different context to refer to any attempt to improve our lives whatsoever (e.g., the pursuit of utility goods, and not just status ones), e.g., in the famous passage about 'the uniform, constant, and uninterrupted effort of every man to better his condition, the principle from which public and national, as well as private opulence, is originally derived, is frequently powerful enough to maintain the natural progress of things toward improvement, in spite both of the extravagance of government and of the greatest errors of administration' (*WN* II.3.31). For discussion of these passages, see Herzog, 'Normative Stakes', 52; Force, *Self-Interest*, 161; Luban, 'Smith on Vanity', 278–84.

frequently work in tandem. Nonetheless, they are capable of analytic distinction, and one can be posited as being more important in some regard (say, effectiveness as an aggregate economic motor) than the other. Which is precisely what Smith argues. The pursuit of riches and rank is about seeking sympathetic approval. The pursuit of the means of utility is about the quirk of rationality. Both tend to complement each other in practice. But as Part IV makes plain, the heavy lifting in terms of aggregate economic activity and resultant prosperity is done by the quirk and not the vanity. There is no contradiction here—only further appreciation of the sophisticated integration, and indeed plausibility, of Smith's ideas.

Conclusion

The aim of this chapter has been purposefully constrained: to examine the extent to which Smith did and did not think that advanced modern European societies were corrupting of the individuals who lived within them, and the extent in turn to which such societies might be normatively compromised. Against prevailing views in the existing scholarship, I contend, first, that for Smith moral corruption was not unique to, nor especially problematic in, 'commercial society' (that of modern Europe, or anywhere else). Second, whilst Smith readily recognised the capacity for moral sentiments to be corrupted in commercial societies in particular, this was due not to *commerce*, but to the division of labour. Third, Smith did not view commerce or markets as presumptively normatively problematic due to the motivations that powered them (which were on his account ordinarily benign), and thus neither in turn were the societies that made extensive use of them.

What this chapter has not sought to enter into is a wider debate over the extent to which *TMS* offers a series of attempted solutions to what Smith views as the potential pitfalls of ethical life, including the capacity for ethical sentiments to be corrupted (from whatever cause).[48] Particularly important here are Smith's attempt to refute Mandeville's claim (picked up directly by

---

48. This wider question is explored in, e.g., Vivienne Brown, *Adam Smith's Discourse: Canonicity, Commerce, and Conscience* (London: Routledge, 1994); Griswold, *Adam Smith and the Virtues of Enlightenment*, chaps. 5 and 8, and *Jean-Jacques Rousseau and Adam Smith: A Philosophical Encounter* (London: Routledge, 2018), chaps. 1, 2, and 4; Hanley, *Adam Smith and the Character of Virtue*; Hill, 'Poor Man's Son'; Leonidas Montes, 'Adam Smith: Self-Interest and the Virtues', in Hanley, *Adam Smith*; Schliesser, *Adam Smith*, chap. 9.

Rousseau) that all human motivations stem from the love of praise, and hence that virtue is revealed as a fraud, as well as the extensive additions to the sixth and final edition of *TMS* in the newly added Part VI, where Smith goes beyond the anatomy of the moral sentiments which compromised the bulk of earlier editions, and offers in addition a picture of what constitutes the properly virtuous life. Standing behind this is a further set of questions over what Smith takes the connection between virtue and true happiness to be, and the extent to which he did and did not take over (for example) Stoic ideas of *ataraxia*, Aristotelian notions of *eudaimonia*, and so forth. The appropriate place for a discussion of these further issues, however, is a book on Smith's moral philosophy. Yet if what I have said above is correct, then any such discussion must absolutely not start from the assumption that whatever Smith had to say about virtue and happiness, it was primarily because his starting point was a belief that 'commercial society', or 'commerce' generally, create unique and especially severe problems in these regards. On the contrary, Smith in *TMS* was engaged more fundamentally with understanding the human condition, and suggesting some ways to help it go better than it otherwise might. Not only does presenting him as offering a 'defence' of 'commercial society' from the 'critique' of Rousseau cause us to misread him in this regard, it also does a disservice to Smith's ambition and achievement as regards the scope and endeavour of his great work of moral philosophy.

5

The Conspiracy of the Merchants

SMITH FAMOUSLY declared that 'people of the same trade seldom meet together, even for merriment and diversion, but the conversation ends in a conspiracy against the publick, or in some contrivance to raise prices' (*WN* I.x.c.27).[1] Given the rhetorical combativeness of this most forthright of accusations, it is unsurprising that it is well known. Less well known, however, is the full extent to which Smith believed such a 'conspiracy' to obtain, how he believed it came about, and why it would prove highly resistant to effective political control. The goal of this chapter is to bring this more plainly into view. In doing so, it reveals the extent to which Smith identified the most pressing challenges to advanced European commercial societies as lying not in the threat of moral corruption—which as we saw in the previous chapter Smith held to be considerably less serious than recent commentary has suggested—but in the *political* dangers arising out of the systemic corruption propagated by the merchant and manufacturing classes.[2] In turn, and in light of what has

---

1. This chapter originally appeared as 'Adam Smith and the Conspiracy of the Merchants', *Global Intellectual History* 6, no. 4 (2021), 463–483. It has been revised to take account of the arguments in chapter 1 above, as the earlier version fell into the mistakes I now identify regarding technical usage of the term 'commercial society' and the true nature of Smith's stages theory.

2. Recall Wallis's definition introduced in the previous chapter: 'a concrete form of political behavior and an idea. In polities plagued with systematic corruption, a group of politicians deliberately create rents by limiting entry into valuable economic activities, through grants of monopoly, restrictive corporate charters, tariffs, quotas, regulations, and the like. These rents bind the interests of the recipients to the politicians who create them. The purpose is to build a coalition that can dominate the government. Manipulating the economy for political ends is systematic corruption. Systematic corruption occurs when politics corrupts economics' (John Joseph Wallis, 'The Concept of Systemic Corruption in American History', in *Corruption and Reform: Lessons from America's Economic History*, ed. E. L. Glaiser and C. Goldin [Chicago:

been said in earlier chapters, the ambition is to present Smith's political thought as a whole as more thoroughly *political* than recent scholarship has treated it as being. For Smith, the most pressing dangers to modern commercial societies arose not from the alleged impacts of markets upon morals, but from the way in which power and wealth could come to be reconfigured in ways that opened the door to the renewed domination of the weak by the powerful. This in turn potentially imperilled the hard-won modern liberty that Smith saw modern European states as having fortuitously stumbled their way into (as discussed in chapter 2).

Whilst nobody even passingly familiar with Smith's works will be surprised to hear that he exhibited a profound hostility to the merchants, what remains unexplained in the specialist literature is why and how Smith thought they were able to exert such disproportionate influence in modern societies.[3] To understand this, we need to place Smith's hostility in the context of his psychological account of authority, as well as the development of different forms of political organization as generated by the convoluted social and economic developments of not just European but global history. In turn, however, we must also come to recognize that Smith's condemnation of the merchants is in the final instance Janus-faced: his hostility is qualified when placed in the context of disastrous political failures, as experienced both in the ancient world and in more recent European imperial expansionism. When it comes to Smith and the conspiracy of the merchants, we must take a deeper look at what appears familiar.

University of Chicago Press, 2006], 25). For an overview of Smith's attitude to this sort of corruption—which preoccupied and concerned him much more than that of moral corruption—see Lisa Hill, *Adam Smith's Pragmatic Liberalism: The Science of Welfare* (Cham: Palgrave Macmillan, 2019), chap. 5.

3. On the central hostility to the merchant classes evinced by Smith in *WN*, see, for example, Donald Winch, *Riches and Poverty: An Intellectual History of Political Economy in Britain, 1750–1834* (Cambridge: Cambridge University Press, 1996), chaps. 2–3; Giovanni Arrighi, *Adam Smith in Beijing: Lineages of the Twenty-First Century* (London: Verso 2007), chap. 2; Siraj Ahmed, *The Stillbirth of Capital: Enlightenment Writing and Colonial India* (Stanford, CA: Stanford University Press, 2012), chap. 4; A. W. Coats, 'Adam Smith and the Mercantile System', in *Essays on Adam Smith*, ed. A. Skinner (Oxford: Clarendon, 1975); Sankar Muthu, 'Adam Smith's Critique of International Trading Companies: Theorizing "Globalization" in the Age of Enlightenment', *Political Theory* 36, no. 2 (2008); Jennifer Pitts, *A Turn to Empire: The Rise of Imperial Liberalism in Britain and France* (Princeton: Princeton University Press, 2005), chap. 2. Vivienne Brown, *Adam Smith's Discourse: Canonicity, Commerce, and Conscience* (London: Routledge, 1994), 168–73, gives a helpfully detailed account of Smith's attack on the merchants in *WN*.

Smith's accusation of conspiracy appears not in Book IV of *WN*—where the bulk of his self-described 'very violent attack' on the whole commercial system of Great Britain takes place—but in Book I's technical discussion of labour and stock accumulation (*CAS* i.251). This by itself is not especially remarkable: the immediate context is Smith's critique of apprenticeships and incorporation, part of his analysis of why the 'Policy of Europe' has generated artificial inequalities in the division of labour and stock, and which he is explicit he will go into more detail regarding after Book III's explanation of the unnatural and retrograde development of modern European economic development. More remarkable is what Smith immediately goes on to say in Book I about what might be done regarding the merchants' conspiratorial activities: 'It is impossible indeed to prevent such meetings, by any law which either could be executed, or would be consistent with liberty and justice. But though the law cannot hinder people of the same trade from sometimes assembling together, it ought to do nothing to facilitate such assemblies; much less to render them necessary' (*WN* I.x.c.27). Smith follows this up with a series of apparently straightforward recommendations for altering policy so as not to provide needless opportunities for the merchants to conspire, principally the abolishing of corporations and the promoting of genuine competition. Yet he then immediately leaves the subject, turning to discuss the distortion of the market via educating too many people in oversubscribed trades. This turning away might be puzzling, however, to those who know what is coming in Book IV. For in Book I Smith appears to suggest that the conspiracy of the merchants can be relatively easily ameliorated: political decision makers should simply reduce opportunities for the merchants to conspire, even if considerations of practicality, as well as 'liberty and justice', mean that total prevention is impossible. But as is well known, in Book IV Smith is highly sceptical of the capacity of legislators to do precisely this. Rather than breaking up the corporations and other monopolistic structures, governments have tended to side with the merchants, turning state policy to their bidding, against the welfare of ordinary people, and thus violating 'that justice and equality of treatment which the sovereign owes to all the different orders of his subjects' (*WN* IV.viii.30).[4] But *why*? Why don't agents of government—for the good of the broader public, whom it is their principal job to serve—see what the merchants are up to and stop them, in just the sorts of ways recommended in Book I?

A full answer to this question turns out to be complex. This is because Smith's account of the conspiracy of the merchants is embedded in his wider

4. Ahmed, *Stillbirth of Capital*, 110–16; Coats, 'Smith and the Mercantile System'.

assessment of the political condition of modern Europe, and the result is an intricate account of why political rulers are systematically liable to capture by special interests, with entire states potentially captured in turn. Recognizing the full scope of Smith's assessment, however, requires us to pull together many threads of his thought, woven into not just *TMS* and *WN*, but also the student lecture notes of *LJ*. Accordingly, this chapter begins by examining what Smith has to say in *WN* regarding the disproportionate influence that the merchants exercise over the policy of Europe, as well as the pernicious effects that this has had upon wider society. The focus is then broadened to consider Smith's claims about the capacity of wealthy elites to psychologically dominate political decision makers, the crucial underlying factor in his explanation of why merchant conspiracies have proved so successful in modern European commercial societies. It next examines Smith's analyses of Athens and Rome, which he believed were ultimately destroyed by worsening misalignments between power and wealth. Yet on Smith's account the subsequent advent of the rule of law in modern Europe ensured a different playing out of political contestation, and the activities of the modern merchants had to be understood in that, very precise, context. In turn, Smith's blistering attack on Britain's imperial exploitation of India is presented as in part a dire warning about just how far merchant conspiracies might go if not subjected to meaningful political control. The chapter concludes by emphasizing the Janus-faced nature of Smith's final assessment, connecting this to the late additions made to the final edition of *TMS* regarding the problem of political judgement. The overall aim is to show that if Smith's famous condemnation of the merchants and the mercantile system in *WN* is to be fully understood, it must be read both backwards and forwards—backwards to see how it is embedded in Smith's underlying conceptualization of European history and the rise of modern European commercial societies, forwards to see his final interventions regarding the centrality of good judgement to the 'science of the statesman or legislator' (*WN* IV.intro.1).

From Private Conspiracy to State Policy: The Merchants and the Mercantile System

Smith's condemnation of the merchant classes is one of the most prominent features of Book IV of *WN*. In particular, he there accuses the merchants of being responsible for the invention of the specious doctrine of the 'balance of trade'—that a nation would grow wealthiest if its exports outstripped imports so as to accrue favourable reserves of money—which despite its economic absurdity constituted the lynchpin of the entire mercantile system. In a claim already debunked by Hume as a self-serving chimera, Smith maintained that the merchant classes had propagated the notion of a 'balance of trade' precisely because it enabled them to deceive political rulers into granting vast networks of monopolies, drawbacks, and bounties, that enriched the merchants whilst retarding the economic development of the rest of the nation.[5] Smith likewise located the primary blame for the rise of what Hume termed 'jealousy of trade'—the introduction of commerce into the arena of reason of state, with decisions about economic production subordinated to political calculations regarding international competition—as lying squarely with the merchants: 'Commerce, which ought naturally to be, among nations, as among individuals, a bond of union and friendship, has become the most fertile source of discord and animosity. The capricious ambition of kings and ministers has not, during the present and preceding century, been more fatal to the repose of Europe, than the impertinent jealousy of merchants and manufacturers' (WN IV.iii.c.9).[6] In other words, the two most pernicious aspects of the mercantile system when considered domestically and internationally could both be traced back to the conspiring activities of the merchant elites.

Smith in turn famously described the entire British colonial enterprise in North America as establishing a 'great empire . . . for the sole purpose of raising up a nation of customers who should be obliged to buy from the shops of our different producers'. The vast expense of the recently concluded Seven Years' War—indeed, the interest on the war debt alone—easily outstripped the entire profit that monopoly trade with the colonies could ever hope to secure. And yet all of this was to be paid for by the 'home-consumers' who had been 'burdened with the whole expense of maintaining and defending that empire', all for the paltry 'little enhancement in price' which the American monopoly might afford British merchants (WN IV.viii.53). In Smith's final judgement, the entire North American colonial enterprise—the consequences of which were exploding spectacularly as Smith was going into print in 1776— was not fit even for a pathetic nation of shopkeepers, but for something worse:

5. David Hume, Essays Moral, Political, and Literary, ed. E. F. Miller (Indianapolis: Liberty Fund, 1985), 308–26; WN IV.i.1–45.

6. Hume, Essays Moral, Political, and Literary, 327–31. For detailed analysis, see István Hont, 'Introduction', in Jealousy of Trade: International Competition and the Nation-State in Historical Perspective (Cambridge, MA: Belknap, 2005).

'a nation whose government is influenced by shopkeepers'. Politicians had come to believe it acceptable to sacrifice 'the blood and treasure of their fellow citizens' to the interests of an elite minority who had captured state policy (*WN* IV.vii.c.63). As Muthu has shown, the result was that the influence of the merchants—in particular through the rise of joint stock companies and the pivotal role that these played in the imperial affairs of Europe both in the West and East—had become so extensive that 'in Smith's view, by the mid-eighteenth century, a state-driven mercantilist system of international political economy had been largely transformed into a company-driven mercantilist system'.[7] Smith's hostility to institutional power structures, and their distorting effect upon commerce and international relations, is thus trained not only on government agents, but also upon the vested private interests who have 'not only colluded with states, but captured state power'.[8] The result was that the laws perpetuating the mercantile system 'like the laws of Draco . . . may be said to be all written in blood' (*WN* IV.viii.17).

It is, of course, in Book IV that Smith introduces his now (in)famous metaphor of the invisible hand. Yet what remains underappreciated is the extent to which he used the invisible hand to single out the activities of the merchant classes for special opprobrium.[9] Smith employs the 'invisible hand' to argue two connected points. First, that individuals often promote the good of wider society by performing actions that seek only to improve their own private lot, and this (surprisingly) tends to be a *more* effective way of promoting collective prosperity than setting out with that latter goal specifically in mind. Second, that because each individual knows their own interests better than a central administrator ever can, it is folly for 'the statesman or lawgiver' to try to make decisions about how to employ capital in domestic industry on behalf of private individuals (*WN* IV.ii.10). What Smith finds notable about the monopolies that the merchants have accrued to themselves is that such measures violate *both* of the maxims attaching to the invisible hand. Whilst aiming to promote the general good, political decision makers inadvertently hinder it, making the mistake of thinking that their interference (undertaken on behalf of the merchants) can be more effective than letting free competition do its work by allowing each to enter and exit competitive markets as directed by private

7. Muthu, 'Smith's Critique', 185.

8. Muthu, 'Smith's Critique', 185.

9. For a partial exception, see Emma Rothschild, *Economic Sentiments: Adam Smith, Condorcet and the Enlightenment* (Cambridge, MA: Harvard University Press, 2002), 126–28.

interest. The result is that 'to give the monopoly of the home-market to the produce of domestick industry, in any particular art or manufacture, is in some measure to direct private people in what manner they ought to employ their capitals, and must, in almost all cases, be either a useless or a hurtful regulation' (*WN* IV.ii.11). Again, this situation was brought about by dominant market actors seeking to rig markets in their own favour. Smith's appeal to the 'invisible hand' was thus directed not simply at overweening governmental administrators—as is often supposed[10]—but against the merchants who had persuaded policy makers to do their private bidding at the expense of wider society. The invisible hand was introduced not simply to make a point about the limits of the knowledge held by administrators, especially as compared to the relative efficiency of the price mechanism (as more recent Hayekian approaches tend to emphasize), but to draw attention to the problem of special-interest lobbying and rent-seeking by those in dominant market positions.

Given all of this it is not surprising that Smith's general hostility towards the merchant classes is already well known. What has not received sufficient attention, however, is the more fundamental question of *why* the merchants are able to succeed with such apparent ease in perpetrating their conspiracies. If, as Smith claims, the doctrine of the balance of trade is so obviously specious, if predictions of national impoverishment should a favourable balance not be maintained have (as he notes) always been proven wrong by the experience of countries and port towns who have opened themselves to trade, and if the interest of a nation is evidently harmed rather than helped by adopting the policies demanded by the merchants, why don't rulers see what is afoot and put a stop to such matters? As Smith states in his discussion of jealousy of trade, 'The violence and injustice of mankind is an ancient evil, for which, I am afraid, the nature of human affairs can scarce admit of a remedy. But the mean rapacity, the monopolizing spirit of the merchants and manufacturers, who neither are, nor ought to be the rulers of mankind, though it cannot perhaps be corrected, may very easily be prevented from disturbing the tranquility of any body but themselves' (*WN* IV.iii.c.9). If it is indeed 'easy' to prevent the disturbances affected by the merchants, why do rulers nonetheless frequently fail to do so, with states instead being captured by their own mercantile elites?

The most immediate and obvious part of Smith's answer, presented most prominently in *WN*, focuses on the structural advantages possessed by the

---

10. For example, James R. Otteson, 'Adam Smith and the Great Mind Fallacy', *Social Philosophy and Policy* 27, no. 1 (2010).

merchants. As the close of Book I explains when discussing the 'three great, original and constituent orders of every civilized society, from whose revenue that of every other order is ultimately derived', those who live from labouring (i.e., the vast bulk of the population) typically lack the education to understand national affairs, and more especially lack the influence and opportunity to have their voices heard at a decision-making level (*WN* I.ix.p.7).[11] The owners of land ought to possess more clout, but 'their indolence, which is the natural effect of the ease and security of their situation, renders them too often, not only ignorant, but incapable of that application of mind which is necessary in order to foresee and understand the consequences of any publick regulation' (*WN* I.xi.p.8). Typically, the final of the great orders—merchants and manufacturers—in fact know no more about the good of the nation as a whole than the other classes of society, but because they spend their lives engaged in 'plans and projects' aimed at furthering their own interests, they understand *those* very well, and much better than the other two orders. As a result, the merchants' 'superiority over the country gentleman is, not so much in their knowledge of the publick interest, as in their having a better knowledge of their own interest than he has of his. It is by this superior knowledge of their own interest that they have frequently imposed upon his generosity, and persuaded him to give up both his own interest and that of the publick, from a very simple but honest conviction, that their interest, and not his, was the interest of the publick' (*WN* I.xi.p.10).

In practice this structural asymmetry between the orders has been extensively compounded by the very success that the merchants have enjoyed in capturing state policies for their own interests. As Smith explains after his remark that 'to expect, indeed, that the freedom of trade should ever be entirely restored in Great Britain, is as absurd as to expect that an Oceana or Utopia should ever be established in it', this is precisely because 'not only the prejudices of the publick, but what is much more unconquerable, the private interests of many individuals, irresistibly oppose it' (*WN* IV.ii.43). The violence with which the merchants oppose the removal of their privileges and the overturning of mercantilist policies is, Smith says, so ferocious that it would be just as dangerous to systematically oppose the merchants as to dismantle Britain's standing army and turn its leading officers out of doors. Explicitly comparing

---

11. The exception to this, ironically, is when large numbers of labourers are manipulated by manufacturers and merchants into organised demonstrations of public outrage, but which are calculated to benefit the employers rather than the employees (*WN* I.xi.p.9).

the 'tribes' of merchants to an 'overgrown standing army', Smith explains that this class has entrenched its power so as to become 'formidable to the government, and upon many occasions intimidate the legislature'. The predicament for politicians is that anybody who goes against the merchants will suffer 'the most infamous abuse and detraction, from personal insults' as well as 'real danger, arising from the insolent outrage of furious and disappointed monopolists'. By contrast, politicians who cozy up to the mercantile classes will not only get an easy ride, but acquire 'the reputation of understanding trade' as well as 'great popularity and influence with an order of men whose numbers and wealth render them of great importance' (WN IV.ii.43). This process of power consolidation was supplemented by jingoistic tub-thumping: merchants ensured that it was against foreign economic competition that 'national animosity' was 'most violently inflamed', further extending their pernicious influence over the policy making of nations (WN IV.iii.c.10).

Yet in addition to these direct answers in WN regarding how the merchants had managed to turn their private conspiracies into the foundations of national political economy and international strategy, Smith had a deeper story to tell. We are pointed in its direction by his remarks that the merchants 'by their wealth draw to themselves the greatest share of the publick consideration', and that it is precisely their 'numbers and wealth' that renders them 'of great importance' (WN I.xi.p.10; WN VI.ii.43). For in Smith's underlying psychological account of the foundations of political societies, it was precisely wealth that had an especially important—and dangerous—role to play.

Lessons from History: Wealth, Power, Law

In order to understand why Smith thought that the merchants were so successful in capturing state policy in modern Europe, it is necessary to locate the analysis of WN in reference to his wider political thought, which is itself dependent upon Smith's assessment of the historical conditions from which differing political conditions arose. In particular, we must here pay attention to Smith's account of the fates of Athens and Rome, as well as the subsequent rise of Europe's modern monarchies. This, however, first requires us to consider Smith's account of how authority operates in the psychologies of the ruled, and his explanation of how politics plays out in different socioeconomic contexts. Once this is done we will be in a position to appreciate the full extent of the 'conspiracy' Smith believed the merchant classes to have perpetrated.

We must here recall what was established in chapter 1 vis-à-vis Smith's technical understanding of 'commercial society'. In particular, that in the first place commercial society is not simply characterized by trade, either internally or externally: all human societies will have engaged in material exchange to varying degrees, both with fellow members and with neighbouring groups. What sets commercial society apart is specifically *how most individuals secure their subsistence*—that they live from exchange due to the advanced progress of the division of labour. Second, commercial society is by no means a uniquely modern, post-feudal, European phenomenon. On the contrary, premodern societies where most individuals 'lived by exchange' eminently qualified as commercial societies, and Smith thought that Athens and Rome were paradigm cases, as were the economically and technologically advanced Chinese dynasties periodically ravaged by Mongol invasion from the eastern steppe before the invention of gunpowder neutered the capacity of nomadic shepherd barbarians to reset the progress of civilization.[12] We shall return to this point about predecessor forms of commercial society momentarily, for it is of considerable significance to understanding Smith's assessment of the place of the merchants in the peculiar instantiation of commercial society that arose in post-feudal Europe.

Before doing so, however, we must also note that Smith, like Hume, took to heart James Harrington's dictum that in political affairs, 'the balance of power depends on that of property'.[13] And also like Hume, Smith founded his political theory on the basis of the 'opinion of mankind': that all large-scale political processes had to be understood through the predominantly voluntary submission of the ruled to rulers (the former always outweighing the latter in strength and number).[14] Smith went beyond Hume, however, in detailing the

12. For details, see chapter 1 above. See also István Hont, 'Adam Smith's History of Law and Government as Political Theory', in *Political Judgement: Essays for John Dunn*, ed. R. Bourke and R. Geuss (Cambridge: Cambridge University Press, 2009); Hont, *Politics in Commercial Society: Jean-Jacques Rousseau and Adam Smith*, ed. B. Kapossy and M. Sonenscher (Cambridge, MA: Harvard University Press, 2015), 3–4, 81; Ryan Patrick Hanley, 'The "Wisdom of the State": Adam Smith on China and Tartary', *American Political Science Review* 108, no. 2 (2014).

13. Hume, *Essays Moral, Political, and Literary*, 47.

14. Hume, *Essays Moral, Political, and Literary*, 33; István Hont, 'Commercial Society and Political Theory in the Eighteenth Century: The Problem of Authority in David Hume and Adam Smith', in *Main Trends in Cultural History: Ten Essays*, ed. W. Melching and W. Velema (Amsterdam: Rodopi, 1994; Paul Sagar, *The Opinion of Mankind: Sociability and the Theory of the State from Hobbes to Smith* (Princeton: Princeton University Press, 2018), chap. 3.

mechanics of how authority operated in the minds of the ruled, leading them to submit to the commands of those who became successfully established as superiors, the phenomenon which the *Theory of Moral Sentiments* described as 'the habitual state of deference' that individuals paid to 'those whom they have been accustomed to look upon as their natural superiors' (*TMS* I.iii.2.3).[15]

The two most basic mechanisms of natural authority were superiority of individual abilities and superiority of age (*WN* V.i.b.5–6; *LJ(B)* 12–13). In primitive hunter societies these were the entire basis of all political authority. But with the advent of shepherding, dramatic increases in the wealth possessed by chieftains meant that *wealth itself* emerged as a predominant source of authority (*WN* V.i.b.7,10–12; *LJ(B)* 20–22). Finally, hereditary lineage—which presupposed economic inequality, and hence authority based in wealth—arose as a claim to other men's submission, something proved by the fact that the histories of shepherding peoples consisted almost entirely of genealogies (*WN* V.i.b.8–13; *LJ(A)* iv.43–44). In all societies advanced beyond the stage of hunters, however, more immediately visible and permanent external signs of authority were needed than the nebulous qualities of age and ability, not least thanks to the rise of the need for government due to increases in wealth inequality, and the invention of laws as a way of protecting the rich from the depredations of the poor (*WN* V.i.b.12; *LJ(B)* 20). Hence wealth and lineage became entrenched as sources of authority not just in shepherding but also in more economically developed societies. For the most part, however, these were attached to the present possessors of political office, and therefore of established political power.

Although Smith does not state the point explicitly, it is central to his analysis of the politics of commercial societies that it is at this most advanced stage of socioeconomic development, when every man is to some extent a merchant because living from exchange, that things become different with regards to the conjunction of wealth, political office, and power. This is because in commercial societies the division of labour, and the resulting processes of exchange from which most individuals live, inaugurate the possibility for individuals who are not the traditional holders of political office to become extremely wealthy. But this means that the newly rich are able to use their wealth in order to exercise authority over the minds of peers—something that was

---

15. See also Jacob Levy, *Rationalism, Pluralism, Freedom* (Oxford: Oxford University Press, 2015), 174–77.

traditionally the preserve of established political leaders (*WN* IV.vii.c.61). And the reconfiguration of power's relation to property through the growth of wealth held by nontraditional elites was, Smith believed, potentially explosive, as indeed the historical record supplied abundant evidence regarding.

To see this, we must look not only to Smith's more famous account in *LJ*, but to his less frequently remarked discussion of the socioeconomic conditions of Athens and Rome in *LRBL*. Smith there claimed that although the dynamics played out differently, both Athens and Rome were fundamentally destabilized by the growth of wealth amongst nontraditional elites who did not have direct access to political office, and so subverted the authority of established power holders. In Athens, the nobility originally dominated: 'The Ballance of Wealth and Rank on their side gave them also the Ballance of Power' (*LRBL* ii.142–43). Expanding economic prosperity, however, meant that in time 'commerce gave the lowest of the people an opportunity of raising themselves fortunes and by that means power'. Because democracy opened offices to all individuals, the *nouveaux riches* grasped for power, their wealth enabling them to have 'equal weight with the People' (*LRBL* ii.143). This ultimately resulted in a loss of martial capacity, as lazy citizens were paid to attend the public law courts and forsook military endeavours and genuine civic engagement, becoming easy prey for the flattery of ambitious orators. When Philip of Macedon threatened the republic, it by that point lacked the capacity to adequately offer resistance, with citizens opting to spend time loudly pontificating about what they would do to Philip after they had defeated him, whilst entirely neglecting to adequately prepare for the war itself. The result was the military subjugation of what had been one of the greatest and most formidable commercial societies in all of Attica (*LRBL* ii.148–50).

The case of Rome was more complex, and played out over a longer period, but Smith's assessment was that the origins of the Republic's destruction lay in the rise of the 'Populares', demagogues who cynically appealed to those citizens left behind by the explosion of wealth generated by successful foreign conquest, but subsequently monopolized by the 'Optimates' (*LRBL* ii.153–66). The internal unrest unleashed by the conflict between these two groups eventually led to the dictatorship of Sulla, and later Caesar's abolition of the Republic after the collapse of the Triumvirate. Thus, alongside Smith's more famous analysis in *LJ* that it was luxury that eventually brought down the Roman Empire due to its enfeebling of military capacity and the rapacious attentions of the German barbarians that it generated, he also maintained that the Roman *Republic* was first destabilized, and ultimately destroyed, by the centrifugal political forces unleashed by advanced economic development—that is, by commercial society (*LJ(A)* iv.87–91; *LJ(B)* 36–43).[16]

Modern Europe, however, was different. This was due to accidents of history having ensured that the dynamics of politics in modern commercial societies played out differently to those of the ancient world. Once we see this, the nature of the merchants' modern conspiracies comes into focus—but also takes on a different aspect. As Smith famously stated in Book III of *WN*, the economic and political development of modern Europe had been 'unnatural and retrograde' (*WN* III.i.9).[17] This was because modern Europe had grown out of the feudal regimes founded on the ruins of Rome. In particular, that in economic terms European states had not followed a 'natural' (i.e., analytically logical, without the influence of real-world contingent historical accidents) process of development, which presupposed a solid agricultural base being established prior to the development of refined manufactures in the towns. Things had instead been the other way around, a product of modern Europe starting midstream in its economic development due to the collapse of Rome having left behind pockets of advanced manufacturing in southern European city-states. These outposts of economic advancement had injected their refined manufactured goods into the rising feudal, agricultural-based monarchies erected by the descendants of the Germanic shepherd conquerors, generating the retrograde progression of modern European development (*WN* III.iii.1–20).[18] This led to serious problems of imbalance in European economies—but these had to be lived with and worked around (rather than, as the French Physiocrats hubristically supposed, being forcibly reversed by the hand of the legislator) (*WN* IV.ix.1–52).

As noted in chapter 2 above, this meant that for Smith modern Europe was therefore a story not of ancient republics, but of the legacy of gothic shepherd nations who had settled on the rubble of Rome. Here Smith broadly agreed with Montesquieu's basic analysis in his 1748 *Spirit of the Laws*: the future of European politics was northern and modern, not southern and ancient.[19] Isolated city-states of the sort found in Italy and Switzerland were not models of correct political formation, but chance survivors of the barbarian holocaust: ancient relics in a modern world, soon to be swept away. The future of

16. See also Hont, 'Commercial Society'.
17. See also Hont, *Jealousy of Trade*, 354–88; Ahmed, *Stillbirth of Capital*, 110–13.
18. See also Hont, *Jealousy of Trade*, 354–88.
19. Sagar, *Opinion of Mankind*, chap. 5.

European politics was not small republics concentrated in individual cities, but large modern monarchies spread across great territories, characterized by large internal inequalities of rank and fortune, whilst operating large commercial trading economies.[20]

This mattered. As discussed in chapter 2, Smith saw modern liberty as in part having arisen via the ironic and unintended effects of luxury, as well as the effects of violence and international warfare, through the way in which these shaped the logic and institutional form of European states. Although luxury brought down the Roman Empire, it later helped to end the backwards and stagnant feudal societies of western Europe after the barons shortsightedly traded all of their political influence for 'trinkets and baubles', that is, swapping the capacity to hold thousands of retainers for the chance to purchase inane status goods (WN III.iv.15). The result was the rise of absolute monarchies across western Europe, which were actually an improvement in terms of liberty for most subjects, insofar as distant kings were typically less oppressive than local baronial tyrants (LJ(A) iv.98–99). England was a peculiar exception to this general story, as its situation as a united island after 1603 meant it could do without a standing army, whilst the unique consequences of its mid-seventeenth-century civil war led to the rapid rise of Parliament, and in turn to the innovation of a constitution which was mixed in form and orientated towards preserving the liberties of subjects. England was politically unique, but this was a recent development. Prior to the Stuarts it had been as much an absolutist regime as its monarchical neighbours still were (LJ(A) iv.157–79, v.1–12; LJ(B) 59–64).

This was the political situation of Europe by the time the merchants rose to prominence and began to use their increasing wealth to influence the political decision makers of European states. From this, however, we can infer the following to be unstated, but crucial, tenets of Smith's background assumptions regarding the place of the merchants in contemporary commercial society.

---

20. Montesquieu, *The Spirit of the Laws*, ed. A. M. Cohler, B. C. Miller, and H. S. Stone (Cambridge: Cambridge University Press, 1989), 17–20, 25–30, 55–58; Hont, *Politics in Commercial Society*, 70–75; Michael Sonenscher, *Before the Deluge: Public Debt, Inequality, and the Intellectual Origins of the French Revolution* (Princeton: Princeton University Press, 2007), chap. 2; Annelien de Dijn, 'Montesquieu's Controversial Context: The Spirit of the Laws as Monarchist Tract', *History of Political Thought* 34, no. 1 (2013); de Dijn, 'Was Montesquieu a Liberal Republican?', *Review of Politics* 76, no. 1 (2014); Robin Douglass, 'Montesquieu and Modern Republicanism', *Political Studies* 60, no. 3 (2012); Samuel Fleischacker, *On Adam Smith's Wealth of Nations: A Philosophical Companion* (Princeton: Princeton University Press, 2004), 246–49.

First, the radically non-ancient political landscape of modern Europe had proved—completely ironically, and without design—to be a relatively *stable* habitat within which the merchants could undertake their nefarious activities. The collapse of the power of the barons, and the undisputed preeminence of absolutist rulers in the wake of the end of feudalism, meant that their private wealth notwithstanding, the merchants could neither replace the barons as alternative sources of domestic power, nor appeal directly to the general population as a way of contesting the authority of the monarch (or in Britain's case, the Crown in Parliament). Instead, the ambition of the merchants had to be directed to attempts at influencing established holders of political power, encouraging them to adopt policies that would benefit the merchant classes. Using wealth as a psychological lever with which to dazzle those who made state policy, as well as exploiting their structural position of advantage with regard to knowledge of their own interests, the merchants ultimately achieved great success in this regard, as Smith made damningly clear in WN. Crucially, however, they did so whilst working with and through, rather than against, established political officeholders. This entailed a sharp contrast with the ancient world, which lacked merchant conspiracies in the modern mode, but where growing misalignments between wealth and power led to the subversion and destruction of liberty-promoting republican institutions.

Second, modern European politics exhibited a vitally important further stabilizing factor that helped to ensure that political forces in modern commercial societies were centripetal rather than (as in the ancient world) centrifugal. This was the (again ironic and unintended) emergence of the rule of law, as discussed in chapter 2 (*WN* V.i.b.13–25). Recall that in *LJ* and *WN* Smith posited that in early periods of society judging was undertaken by political leaders not out of a sense of public duty, but to extract gifts from those seeking redress, with predictably problematic results (*WN* V.i.b.13–17; *LJ(A)* iv.15–19). With the innovation of legislatures to control such practices, and the resulting evolution of standards of equitable and impartial treatment in matters of law, judges became upholders of individual liberty, as well as acting as checks to sovereign power, rather than being the 'terrible sight' signalling extractive demands in return for crooked justice that they were to primitive peoples (*LJ(B)* 92; *WN* V.i.b.13–25). The phenomenon of the rule of law—the long-run outcome of judicial independence—was, however, largely unknown in the ancient world, where justice was much more unreliable and irregularly dispensed, and where the courts were frequently extensions of, rather than restraints on, executive power. Yet as Smith explained in *WN*, and as was discussed in chapter 2, for each individual to be secure in their liberty, 'it is not only necessary that the judicial should be separated from the executive power, but that it should be rendered as much as possible independent of that power' (*WN* V.i.b.25). This was an innovation perfected only under modern European conditions.

The nation where the securing of liberty via the rule of law had progressed the furthest was, of course, Britain. This was another accident of history. As Smith explained in the section of *LRBL* dealing with modern judicial eloquence, British monarchs had, like their continental counterparts, quickly grown uninterested in the tedious task of the administration of justice, and had delegated it to paid officials. Over time the stature and status of individual judges had grown dramatically, and they in turn vigorously asserted their independence from sovereign direction. What was unique to Britain, however, was the practice of ruling on cases based on precedent. This was the birth of the English common law, which turned out to be a remarkably effective restraint on executive decision making whilst providing a stable framework of evolving rules within which all of society could operate predictably and transparently. Smith thus declared that the common law 'may be looked on as one of the most happy parts of the British Constitution tho introduced merely by chance and to ease the men in power that this Office of Judging causes is committed into the hands of a few persons whose sole employment it is to determine them' (*LRBL* ii.203; cf. *WN* V.i.b.13–25). Yet whilst Britain was most advanced in this regard, the benefits of living under impartial systems of justice were not confined to Britain alone, insofar as judiciaries separate from the direct control of executive powers also existed in the continental monarchies:

> This Separation of the province of distributing Justice between man and man from that of conducting publick affairs and leading Armies is the great advantage which modern times have over antient, and the foundation of that greater Security which we now enjoy both with regard to Liberty, property, and Life. It was introduced only by chance and to ease the Supreme Magistrate of this the most Laborious and least Glorious part of his Power, and has never taken place until the Refinement and the Growth of Society have multiplied business immensely. (*LRBL* ii.203; cf. *WN* V.i.b.24)

The rule of law was a central plank of modern liberty, and yet it was a historical accident found only in modern—and crucially not ancient, or non-European—commercial societies. It was in *this* context that modern merchants had needed to operate. The result, however, is that Smith's wider analysis of the conspiracy of the merchants is therefore ultimately Janus-faced.

Whilst there was no doubt that the merchants had degraded the policies and polities of modern Europe through their conspiracies against the public, it was also the case that modern Europeans had gotten off comparatively lightly. Furthermore, although the merchants served to degrade the quality of much political decision making, they had also inadvertently helped promote the shift in power that enabled the rule of law to operate by supplying the luxury goods that the barons traded for power, and thus promoted a wider social system of decentralized legal arbitration that ultimately kept their own degradations from becoming politically destabilizing. The unnatural and retrograde path of the historical development of modern European states had chanced to create political and legal structures within which the potentially destructive effects of wealth's becoming separated from established political power could be effectively contained. The merchants certainly used their wealth and structural informational and positional advantages to dazzle and manipulate policy makers, using the power of wealth-generated authority to bend national policy to their sectional demands. But they did so by operating broadly within the rule of law, and thus avoided (not that they intended this; but no matter) undermining the stability of post-feudal commercial societies. This was no small blessing, as the fates of independent Athens and republican Rome showed.

Warnings from India: When Merchants Turn Sovereign

Such was the situation of modern western Europeans. Alas, by the close of the eighteenth century the merchants had not confined their attentions to western Europe. Non-European peoples, Smith knew, had not gotten off so lightly, and *WN* accordingly contains his blistering, and justly famous, condemnation of British imperial policy in India. In the light of the above, however, we can read his polemic as not only a denunciation of imperial exploitation (which it most certainly was), but also a warning about what the merchants were capable of if left to their own devices.[21] India represents, in Smith's thought, a limit case regarding how far the conspiracy of the merchants against the well-being of the public could be taken absent the stabilizing controls provided by the rule of law.

21. Pitts, *Turn to Empire*, chap. 2; Muthu, 'Smith's Critique'.

Smith was under no illusions about the destructive and oppressive nature of European imperial projects.[22] The consequences of the British East India Company for the territories it governed were listed in Book I as 'want, famine, and mortality', themselves the results of 'tyranny' and 'calamity' (*WN* I.viii.26). In Book IV, Smith described the mercantile system's manifestation in the East Indies as constituting an 'oppressive authority' based on force and injustice, which 'deranged' the allocation of stock both at home and abroad, and whose joint stock companies (the principal engine of mercantile colonialism) operated exclusive monopolies that were 'destructive' to those countries 'which have the misfortune to fall under their government' (*WN* IV.vii.c.80; cf. *WN* IV.vii.c.92; *WN* IV.vii.c.108). Smith was well aware that the *Western* territories not had gotten off any lighter—indeed arguably the reverse. This was easily forgotten by contemporary observers thanks to the differing histories of colonialism having produced different results and states of oppression in the observable present. But remembering these differing histories was crucial to understanding why the experiences of the East and West diverged by the late eighteenth century.

When the Europeans discovered North America, they found a people who were less economically advanced than those of the East Indies. The Native Americans were mostly in the condition of hunters, the Indians mostly shepherds—'and the difference is very great between the number of shepherds and that of hunters whom the exact same extent of equally fertile territory can maintain' (*WN* IV.vii.c.100). The result was that Europeans were able to easily apply their superior military force against the indigenous North American populations, rapidly committing genocide, forcing survivors west, and clearing indigenous lands for settlement by Europeans. In the East, by contrast, larger and more robust native populations could not be so easily wiped out or displaced, and instead had to be ruled over directly. This led to the different 'genius' of the mercantile system's colonial manifestations in West and East under British rule, founded on different species of original injustice (*WN* IV.vii.c.100–101). In the West, the 'savage' policy of murder and displacement paradoxically gave way to a more gentle (if highly economically inefficient and unjustifiable) form of colonial settler rule, where the European merchants and sovereigns saw these colonial populations as fellow citizens of the mother

22. Ahmed, *Stillbirth of Capital*, chap. 4; Robert Travers, 'British India as a Problem in Political Economy: Comparing James Steuart and Adam Smith', in *Lineages of Empire: The Historical Roots of British Imperial Thought*, ed. D. Kelly (New York: Oxford University Press, 2009).

country, and entitled thereby to comparable levels of defence and care (*WN* IV.vii.c.101). By contrast, the subjugated populations of the East were viewed not as fellow citizens deserving equitable treatment, but as mere resources for the extraction of gain by the merchant monopolies granted authority over conquered territories. The results were ultimately also catastrophic for the indigenous populations of the East, even if they played out more slowly than they had in the West.

Part of the problem was an outgrowth of the general misalignment between the interests of the wider people versus those of the merchants. Employees of the East India Company—private merchants—aimed simply to extract as much short-term profit from their administrations as possible. What they failed to realise was that in ruling over subjugated populations they ceased to be just merchants and instead became de facto sovereigns. This meant that their real interest was in improving the value of land, and thus in turn the growth of wages and stock, so that the territory that they ruled over could prosper, and they in turn could reap the benefits of an economy in which opulence was increasing. Yet because the merchants saw themselves as British, and India as simply a foreign place from which to extract profit before leaving for home, they failed to make this connection. For this reason in particular, 'a company of merchants are, it seems, incapable of considering themselves as sovereigns, ever after they have become such' (*WN* IV.vii.c.102). This incapacity to switch from a merchant perspective to that of a sovereign virtually guaranteed the unjust exploitation of subject populations, who were viewed not as fellow citizens, or even as humans, but merely as resources.

In fact the problem ran deeper still. In the first place, because the administrators of the East India Company were precisely 'a council of merchants', and not a genuine political organization, they found it virtually impossible to exercise legitimate authority over the Eastern territories (*WN* IV.vii.c.104).[23] The merchants may have possessed wealth, but they shipped this straight home, or kept it conspicuously apart from those they ruled over, making no pretence that its basis was in anything other than rapine targeted at the ruled. As the operatives of the East India Company held no office other than that granted through superior force, their authority could not extend beyond naked power—making it barely authority at all. The result was that the entire colonial system could ultimately be sustained *only* by violent oppression,

23. Richard Bourke, *Empire and Revolution: The Political Life of Edmund Burke* (Princeton: Princeton University Press, 2015), 524.

meaning its rule was 'necessarily military and despotical' (*WN* VI.vii.c.104). Even worse, there were yet further structural predicaments ensuring that corruption and exploitation were virtually inevitable in colonies ruled this way. Whilst leading administrators, or indeed the British government, might from afar command a more equitable policy towards the Indians, company servants located in the territories would always find—in their private or official capacities—opportunities and excuses to secure themselves monopolies and unfair advantages, employing force to maintain their profits, and extracting what they could from those they found themselves in a position of domination over. Because the merchants had no connection with the territories they administered beyond the seeking of profit, even well-meaning directives from above (which were in practice anyway lacking) would come to little, as the individual imperative at street level was to seek private gain, in a context untethered by any proper system of domestic justice enforced by meaningful political authority (*WN* IV.vi.c.105). The result was an abomination: 'a very singular government in which every member of the administration wishes to get out of the country, and consequently to have done with the government, as soon as he can, and to whose interest, the day after he has left it and carried his whole fortune with him, it is perfectly indifferent though the whole country was swallowed by an earthquake' (*WN* IV.vii.c.106). No wonder Smith's famous remark that 'the government of an exclusive company of merchants is, perhaps, the worst of all governments for any country whatsoever' (*WN* IV.vii.b.11).

Whilst Smith's assessment of the condition of India has long been recognized for its condemnation of oppression and injustice, what also needs to be appreciated is that India served as a limit case in Smith's analysis of the merchants as a central, albeit highly problematic, feature of commercial modernity. Due to the Indians being viewed not as citizens in need of defence and maintenance by regular political authority, but as mere resources for exploitation, the merchants were structurally and psychologically enabled to prey upon them, with no institutional or normative system in place to impose meaningful restraint. In a state like Britain, by contrast, administered by domestic sovereign authority operating under the rule of law, such behaviour could occur only on much smaller scales, and where meaningful (if imperfect) mechanisms for redress existed thanks to the accidents of preceding history. Nonetheless, one way to read Smith's polemic against the injustices committed in the East is to see that there but for the grace of history, and the benefits reaped from past injustices committed, go we—and might go ourselves to greater degrees if vigilance is not maintained.

Yet once again Smith's final position is replete with complexity. For when he wrote that 'no two characters seem more inconsistent than those of trader and sovereign', this point was intended to cut both ways (*WN* V.ii.a.7). Whilst merchants made for terrible sovereigns, it was also the case that sovereigns are in general very poor merchants. On the one hand this was a product of the structural predicament of 'Princes', whom Smith claimed have 'scarce ever succeeded' in becoming 'adventurers in the common branches of trade', despite often having been tempted to try from a genuine desire to better their nation's condition (*WN* V.ii.a.6). In the first place, 'The profusion with which the affairs of princes are always managed, renders it almost impossible' that sovereigns should be capable of dedicating themselves with the singularity of purpose, and narrowness of focus, required to secure reliable profits in commercial endeavours. Furthermore, their own servants were highly unreliable agents of commerce: they 'regard the wealth of their master as inexhaustible; are careless at what price they buy; are careless at what price they sell; are carless at what expence they transport his goods from one place to another' (*WN* V.ii.a.6). And of course behind this lay the ironical workings of the invisible hand: sovereigns were much poorer judges of where and how to allocate resources so as to secure national prosperity than the aggregated but uncoordinated outcome of disparate judgements of utility made by individual agents themselves. In other words, sovereigns in modern commercial societies could not help but rely upon merchants to a significant degree if they were to genuinely attempt to secure the *salus populi* it was their duty as rulers to pursue.

Political Judgement in Commercial Conditions

In Smith's final analysis merchants are dangerous to a modern commercial society, and yet entirely necessary to its continued operation and flourishing. It was commercial activity that generated opulence and freedom, and so the true 'science of the statesman or legislator' consisted in deciding how best to govern the merchants' activities, striking a balance between granting them liberties to pursue legitimate commercial activities that promoted the general well-being of the nation, yet applying control when such activities became vehicles for sectional private gain at public expense (*WN* IV.intro.I). We thus find a direct point of synthesis between Smith's complex evaluation of the conspiracy of the merchants in *WN*, and his striking addition to the sixth and final edition of *TMS* in 1790, where he discusses the ineliminable role of judgement in good statecraft. Although often read as Smith's late-in-life response to the French Revolution—which it may well be—Smith's argument about the intractability of judgement goes far deeper than a passing commentary on contemporary events.

Underlying his famous disdain for the 'man of system', who is 'apt to be wise in his own conceit', arrogantly believing that he can reorder society as though the individuals that compose it are mere pieces upon a chessboard, but failing to recognise that each 'piece' has its own principle of motion that inevitably upsets the system maker's plan, Smith was drawing attention to problems facing any ruler who aspired to govern well (*TMS* VI.ii.2.17).[24] All good leaders, according to Smith, were animated by two principles. First, a 'certain respect and reverence for that constitution or form of government which is actually established'. But second, 'an earnest desire to render the condition of our fellow-citizens as safe, respectable, and happy as we can' (*TMS* VI.ii.2.11). When taken by the latter spirit of reform, however, the human psyche was apt to become enamoured with abstract plans promising to sweep away the complex problems of the real world, replacing these with an allegedly improved, putatively more rational and ethical, alternative. Unfortunately, such plans were invariably chimerical: a preconceived system could never cope with the difficulties and complexities of the real world, and imposition would usually do more harm than good. Such chimeras were particularly dangerous, however, due to their capacity to enrage party fanaticism and impose policy via the power of faction and groupthink mentality. 'The great body of the party are commonly intoxicated with the imaginary beauty of this ideal system', meaning that even individual leaders who were wise enough to appreciate the great difficulties and dangers of introducing reform 'dare not always to disappoint the expectation of their followers; but are often obliged, though contrary to their principle and their conscience, to act as if they were under the common delusion' (*TMS* VI.ii.2.15). The good political leader had to exercise judgement as to when reform was necessary versus a continuation of the existing order, whilst also attempting to hold themselves independent from the spirit not just of system, but of faction, which were both apt to distort or even subjugate good judgement—with potentially disastrous results.

When we recall Smith's analysis in *TMS*, however, the conspiracy of the merchants emerges as posing an even more acute problem than has already been noted. For *WN* suggests that it is precisely the merchant classes who are amongst those most likely to attempt to exercise power and influence over

---

24. Levy, *Rationalism*, 173–77.

modern rulers. The mercantile elites form factions and cabals, attempting to direct government policy to their own private interests—and furthermore, are precisely the sorts of actors most likely to celebrate the adoption of abstract plans that reorder society in ways that putatively serve the common good, but are in fact calculated to serve sectional mercantile interests. Smith's two prime threats to good political judgement—the spirit of system and the spirit of faction—are thus particularly acute in the context of the influence exercised by merchant elites. Thus, whilst Smith may have had France and radical reform foremost in his mind when he wrote his late remarks, the depth of his insight suggests a longer period of gestation. In which case, his wider analysis of the capture of the British state by the mercantile class represents a plausible site of intellectual origin for his account of political judgement. In any case, for Smith a good ruler in a modern European commercial society—she who understands the 'divine maxim of Plato' that one is made for the state, not the state for oneself—will be faced with the extremely difficult task of not falling for the flattery and wealth-generated authority of mercantile power, and thus of preventing state policy from being bent towards private interests (*TMS* VI.ii.2.12). On the other hand, a considerable degree of mercantile freedom would continue to be necessary to secure the prosperity of the nation insofar as princes made for terrible merchants. On Smith's analysis, deciding where the balance falls is a task demanding an acute capacity for judgement, one that cannot be taught through theory, is likely to be possessed only by a very few, and yet is essential for good statecraft in a world shaped by the turbulent currents of history, politics, and economic exchange.

The picture that emerges of Smith's final position is therefore altogether less sanguine than the still common depiction of him as a relatively blasé believer in the inevitable conjunction of commerce with liberty, and the upwards progress of human civilization powered by the benign engine of market exchange.[25] On the contrary, Smith warned that in conditions of European modernity the conspiracy of the merchants was hemmed in mostly by fortunate and unintended accidents of history, which neither politicians nor manufacturers themselves understood. Nor did they appreciate how disastrous the consequences might be—for the general population, and indeed for the long-run survival of the state itself—if that hemming in was not continuously maintained. Furthermore, any appeal to wise legislators who might see this truth

25. On which see especially Muthu, 'Smith's Critique'; Ahmed, *Stillbirth of Capital*; Jennifer Pitts, 'Irony in Adam Smith's Critical Global History', *Political Theory* 45, no. 2 (2015).

and govern in the light of it was hobbled by the manifest infrequency with which political power comes to rest in the hands of good judges, and the myriad obstacles that stand in the way of being able to act on good judgement even for the best of leaders. Likewise, the sheer complexity of Smith's analysis of commercial societies, the Janus-faced place he ascribes to the merchants within the historical development of European states, the further complicating factor of their behaviour beyond the metropole, as well as the demands and burdens of judgement imposed upon rulers, ought all to indicate that—as Craig Smith and Ryan Patrick Hanley have urged—when it comes to politics Smith is not helpfully reduced to either side of a contemporary debate about whether his politics is 'left' or 'right'.[26] Ultimately, Smith's thought is too subtle for such a crude binary to do justice to, whilst his emphasis on the necessity of careful judgement to good political decision making is diametrically opposed to the prescriptive certainty that is the hallmark of ideology.[27] Smith is neither 'left' nor 'right', precisely because his analysis cuts deeper than such superficial labels can hope to make sense of.

Conclusion

This chapter has sought to demonstrate that insofar as Smith worried about the status and prospects of modern European commercial societies, he was principally preoccupied not with their alleged moral failings (which he largely denied, or thought to be fundamentally no different to those found in other times and places), but with the political threat that emanated from the systemic corruption propagated by the conspiracy of the merchants, and the dangers of allowing established political power to become decoupled from the possession of wealth. In other words, much of the recent scholarship on Smith

26. Against left or right readings of Smith, see Craig Smith, 'Adam Smith: Left or Right?', *Political Studies* 61, no. 4 (2013); Hanley, 'Wisdom of the State', 381. For a 'left' Smith, see Michael Frazer, *The Enlightenment of Sympathy: Justice and the Moral Sentiments* (Oxford: Oxford University Press, 2010), chap. 4; Samuel Fleischacker, 'Adam Smith and the Left', in *Adam Smith: His Life, Thought, and Legacy*, ed. R. P. Hanley (Princeton: Princeton University Press, 2016). For a 'right' Smith, see Otteson, 'Adam Smith and the Great Mind Fallacy' and 'Adam Smith and the Right', in Hanley, *Adam Smith*.

27. This does not make Smith a reactionary conservative always in favour of the status quo. As he makes clear, *some* reform will always be required to promote *salus populi*—the difficulty is knowing how and when to undertake it, and to what extent.

as theorist of 'commercial society' has erred by failing to appreciate how *political* Smith's political thought really is.

We no longer live under the mercantile system, having moved to something more like the 'system of natural liberty' that Smith himself supposed was a mere 'Utopia', both 'useless and chimerical' (*WN* V.iii.68).[28] The story of how *that* happened has been debated elsewhere.[29] But even if we now live in something more closely approximating Smith's system of natural liberty—insofar as monopolies held by state-backed joint stock companies are no longer the 'genius' of our present commercial system—none ought to deny the continued outsized influence of mercantile, or, as we now say, corporate, interests in political decision making.[30] We are not as far removed from Smith's world, in this regard at least, as we might like to think. Politicians remain highly vulnerable to the influence of merchant elites, and whilst liberal capitalist democracies are dependent upon extensive commercial freedoms for their continued operation and success, it also remains true (as Smith emphasized) that the immediate interests of the merchants frequently diverge from those of the other 'orders' of society, often to the significant disadvantage of the latter. Good political judgement regarding how to manage this state of affairs remains as desirable as ever. Smith helps us to see why such judgement is nonetheless always likely to be in acutely short supply, and why we have much to fear from that fact. This is one of his enduring lessons to us today. We would do better to heed it than to go on indulging anxieties over luxury consumption and the status of morality amidst markets, the very anxieties which Smith helps us to see are largely misguided, and not where the true threat lies. Morality, Smith wants us to realise, will mostly look after itself, as indeed it has always done. Politics will not.

28. Coats, 'Smith and the Mercantile System', 231–36.

29. Lucy M. Brown, *The Board of Trade and the Free Trade Movement, 1830–42* (Oxford: Clarendon, 1958); Boyd Hilton, *Corn, Cash, Commerce* (Oxford: Oxford University Press, 1977); Anthony Howe, *Free Trade and Liberal England, 1846–1946* (Oxford: Clarendon, 1997).

30. The scope of the problem is sobering, as laid out in, for example, Francis Fukuyama, *Political Order and Political Decay: From the Industrial Revolution to the Globalization of Democracy* (London: Profile Books, 2014); Jacob S. Hacker and Paul Pierson, *Winner-Take-All Politics* (New York: Simon & Schuster, 2010); Martin Gilens, *Affluence and Influence: Economic Inequality and Political Power in America* (Princeton: Princeton University Press, 2012); Lee Drutman, *The Business of America Is Lobbying: How Corporations Became Politicized and Politics Became Corporate* (Oxford: Oxford University Press, 2015).

Conclusion

THIS BOOK has attempted to offer a series of revisions to our understanding of both the foundations and implications of Adam Smith's political thought. By way of conclusion, I wish to make explicit and develop a final point that has been implicit in the above but is now worth bringing out fully. This is that Adam Smith is *not a theorist of capitalism*. For despite commentators frequently treating Smith's idea of 'commercial society' as synonymous with what we now call capitalism,[1] and despite the apparently obvious equation that as Smith theorised markets, and as capitalism rests on market exchange, so therefore must Smith have theorized capitalism, this is not right.[2] The reasons are as follows.

First, our understanding of capitalism in the early twenty-first century now necessarily incorporates reference to the idea of 'the economy'.[3] Capitalism is a mode of managing what is conceived of as a discrete (if to some degree necessarily abstract) unit of analysis, one that can be manipulated in more or less successful ways, and which it is now firmly the prerogative of sovereign decision-making powers in relevant states to have final discretionary authority over. Specifically, capitalism is a mixed mode of managing the economy which combines extensive levels of private property ownership, relatively open market transactions, and varying degrees of governmental direction, control, and

1. For example, Samuel Fleischacker, *On Adam Smith's* Wealth of Nations: *A Philosophical Companion* (Princeton: Princeton University Press, 2005), 55; Dennis Rasmussen, *The Problems and Promise of Commercial Society: Adam Smith's Response to Rousseau* (University Park: Pennsylvania State University Press, 2008), 161–75.

2. See also Keith Tribe, 'Adam Smith: Critical Theorist?', *Journal of Economic Literature* 37, no. 2 (1999): esp. 627–29.

3. On this see especially Timothy Mitchell, 'Fixing the Economy', *Cultural Studies* 12, no. 1 (1998).

interference, with the basic objective of improving the overall economic productivity of a given political unit (typically, a state).[4] Smith did not—indeed, could not—think in these terms, for the simple reason that he did not possess any concept of 'the economy'.[5] Certainly, he was a major innovator in the emergent discipline of political economy, which was an intellectual precondition for the later emergence of the idea of the economy as a discrete object of analysis and control (and *pari passu*, of economic management). But Smith cannot have thought or written about what we now mean by capitalism, because in the eighteenth century the intellectual apparatus for conceptualising this idea did not yet exist.

This point may seem to be one of merely—indeed, excessive—historicist pedantry. Surely what Smith called 'commercial society' became in time what we call 'capitalism', the latter being an augmented version of the former, fleshed out with subsequently evolved concepts ('the economy', 'gross domestic product', 'the unemployment rate', etc.) and subsequent historical experience (especially from the nineteenth century about the rise of mass industry, and from the twentieth regarding the outcome of the socialist calculation debate and the capacity for states to engage in certain kinds of economic management).[6] In which case, what is the harm in using 'commercial society' and 'capitalism' as (rough) synonyms?

The answer is that, at least when regarding Smith's ideas specifically, it constitutes a category error. This is because on Smith's understanding capitalism properly qualifies as a *mode of managing a commercial society*, rather than being

4. It is a mistake, as some maintain, to posit the 'mixed economy' as some sort of midway point between capitalism understood as pure free-market economics on the one hand, and total *dirigist* state planning on the other. *All* capitalist systems involve significant governmental interference and influence because all capitalist systems exist by permission, and with the assistance of, sovereign states, via the coercive implementation of rules about (at the very least) private property and how it may legitimately be transferred, as well as a codified system of legal arbitration for deciding when those rules have been broken and what consequences will follow as a result. On this see Paul Sagar, 'István Hont and Political Theory', *European Journal of Political Theory* 17, no. 4 (2018): 481–84.

5. On the historical context surrounding Smith's use of this term, and what this means in turn for his own usage in *WN*, see Luigi Alonzi, 'The Term "Political Economy" in Adam Smith', *Intellectual History Review* 31, no.2 (2021), 321–339.

6. Or to speak more accurately, of the *many* socialist calculation debates—on which see John O'Neill, 'Who Won the Socialist Calculation Debate?', *History of Political Thought* 17, no. 3 (1996). See also Don Lavoie, *Rivalry and Central Planning: The Socialist Calculation Debate Reconsidered* (Cambridge: Cambridge University Press, 1985).

identical with commercial society itself. To see this recall—one final time—Smith's full definition of commercial society:

> When the division of labour has been once thoroughly established, it is but a very small part of a man's wants which the produce of his own labour can supply. He supplies the far greater part of them by exchanging that surplus part of the produce of his own labour, which is over and above his own consumption, for such parts of the produce of other men's labour as he has occasion for. Every man thus lives by exchanging, or becomes in some measure a merchant, and the society itself grows to be what is properly a commercial society. (*WN* I.iv.1)

A society is 'commercial' when individuals secure their subsistence (and beyond) via exchange. For Smith, the only historically known—and at the time he was writing, probably the only intellectually conceivable—method for facilitating such exchange was via markets. Those markets could however operate well or badly, as represented for example by the disparity between Smith's proposed 'system of natural liberty', and the actually existing mercantile system of drawbacks and monopolies (which were still market exchange mechanisms, just highly inefficient and politically corrupted ones).[7] But this identity of markets and commercial society is best thought of as an *empirical* and not an *analytic* relationship in Smith's schema. The two could in principle—even if they hadn't yet in practice—come apart.

Indeed, after Smith wrote it became entirely possible to conceive of facilitating 'exchange' without relying primarily on markets. Most obviously: state planning based on centralised calculation of both supply and demand. In its most extreme form, state communism on an ultra-*dirigist* Soviet model. Strictly speaking, on a fully Smithean analysis Soviet Union–style state communism as attempted in the twentieth century *was still a kind of commercial society.* After all, the individuals therein lived from exchange due to the advanced progress of the division of labour (most Soviet citizens didn't grow their own food, nor herd their own flocks, but worked for a wage which they transacted with in order to survive). However, centralised state planning largely replaced the market as the nexus of economic exchange. Of course, Smith had no knowledge of state communism either in theory or in practice: its emergence as both a conceptual and then a practical possibility first required massive growth in both the

---

7. On the system of natural liberty as precisely *a system*, one pertaining specifically to economic management, see appendix 2 to chapter 2 above.

power and capacity of the modern state, which happened only during the next century, being importantly inflected through the writings of Karl Marx (more on which momentarily).[8] And as Smith's famous remark about the invisible hand in *WN* indicates, he would not have been at all surprised by what we now know to be the facts regarding the extensive superiority of relative market freedom over planning when it comes to facilitating efficient resource exchange and overall productivity and prosperity. Nonetheless, the point is that capitalism—just like real-world state communism—is a mode of managing a commercial society, but is not identical with commercial society itself. To reprise in turn a point made in chapter 1, we see again therefore that the designator 'commercial society' radically underdetermines what kind of politics (and we can also now say, economics) may turn out to supervene upon it. 'Commercial society' on Smith's technical definition is compatible, at least in principle, with both capitalism *and* real-world communism—just as it was with ancient Mediterranean republicanism, and various forms of historical Chinese sociopolitical organisation. Furthermore, not only can commercial societies therefore take many, and in some ways fundamentally opposed, forms, but even *within* the broad designator of 'capitalism' there remains the wide spectrum of choices about which kind of capitalism might be pursued by a particular commercial society: Anglo-liberal, Scandinavian, European social democratic, East Asian, and so forth.[9] For Smith, it was an empirical truth that commercial societies were market societies. It is a mistake about the structure of his thought, however, to conclude that the truth is also analytic.

It is here illuminating to briefly consider and compare the thought of Marx, both to Smith's ideas, and also to what came to be called communism in twentieth-century practice (but which would have been unrecognisable as such to Marx himself). Marx would likely have fully understood the Smithian

8. For an overview of how long, complex, and in many ways slow the process of this emergent modern state power was, and just how recently it was that the modern state finally appeared onto the world stage, see Francis Fukuyama, *Political Order and Political Decay: From the French Revolution to the Globalisation of Democracy* (London: Profile, 2014).

9. Hence even if it is true, as might be maintained, that Smith's 'system of natural liberty' is a prototype vision of what we call capitalism, too much remains undetermined about *which kind* of capitalism it would translate to today—for there are many, and understanding and evaluating them requires extensive historical knowledge and experience that Smith did not possess. That the 'system of natural liberty' does not automatically translate, for Smith, into a preference for unregulated free markets, see Eric Schliesser, *Adam Smith: Systematic Philosopher and Public Thinker* (Oxford: Oxford University Press, 2017), 220–24.

framework when he first encountered it. This is because Marx's prediction of communism as consisting of a superior and succeeding form of economic organisation functions very precisely as an alternative to what Smith called commercial society, and which Marx in his own lexicon identified as the *capitalist mode of production*, that is, economic organisation based on the division of labour, private property, market exchange, and (as Marx saw it) the exploitation of workers who were required to sell their labour in return for wages paid by those who owned the means of production (i.e., the capitalist bourgeois class).[10] Marx's vision of communism was one in which technological advancement would provide such high levels of material abundance that private property, the market as an exchange mechanism, and ultimately the state itself ('the committee for managing the common affairs of the whole bourgeoisie')[11] would simply become defunct, and hence more or less spontaneously go out of existence, even if a revolution was first required to help the process along, insofar as capitalist power holders were unlikely to give up their power without a fight. Marx's vision of communism *is* an alternative to Smith's commercial society, because it is a vision in which living from exchange has been entirely superseded (hence why one might under communism be free to hunt in the morning, fish in the afternoon, and criticise after dinner, and where distribution would operate not according to market incentives but 'from each according to his ability, to each according to his needs').[12] What came to be

10. One does not need to be a specialist reader of Marx to appreciate this point; familiarity with even just the early writings is enough to make it clear. See, for example, 'On the Jewish Question', 'Economic and Philosophical Manuscripts', 'The German Ideology', and 'The Communist Manifesto', in *Karl Marx: Selected Writings*, ed. D. McLellan (Oxford: Oxford University Press, 2000). As Keith Tribe has recently shown, what Marx discussed was specifically *the capitalist mode of production*—i.e., a mode of industrial organisation—whereas what we call 'capitalism', referring to a socioeconomic condition whose rationality eventually pervades all areas of life, is in fact a twentieth-century invention, whose first sustained elucidation comes not from Marx but from Max Weber. In other words, *Marx is not a theorist of capitalism, either*. See especially Keith Tribe, 'Capitalism and Its Critics', in *The Cambridge Companion to Nineteenth-Century Thought*, ed. G. Claeys (Cambridge: Cambridge University Press, 2019), and also Tribe, *The Economy of the Word* (Oxford: Oxford University Press, 2015), chap. 6. For 'commercial society' as effectively synonymous in Marx's thought with 'the capitalist mode of production', see also Gareth Stedman Jones, 'Marx's Critique of Political Economy: A Theory of History or Theory of Communism?', in *Marxist History: Writing for the Twenty-First Century* (Oxford: Oxford University Press, 2007), 152.

11. Marx, 'Communist Manifesto', 247.

12. Marx, 'The German Ideology', 185, and 'Critique of the Gotha Programme', in McLellan, *Karl Marx: Selected Writings*, 615.

called communism in the twentieth century is, in this sense, not Marxist at all: it is an attempt to replace the market with centralised planning, but absent the technological advancement and material abundance that for Marx was a necessary precondition of being able to supersede reliance on markets. Again, therefore, we see that real-world twentieth-century communism was a very inefficient (as well as extraordinarily politically brutal) *forcible restructuring of commercial society* (to put it in Smith's terms), wherein (to speak now in Marx's) the capitalist mode of production via the division of labour became monopolised by the state (now a hyper-concentrated cabal of the ruling class) but continued to rest on a (corrupted, but still functional) notion of private property, and the continuing mass exploitation of workers who had only their labour to exchange, this time not in the market, but via bureaucratic tyranny.[13]

In light of these considerations we may conclude by turning back to Smith and asking how we ought to understand his political project as a whole. One way to make progress is to recognise, as suggested in chapter 4, that it is a subtle but important mistake to read Smith as offering a 'defence' of commercial society. In the first place, the suggestion that a thinker is offering a 'defence' implies that there has first been an attack, or critique. Standardly, commentators locate this as emanating from Rousseau, with Smith 'replying' in turn. I have argued in chapters 3 and 4 that this is implausible. Smith *already* knew what he thought was wrong with Rousseau's polemic by the time he encountered it, and in turn he did not think there was any defence needed, because the critique was so far off base as to not be a challenge (hence why it could be dealt with incidentally and in passing).

Second, a 'defence' implies that there is some kind of alternative that might be pursued instead, but which the defence argues against. Yet as I have tried to show in the above chapters, from Smith's perspective insofar as one desires to live in some form of advanced civilization—that is, assuming, as is plausible, that nobody sanely wants to try to go back to less developed earlier modes of living, not least because these have always been characterised by extreme indigence and/or violent domination—then one has to live in a 'commercial society' of some sort. *All* advanced civilizations are commercial societies, on

---

13. It is thus true, as the old Marxist defence goes, that what was tried in Russia and other states in the twentieth century 'wasn't real Marxism'. Indeed—but that by itself is to miss the more fundamental point: that 'real Marxism' will *never* be achieved, precisely because there is no good reason to believe in Marx's (Hegelian) prediction of a postcapitalist future of technological abundance as part of the upward sweep of material progress.

Smith's view.[14] The question therefore is not one of 'defending' commercial society from some putative alternative, but one of encouraging us to see that our choices relate to *what kind* of commercial society we want to try to live in.

The mercantile system was a very bad way of organising commercial society, Smith attempted to make his readers understand, whilst the system of natural liberty would be an improvement in many regards. Similarly, Smith would have been horrified by twentieth-century real-world state communism, and deeply sceptical about the purported benefits of replacing markets with extensive central planning.[15] On the other hand, asking which variety of capitalism found in the world today he would have been most likely to support is a fool's errand, demanding more from his texts than can plausibly be delivered at this range of historical distance. Having said that, we can nonetheless be sure that the complexity of his political, social, historical, and economic judgements precludes any possibility that he would have endorsed the sort of simplistic—and highly politically motivated (with the merchants and manufacturers lurking conspicuously in the background)—market fundamentalism that has in more recent history sometimes been tied to his name. Such ideological dogma is, after all, one of the most dramatic and influential recent manifestations of the simplifying and totalising 'spirit of system' which Smith explicitly warned against (*TMS* VI.ii.2.15).[16]

14. For a recent riposte to Smith's view, which argues that in fact humanity was far better off before what is now known as the agricultural revolution, see James C. Scott, *Against the Grain: A Deep History of the Earliest States* (New Haven, CT: Yale University Press, 2017). Of course, even if it is Scott and not Smith who is right about what it was like back then, this doesn't change the fact that for us there is no going back.

15. Rasmussen, *Problems and Promise*, 'Conclusion', helpfully details the reasons why— although I urge that Rasmussen's presentation of Smith as offering a 'defence' of commercial society from historical and more recent alternatives is not right; Smith's position is that *there is no alternative*. Rasmussen misses this, at least in part, because he largely equates commercial society with capitalism.

16. I argue this case in more detail in 'The Real Adam Smith', *Aeon.co*, 16 January 2018, https://aeon.co/essays/we-should-look-closely-at-what-adam-smith-actually-believed. This is not to deny—as Glory Liu and Craig Smith have shown—that twentieth-century 'Chicago' interpretations of Smith by working economists were themselves intellectually serious engagements, whatever political uses his name has subsequently been put to: Glory Liu, 'Rethinking the "Chicago Smith" Problem: Adam Smith and the Chicago School, 1929–1980', *Modern Intellectual History* 17, no. 4 (2020), 1041–1068; Craig Smith, 'Adam Smith and the New Right', in *The Oxford Handbook of Adam Smith*, ed. C. J. Berry, M. P. Paganelli, and C. Smith (Oxford: Oxford University Press, 2013).

Yet Smith would surely have been highly sceptical of Marx's assured (ulti-mately, Hegelian) predictions that commercial society would inevitably be transcended due to technological progress generating mass abundance—and we now know that he would have been entirely correct.[17] Beyond this, how-ever, we have to do our own thinking for ourselves, and cannot look to Smith expecting ready-made answers. Nonetheless, reading him properly at least encourages us to think about the right things, at the right level. As chapters 4 and 5 tried to show, Smith's assessment is that the real dangers to commercial societies lie not in the moral but in the political threats that they face. If he is indeed correct, we have good reason to take the lesson to heart.

Smith's attitude towards commercial society is best thought of as akin to how a fish might think about water. To the fish, offering a *defence* of water is ultimately beside the point. Some version of this thing has to be lived in, one way or another. From this it does not follow, however, that the fish can or should be indifferent to the water's quality. At a bare minimum, clean water is better than dirty, and ipso facto the fish has reasons to prefer that over the al-ternatives. Likewise, we have good reasons to try to live in some kinds of com-mercial societies rather than others, and hence to take steps to try to secure what we take the better outcomes therein to be. As chapter 2 argued, for Smith one of the greatest and most substantive achievements of modern European commercial society was the establishment of modern liberty as an outgrowth of the unintended development of the rule of law. As chapter 5 argued, accord-ing to Smith the same rule of law that undergirded modern liberty had also stabilized the otherwise potentially explosive divergence of wealth and power in recent history, and allowed the moderns (at least in Europe) to avoid repeat-ing the fate of the ancients. These were real and tangible benefits, Smith wanted his readers to see. But they were benefits that could be lost.

Smith's thought thus retains real relevance for us today. It urges us to resist the siren song of those who think that the choice we face is between commer-cial society and some impossible alternative, as well as (on the other side) those who claim that commercial society can be composed only in one very particu-lar way if it is to function correctly (regarding whom, Smith reminds us always to ask: *cui bono?*). At the very least, such siren songs will lead us into intellectual error. At the very worst, they risk destroying much that we rightly hold dear.

17. This crucial point has been conceded even by leading Marxist thinkers, for example G. A. Cohen, *Self-Ownership, Freedom, and Equality* (Cambridge: Cambridge University Press, 1995), chaps. 5 and 11.

INDEX

absolute poverty reduction, 170

age of agriculture, 22, 25, 34, 43

age of commerce, 22, 26, 32, 43, 46; as fourth stage of model, 48–49

age of hunters, 18, 21n12, 22

age of shepherds, 21n12, 22, 25

agriculture: age of, 22, 25, 34, 43; commerce and, 31–32; development of, 31; nations of husbandmen, 35, 36

Aisin-Gioro clan, 42

allodialism, 73; allodial rule, 34, 162n29

America: rule-of-law-based system, 91; slaves in North, 65n18. *See also* North America

amour propre: corruption as function of, 165, 167; as driver for material consumption, 135; gratification of, 127; Mandeville's term, 130, 141; Rousseau on pity, 123–24; Rousseau's claim about, 135, 137, 140, 181

Arabs, 25, 26, 32, 35; organisation, 71; shepherd nation, 37, 71; tribes, 18, 18n9

Aristotle, 148, 151; on corruption, 148; eudaimonia, 186; slavery argument, 66

ataraxia, Stoic ideas of, 186

Athens, 49, 50, 82; fates of, 195–96; Rome and, 72, 107, 144, 190, 195–96, 198, 203

Augustus, 72

authority: Hume's account of natural, 138–39; mechanisms of natural, 197; political, and vanity, 156–57; utility and, 138

balance of trade: doctrine of, 47n42, 190, 193; notion of, 191

barbarians: destruction of European civilisation, 38n32; invasions from

shepherding peoples, 37–38; as media of exchange, 46–47n42

benevolence, 1, 2, 107, 122

Berlin, Isaiah, on negative and positive freedom, 102

Berry, Christopher J.: on feudalism as third stage, 33; on Smith's modern liberty, 83–84, 86, 92; standard model and four stages, 14n6

bettering our condition: Smith on, 183–84; spending versus saving, 183–84n47

British Constitution, 202

British East India Company, 204; administrators of, 205–6

Butler, Bishop, 150; 1726 *Fifteen Sermon's Preached at the Rolls Chapel*, 120

Caesar, 50, 72–73; abolition of Republic, 198

Cambridge School, 117

Campbell, Archibald, *An Enquiry into the Original of Moral Virtues*, 121

capitalism: commercial society versus, 145n2; economy and, 212; mode of managing commercial society, 212–14, 215

Carlyle Lectures (2009), 114–16

Catholic Church, 62, 76

Charles I (King), 77

China: agricultural and manufacturing sectors, 43; corruption of officials, 44–45; dynasties, 42, 196; exchange in society, 50; inland navigation, 43–44; of Smith's day, 108; Smith's view of, 49, 49n48; understanding commercial society in, 41–45